Collins | English for Exams

Cambridge English Qualifications
B1 Preliminary for Schools 2
8 practice tests

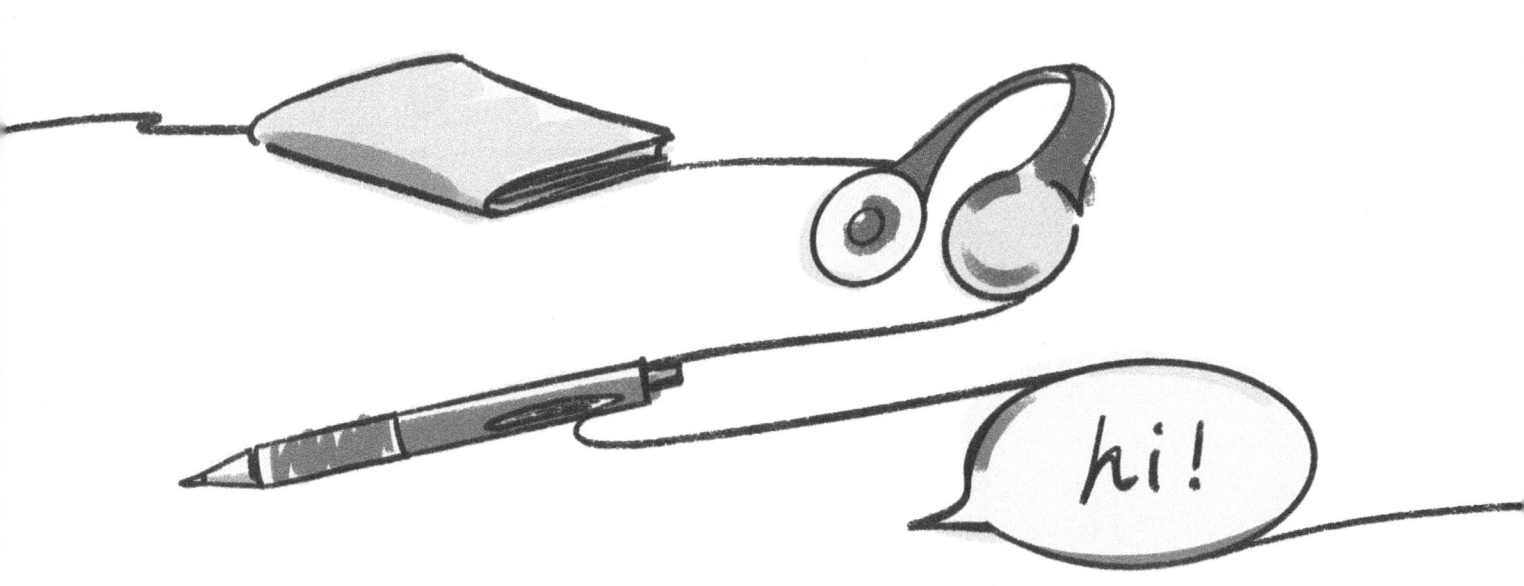

Published by Collins
An imprint of HarperCollins Publishers
Westerhill Road
Bishopbriggs
Glasgow
G64 2QT

HarperCollins Publishers
Macken House
39/40 Mayor Street Upper
Dublin 1
D01 C9W8
Ireland

First edition 2022

10 9 8 7 6 5

© HarperCollins Publishers 2022

ISBN 978-0-00-848417-0

Collins® and COBUILD® are registered trademarks of HarperCollins Publishers Limited

collins.co.uk/elt

A catalogue record for this book is available from the British Library.
All rights reserved. No part of this book may be reproduced, stored in a retrieval system, or transmitted in any form or by any means, electronic, mechanical, photocopying, recording or otherwise, without the prior permission in writing of the Publisher. This book is sold subject to the conditions that it shall not, by way of trade or otherwise, be lent, re-sold, hired out or otherwise circulated without the Publisher's prior consent in any form of binding or cover other than that in which it is published and without a similar condition including this condition being imposed on the subsequent purchaser.

Entered words that we have reason to believe constitute trademarks have been designated as such. However, neither the presence nor absence of such designation should be regarded as affecting the legal status of any trademark.

The contents of this publication are believed correct at the time of printing. Nevertheless, the Publisher can accept no responsibility for errors or omissions, changes in the detail given or for any expense or loss thereby caused.

HarperCollins does not warrant that any website mentioned in this title will be provided uninterrupted, that any website will be error-free, that defects will be corrected, or that the website or the server that makes it available are free of viruses or bugs. For full terms and conditions please refer to the site terms provided on the website.

If you would like to comment on any aspect of this book, please contact us at the given address or online.
E-mail: collins.elt@harpercollins.co.uk

Author: Peter Travis
Series editor: Celia Wigley
For the Publisher: Lisa Todd, Gillian Bowman and Kerry Ferguson
Editor: Alison Macaulay
Typesetter: Jouve, India
Illustrations: Jouve, India
Photographs: All photos from Shutterstock.com
Printer: Printed and bound by Ashford Colour Press Ltd.
Audio recorded and produced by ID Audio, London
Cover designer: Gordon McGilp
Cover illustration: Maria Herbert-Liew
Sample Answer sheets (pages 217–9): Reproduced with permission of Cambridge Assessment English © UCLES 2022

The Publishers gratefully acknowledge the permission granted to reproduce the copyright material in this book. Whilst every effort has been made to trace the copyright holders, in cases where this has been unsuccessful, or if any have inadvertently been overlooked, the Publishers would gladly receive any information enabling them to rectify any error or omission at the first opportunity.

All exam-style questions and sample answers in this title were written by the author.

About the author

Peter Travis has taught English in various European countries including Greece, Portugal and the UK and authored course books and workbooks for major ELT publishers. Peter is co-founder of Flo-Joe, the award-winning portal for Cambridge English exams and runs other popular ELT websites. Peter is also the author of Collins Practice Tests for Cambridge English: First (FCE), Collins Practice Tests for B1 Preliminary and Collins Practice Tests for B1 Preliminary for Schools, volume 1.

This book contains FSC™ certified paper and other controlled sources to ensure responsible forest management.

For more information visit: www.harpercollins.co.uk/green

Contents

How to use this book		4
About B1 Preliminary for Schools		6
How to prepare for the test		10
Test 1		19
Test 2		39
Test 3		59
Test 4		79
Test 5		99
Test 6		119
Test 7		139
Test 8		159
Mini-dictionary		179
Audio scripts		183
Sample answer sheets		217
Answer key for the Reading and Listening papers		220
Model answers for the Writing papers		228
Model answers for the Speaking papers		234
Speaking paper: Additional practice by topic		250

How to use this book

How to use this book

Who is this book for?
This book will help you to prepare for the *Cambridge Assessment English B1 Preliminary for Schools* exam. The exam is also known as the *PET for Schools* exam. The exam was updated for 2020 and this book has been written for the new exam. This book will be useful if you are preparing for the exam for the first time or taking it again. It has been designed so that you can use it to study on your own. However, you can also use it if you are preparing for the *B1 Preliminary for Schools* exam in a class.

The book contains:
- **Tips for success** – important advice to help you to do well in the exam
- **About** *B1 Preliminary for Schools* – a guide to the exam
- **How to prepare for the test** – advice to help you to succeed in each paper
- **Practice tests** – eight complete practice tests
- **Mini-dictionary** – definitions of the more difficult words from the practice tests
- **Audio scripts** – the texts of the audio for the Listening and Speaking papers
- **Sample answer sheets** – make sure you know what the answer sheets look like
- **Answer key** – the answers for the Reading and Listening papers
- **Model answers** – examples of good answers for the Writing and Speaking papers
- **Speaking paper: Additional practice by topic** – more sample questions to help you prepare for the Speaking paper
- **Audio** – all the recordings for the practice tests as well as model answers for the Speaking papers are available online at www.collins.co.uk/eltresources

Tips for success
- **Start studying early** – The more you practise, the better your English will become. Give yourself at least two months to revise and complete all the practice tests in this book. Spend at least one hour a day studying.
- **Time yourself** when you do the practice tests. This will help you to feel more confident when you do the real exam.
- **Do every part** of each practice test. Don't be afraid to make notes in the book. For example, writing down the meaning of words you don't know on the page itself will help you to remember them later on.

Using the book for self-study
If you haven't studied for the *B1 Preliminary for Schools* exam before, it is a good idea to do all the tests in this book in order. If you have a teacher or friend who can help you with your speaking and writing, that would be very useful. It is also a good idea to meet up with other students who are preparing for the exam or who want to improve their English. Having a study partner will help you to stay motivated. You can also help each other with areas of English you might find difficult.

Begin preparing for the *B1 Preliminary for Schools* exam by getting to know the different parts of each paper, what each part tests and how many marks there are for each part. Use the information in the **About B1 Preliminary for Schools** section to find out all you can. You can also download the *B1 Preliminary for Schools Handbook* from the Cambridge Assessment English website for more details. You need to know how to prepare for each of the papers in the best way possible. The **How to prepare for the test** section in this book will be useful. Try to follow the advice as it will help you to develop the skills you need.

In the practice tests in this book, you will see certain words highlighted in grey. These are the more difficult words and you can find definitions of these in the *Mini-dictionary* at the back of the book. The definitions are from *Collins COBUILD* dictionaries. It is a good idea to download the *Cambridge B1 Preliminary Vocabulary List* from the Cambridge Assessment English website. This is a list of words that you should understand at B1 level. Search 'B1 Preliminary Vocabulary List 2020' online. Look through the list and make a note of the words you don't know. Then look up their meaning in a dictionary. Knowing these words will help you to do better in the exam. You could use the Collins online dictionary: www.collinsdictionary.com

Preparing for the Writing and Speaking papers
When you are ready to try the practice tests, make sure you do the tasks in the Writing papers as well as the Speaking papers. You can only improve your skills by practising a lot. Practise writing to a time limit. If you find this difficult at first, start by writing a very good answer of the correct length without worrying about time. Then try to complete the tasks faster until you can write a good answer within the time limit. Learn to estimate the number of words you have written without counting them. Study the model answers at the back of the book. This will give you a clear idea of the standard your answers need to be. Don't try to memorise emails, articles or stories for the Writing paper or answers to the questions in the Speaking paper. If you work your way through the book, you should develop the skills and language you need to give good answers in the real exam.

The Speaking paper in this book has accompanying audio so that you can practise answering the examiner's questions. You will be Candidate B, so if you hear the examiner ask Candidate B a question, this means you should answer by pausing the audio on your computer and answering the question. In Parts 3 and 4 of the Speaking paper, you are expected to have a conversation with Candidate A. Again, you will be Candidate B and will respond to Candidate A's statements or questions. This experience will not be 100% authentic as Candidate A cannot respond to your statements or questions. However, this book and the audio have been designed to give you an excellent opportunity to practise answering questions through the eight practice tests. Once you have finished the Speaking paper, you can listen to the model answers for Candidate B that have been provided for you. Another option is that you record your answers and then compare these with the model answers.

Please note that there are two versions of the Speaking Test audio:
- The first version contains the pauses for you to practise answering the questions in the Speaking tests. This is when you have to answer the questions for Candidate B. The scripts for this audio can be found from page 186 onwards in your book. For example, you will see on page 186 that Test 1 Speaking audio track is labelled 'Track 05'. Look for Track 05 when you search for the audio online.
- The second version of the audio contains the model answers for the Speaking tests. These are for you to listen to, to see how a good student might answer the questions in the Speaking test. The scripts for this audio can be found from page 234 onwards in your book. You will see that these audio files are labelled with an 'a' at the end of the audio track number, for example, Track 05a. Look for Track 05a when you search for the audio online.

At the back of the book you will find more sample questions for the Speaking paper. These provide another opportunity to practise answering questions that an examiner might ask you. There are 24 topics and all the questions have been recorded. Try answering these questions as fully as possible. Don't just give a 'yes/no' answer, but try to give a reason or an example in your answer.

Finally, read as much as possible in English; this is the best way to learn new vocabulary and improve your English.

About B1 Preliminary for Schools

About B1 Preliminary for Schools

The *Cambridge B1 Preliminary for Schools* test is an intermediate-level English exam delivered by Cambridge Assessment English. It is for school students who need to show that they can deal with everyday English at an intermediate level. In other words, you have to be able to:
- read simple textbooks and articles in English.
- write emails and articles on everyday subjects.
- understand factual information.
- show awareness of opinions and mood in spoken and written English.

The exam is one of several offered by Cambridge Assessment English at different levels. The table below shows how *B1 Preliminary for Schools* fits into the Cambridge English Qualifications. The level of this exam is described as being at B1 on the Common European Framework of Reference (CEFR).

	CEFR	Cambridge English Scale	Cambridge qualification
Proficient user	C2	200–230	C2 Proficiency
	C1	180–199	C1 Advanced
Independent user	B2	160–179	B2 First for Schools
	B1	140–159	B1 Preliminary for Schools
Basic user	A2	120–139	A2 Key for Schools / A2 Flyers
	A1	100–119	A1 Movers
	Pre A1	80–99	Pre A1 Starters

The *B1 Preliminary for Schools* qualification is for school students studying general English. Cambridge Assessment English also offers a *B1 Preliminary* qualification. These two qualifications follow exactly the same format, the level of the exams is the same and the candidates are tested in the same skills. However, the content of the exams is a bit different. The 'for Schools' version is specifically designed to suit the interests and experiences of school-age candidates. If you are an adult learner, it would be better for you to take the *B1 Preliminary* qualification and use the *Collins Practice Tests for B1 Preliminary* to prepare for the exam.

There are four papers in *B1 Preliminary for Schools* (each is worth 25% of the total mark):
- Paper 1: Reading (45 minutes)
- Paper 2: Writing (45 minutes)
- Paper 3: Listening (approximately 30 minutes)
- Paper 4: Speaking (12–17 minutes)

Timetabling
You usually take the Reading, Writing and Listening papers on the same day. The Speaking test may take place on a different day and it may be before or after the other papers. If you are studying on your own, you should contact your exam centre for dates. The exam is paper based. You can also take the exam on a computer in some countries. For more information, see: https://www.cambridge-exams.ch/exams/CB_exams.php

Paper 1 Reading (45 minutes)

What is it?
The Reading paper tests how well you can understand general English texts. It includes different types of texts about lots of different subjects.

Skills needed
In order to do well in the Reading paper, you must be able to:
- read real-world texts such as emails, notices and articles and understand the main ideas; understand details about the writer's opinion and their reason for writing; and scan texts of different lengths to find a particular piece of information.
- answer questions within the given time.

About B1 Preliminary for Schools

The Reading paper has six parts:

Part 1 has five short real-world texts, for example, notices, messages, emails and signs, and five multiple-choice questions with three options, A, B or C. You have to read each text and choose the correct answer. (Total marks: 5)

Part 2 has five short descriptions of people and eight short texts. You have to match each of the descriptions with the correct text. (Total marks: 5)

Part 3 has a longer text and five multiple-choice questions with three options, A, B or C. You have to understand details about the text as well as the writer's attitude or opinion on a particular issue and their purpose for writing. (Total marks: 5)

Part 4 has a longer text with five sentences removed. Following the text are eight sentences, which include the five that have been removed. You have to find the missing sentences. (Total marks: 5)

Part 5 has a shorter text with six gaps followed by six multiple-choice questions. You have to fill the gaps by choosing the correct word from four options, A, B, C or D. (Total marks: 6)

Part 6 has a short text with six gaps. You have to fill the gaps by deciding what the missing word is. (Total marks: 6)

Paper 2 Writing (45 minutes)

What is it?
The Writing paper tests how well you can write an answer to a question using a good range of vocabulary and grammatical structures.

Skills needed
In order to do well in the Writing paper, you must be able to:
- understand the instructions and identify the key points that you have to include in your answer.
- use a good range of B1-level vocabulary and grammatical structures.
- write emails, articles and/or stories.
- write a well-organised text that is easy for the reader to follow.
- rephrase information given in the instructions.
- write your answers within the word limits given in the instructions.
- write your answers within the given time.

The Writing paper has two parts.

Part 1 tests how well you can communicate information clearly. You will need to write a short email (100 words). The instructions ask you to include four important points in your message. (Total marks: 20)

Part 2 tests how well you can communicate, organise your ideas and use a range of language. This part gives you a choice of two different tasks: an article or a story. Your answer must be about 100 words. For the article, you read an announcement from a magazine or website. For the story, you are given a sentence which you have to use at the beginning of your answer. (Total marks: 20)

In each part, marks are awarded in the following ways:
- five marks if you include all the necessary information.
- five marks if you express your message clearly.
- five marks if you organise your message so a reader can follow it easily.
- five marks if you use a good range of grammatical structures and vocabulary.

About B1 Preliminary for Schools

Paper 3 Listening (about 30 minutes)

What is it?
The Listening paper tests how well you can understand conversations, talks and recorded messages.

Skills needed
In order to do well in the Listening paper, you must be able to:
- understand main ideas and details.
- understand a speaker's opinion and attitude.
- answer questions within the given time.

The Listening paper has four parts.

Part 1 has seven short extracts from monologues (= a speech by one person) or dialogues (= speech by two people) such as conversations, recorded messages or radio programmes, and seven questions. For each question, you have to listen and choose the correct answer from three options, A, B or C. The options are pictures. (Total marks: 7)

Part 2 has six dialogues and six questions. You have to listen and choose the correct answer to a question from three options, A, B or C. (Total marks: 6)

Part 3 has a longer monologue and six questions. You have to listen and complete six gaps in a text. (Total marks: 6)

Part 4 has an interview and six questions. You have to listen and choose the correct answer from three options, A, B or C. (Total marks: 6)

Paper 4 Speaking (12–17 minutes)

What is it?
The Speaking paper tests your ability to use spoken English. You take the Speaking test with another candidate (your partner) or sometimes in a group of three. You can't take it alone. There are two examiners: one asks you and your partner(s) questions, the other (the assessor) has the marksheets. They both listen carefully and give you marks. If you are taking the exam in a pair, it lasts about 12 minutes; if you are taking it in a group of three, it lasts about 17 minutes.

You can only take the exam in a group of three if there is an uneven number of candidates in the session; the group of three is always the last to be examined in the session. You can't choose to take the exam in a group of three and you can't take the exam on your own.

Depending where you are taking the exam, you may already know the person you are taking the exam with, or you may meet them for the first time when you go into the exam. It doesn't make any difference to how well you do in the exam. The examiners listen to each of you very carefully.

Skills needed
In order to do well in the Speaking paper, you must be able to:
- talk about everyday subjects and express your opinions.
- ask and answer questions during a conversation.
- speak clearly for about a minute.
- speak using a good range of B1-level vocabulary and grammatical structures.

The Speaking paper has four parts.

In **Part 1** the examiner asks you questions about your personal details, daily routine, past experiences, future plans, etc. (Time: 2 minutes)

In **Part 2** the examiner asks each candidate to talk in turn. He/She will give you a photo and ask you to describe it. You have to talk for about a minute. The examiner then gives your partner a different photo. Your partner also has to talk for about a minute. (Time: 3 minutes)

About B1 Preliminary for Schools

In **Part 3** the examiner describes a situation and gives you and your partner instructions to talk about it. He/She also gives you a picture showing you the situation and different things to discuss. You have to make suggestions to your partner and reply to his/her suggestions, talk about different possibilities and agree about the situation. (Time: 4 minutes)

In **Part 4** the examiner asks you and your partner questions related to the theme in Part 3. You have to talk to the examiner and each other and discuss the questions. (Time: 3 minutes)

Marks and results

After the exam, all candidates receive a Statement of Results. Candidates whose performance ranges between CEFR Levels A2 and B2 (Cambridge English Scale scores of 140–170) also receive a certificate.

The Statement of Results shows the candidate's:

- score on the Cambridge English Scale for their performance in each of the four language skills (reading, writing, listening and speaking).
- score on the Cambridge English Scale for their overall performance in the exam. This overall score is the average of their scores for the four skills.
- grade – this is based on the candidate's overall score.
- level on the CEFR – this is also based on the overall score.

The certificate shows the candidate's:

- score on the Cambridge English Scale for each of the four skills.
- overall score on the Cambridge English Scale.
- grade.
- level on the CEFR.
- level on the UK National Qualifications Framework (NQF).

For *B1 Preliminary for Schools*, the following scores will be used to report results:

Cambridge English Scale Score	Grade	CEFR level
160–170	A	B2
153–159	B	B1
140–152	C	B1
120–139	Level A2	A2

Grade A: Cambridge English Scale scores of 160–170

Candidates sometimes show ability beyond Level B1. If a candidate achieves a Grade A in their exam, they will receive the *Preliminary English Test for Schools* certificate stating that they demonstrated ability at Level B2.

Grades B and C: Cambridge English Scale scores of 140–159

If a candidate achieves a Grade B or Grade C in their exam, they will receive the *Preliminary English Test for Schools* certificate at Level B1.

CEFR Level A2: Cambridge English Scale scores of 120–139

If a candidate's performance is below Level B1, but falls within Level A2, they will receive a *Cambridge English* certificate stating that they demonstrated ability at Level A2.

Scores between 102 and 119 are also reported on your Statement of Results, but you will not receive the *Preliminary English Test for Schools* certificate.

For more information on how the exam is marked, go to: http://www.cambridgeenglish.org

Working through the practice tests in this book will improve your exam skills, help you with timing for the exam, give you confidence and help you get a better result in the exam.

Good luck!

How to prepare for the test

This section of the book looks at each part of the test in detail. It describes common mistakes that students make, and suggests what you can do to improve your chances of doing well in that part.

B1 Preliminary for Schools is a test of your general level of English. This means that you should continue to work on your English as you prepare for the test. Practice tests will help you understand the types of question you have to answer and how long you can spend on them, but you should also do activities which will improve the four skills of reading, writing, listening and speaking, as well as improving your knowledge of grammar and vocabulary.

Reading Part 1

In this part of the test, you read five short texts (1–5): notices, signs, pieces of packaging information, notes, emails, or phone texts. There are three sentences (A–C) about each text, and you have to choose the one that matches its meaning. Here is a short example:

> Are you going on the school trip to London on 19th May? Please pay a deposit of £10 before Friday.

A The trip costs £10.

B Students must pay part of the money for the trip by Friday.

C The students get back on Friday.

This part tests your understanding of different kinds of short texts. Read the text before you read the three sentences A–C. If the text is an email or phone text, think about who is writing it, who they are writing to, and what the relationship is between them. If the text is a sign or notice, think about where it is, and who it is for. Be careful: sentences often mix up the names of the people in an email or phone text, so a sentence might look right, but the wrong person says or does something, so the sentence is the wrong answer. Also, be careful if a sentence uses a lot of words from the text; the words might be the same, but they might be used to say something different. You have to find the sentence that has the same meaning as the text, but perhaps using different words.

In the example above, B is the correct answer. It explains the reason for the message, but it uses different words from the text.

COMMON MISTAKES: Choosing an answer because it has the same words as the text. / Choosing an answer which is nearly but not completely correct.

YOU SHOULD: Look out for words in the text and the questions that have a similar meaning as the correct answer will often contain a synonym. / Read signs and notices in English and short messages on social media. Do an IMAGE SEARCH with an internet search engine using the words 'school notices' or 'packaging information' and read the results.

Reading Part 2

In this part of the test, you have five short descriptions of different people (6–10) and eight short texts (A–H), often describing things people can do or buy. You have to match the person with the correct text. Here is a short example:

How to prepare for the test

These teenagers want to go somewhere this Saturday.

6

Matt is thirteen and is keen on watching sport. He is busy on Saturday morning, but would like to find something to do in the afternoon. He doesn't have much money.

G

We're looking for young people from the ages of twelve to fifteen to join our football competition. We start on Saturday at 1.00 in the afternoon. Nothing to pay, but please wear suitable clothing.

H

Come to the city centre this Saturday and see the big match in the main square on our big screen. Entry is free, and the game starts at 2.00 p.m., so come early to get your seat.

This part tests to see if you can find the correct information quickly in a text and then understand the detail.

First, read the texts for general understanding. Then read the first question (6) and underline the key words. Next, read each text (G, H) quickly again to find which part might answer the question. Circle the key sentences. Read these sentences again carefully, and choose the one that matches the question. Be careful: a text might use the same words as the question, but not give the right answer. You must find the text that matches the question using different words.

In the example above, G has the words *Saturday at 1.00 in the afternoon; nothing to pay*, and *ages of twelve to fifteen*, but this is not the correct answer. Matt likes *watching sport*, but G describes an event where you can play football. In H, the description explains that you can *see the big match*, another way of saying *watch*. H states *Entry is free* and the event happens on *Saturday* at *2.00 p.m*. So, H is the correct answer.

COMMON MISTAKES: Choosing a text because it uses the same words as the question. / Choosing a text when only part of the text is correct.

YOU SHOULD: Look out for synonyms, which will quite often help you match the correct answers.

Reading Part 3

In this part of the test, you read one longer text in the style of a magazine or newspaper article, a leaflet or a text describing facts. Then you must answer five multiple-choice questions (A–D). Here is a short example:

Is the printed book dead?
Michelle Adams tells us what she thinks.

A few years ago, I read an article that said printed books would no longer be something we used. Now, when I see so many people reading books on the train to work, I often wonder if the author has changed his mind. He was so sure of his view that I imagine he still feels confident, but I have a different opinion.

11 Michelle explains that

   A she no longer reads articles by the author.

   B she agrees with the author of the article.

   C she thinks the author has changed his mind.

   D printed books still seem to be popular.

This part tests your understanding of the writer's opinion, and also your understanding of details.

11

How to prepare for the test

First, read the text very quickly for general understanding. Then read it again more slowly to understand it in detail. Next, read the first question or sentence and find the part of the text that answers or completes it. The questions follow the order of the text, so the answer for the first question is usually in the first paragraph. Sometimes two questions are answered in the same paragraph. Read the questions carefully, underline the key words in the questions, and check options A–D against the text. Choose the option with the same meaning as the text. Be careful, because the options might use words from the text but mean something different.

In the question above, A contains the words *no longer* and these words appear in the text but with a different meaning. B is wrong because in the final sentence she writes *I have a different opinion*. C contains the words *has changed his mind*, but Michelle is just wondering if this has happened. The correct answer is D as Michelle sees *so many people reading books on the train*, which means she thinks *they still seem popular*.

COMMON MISTAKES: Reading the questions before the text. You need to have an understanding of the whole text before trying to answer questions on it. / Choosing an answer because it uses the same words as the text.

YOU SHOULD: Read as much English as you can to improve your general reading skills. / Do test practice nearer the time of your test, but don't stop developing your general reading skills.

Reading Part 4
In this part of the test, you read one long text in the style of an article. There will be five spaces (16–20) in the article where sentences are missing and eight sentences (A–H). You have to complete the text by adding the correct sentences. Here is a short example:

The Problem with Litter

Everybody knows how important it is not to drop litter. It makes the area look untidy and can be dangerous for wildlife. **(16)** .... How can we deal with this problem?

A In many countries these people are fined.

B However, lots of people still throw away their rubbish without thinking.

This part tests your understanding of the writer's opinion and of how a text is structured.

First, read the text very quickly for general understanding. Then work on each gap one at a time. Find a sentence that fits the gap in terms of meaning, but which is also grammatical. Pay attention to linking words like *yet* or *in addition*, and to words like *this*, *that* and *they* that may help you choose the correct sentence.

In the question above, A contains the words *these people*, but the author hasn't mentioned any people, so the sentence is incorrect. The correct answer is B. *However* shows there is a contrast with the previous sentence, and the content of the sentence fits the subject of the paragraph.

COMMON MISTAKES: Choosing a sentence that doesn't fit grammatically. / Choosing a sentence that has the wrong meaning.

YOU SHOULD: Read the text first and then the sentences. Make a note of sentences that seem to fit the subject. / Pay attention to the words near the beginning of the sentences as these may be linking words that might help you choose.

Reading Part 5
In this part of the test, you must fill in six gaps (21–26) in a text that gives information on a topic. You are given four words to choose from for each gap and you must choose the right one.
Here is a short example:

George Best

George Best was a famous Irish footballer who **(21)** .... for Manchester United in the 1960s and 1970s.

---

21   **A** joined   **B** presented   **C** made   **D** played

How to prepare for the test

This part mainly tests your vocabulary. First, read the text to understand its general meaning. Then read the sentence with the gap again carefully and choose the correct word to complete it. In the example above, the correct answer is D. If you are not sure, read the sentence with each of the words A–D. This might help you choose the correct one. Then read the text again to check your answers.

COMMON MISTAKE: Trying to fill in the gaps without reading the whole text first.

YOU SHOULD: Read the text for general understanding before you fill in the gaps. Then read the text again with your answers for a final check. / Check for words like prepositions or articles before or after the gap. In the question above, *for* helps us choose the correct answer.

Reading Part 6

In this part of the test, you have to fill in six gaps (27–32) in a text with one word in each gap. The text is often in the style of an email or message that you might write to a friend or someone you know. Here is a short example:

> I'm with my family **(27)** .... holiday in Greece and we're having a fantastic time.

This part mainly tests your grammar. First, read the text for general understanding. Then try to think of words to fill in the gaps. The missing words are often small words, like pronouns, prepositions, articles and auxiliary verbs. Do the easy gaps first and then try your best with the harder ones. Remember to use only one word and spell it correctly.

In the example above, the correct answer is *on*. The following word, *holiday*, is part of the set expression *on holiday*.

COMMON MISTAKE: Trying to fill in the gaps without reading the whole text first.

YOU SHOULD: Read the whole text first to get an understanding of the subject. / Identify what kind of word is missing. Check the words around each gap as these will often help. If the gap follows a verb, it might be a preposition. If there is a comma before the gap, the missing word might be a relative pronoun like *who* or *which*.

Writing Part 1

In this part of the test, you have to reply to an email from a friend or someone you know. The situation and the four points you must include are given to you. Here is an example:

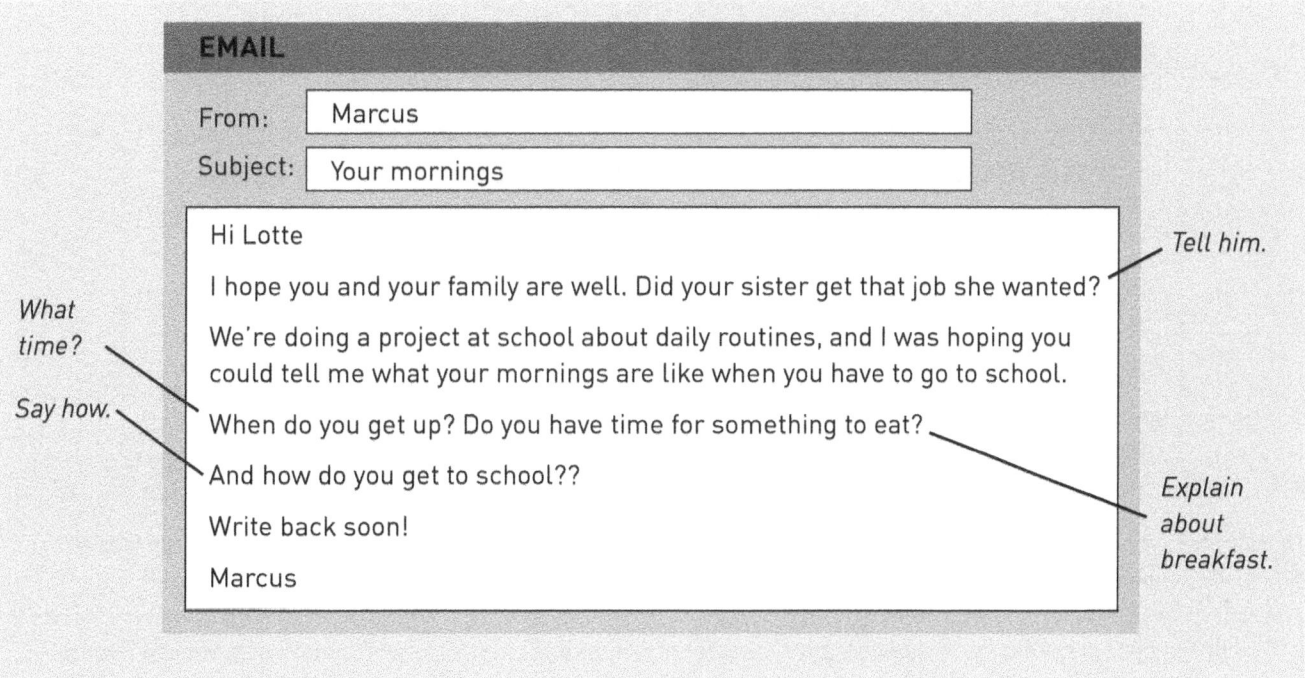

Write **about 100 words**.

In this part, you have to show that you can write a short clear message. Think carefully about the kind of language you will need, e.g. do you have to offer something to someone (e.g. *Would you like* a cup of tea?), make a suggestion (e.g. *Why don't we* go to the cinema?) or ask someone for their opinion (e.g. *What do you*

How to prepare for the test

think?)? You have to use the right kind of language and include all four points in your answer. Here is a good answer to the question above:

> Hi Marcus,
>
> It's good to hear from you! Yes, my sister got the job and she starts next week.
>
> I'm very happy to help you with your project. I'm quite busy in the morning. I have to get up early, about 6.30. I like to have something to eat before I leave, but it's only something simple like a bowl of cereal and a drink, a cup of tea or something like that. Then I catch the bus to school. Luckily, it stops near my house and doesn't take long.
>
> I hope this helps. Good luck with your project!
>
> Write back soon.
>
> Lotte

This is a good answer because:
- it uses the right kind of language when writing to a friend (*It's good to hear from you! ... Good luck with your project! ... Write back soon.*)
- it answers all four points.
- it is about 100 words long.

COMMON MISTAKE: Not including one of the points in your answer.

YOU SHOULD: When you prepare for your test, revise language for talking about yourself and other people, asking for and giving information, giving advice, agreeing and disagreeing, etc.

Writing Part 2

In this part of the test, you have a choice. You can write an article on a topic you are given or a short story. Your answer should be about 100 words long.

Question 2: Article

Here is an example article question:

> You see this notice in an English-language magazine.
>
> **CAN YOU REMEMBER A FAVOURITE PRESENT SOMEONE GAVE YOU WHEN YOU WERE YOUNGER?**
>
> What was the present?
>
> Why were you given it?
>
> **Write an article answering these questions and we will put it in our magazine.**

In this part, you have to show that you can write a short article using suitable vocabulary and grammatical structures. Here is a good answer to the question above:

> *One of the best presents I received was a bicycle that my mum and dad got for me when I was about 11 years old. I was really surprised when they gave it to me. I had just finished junior school and I was looking forward to going to high school. My parents decided it would be good exercise if I cycled to school and so they bought me the bike the week before school started. Cycling to school on my first day helped me feel less nervous about everything, and I soon became a very keen cyclist.*

How to prepare for the test

This is a good answer because:
- it talks about both of the points in the question and is about 100 words long.
- it uses a range of tenses (e.g. *had finished, was looking forward to, helped*).
- it uses words that create good sentence structures (e.g. *that, when, and, if, so*).
- it uses different words to talk about the same topic (*bike, bicycle, cycled, cycling, cyclist*).

COMMON MISTAKES: Only writing about one of the points. / Making mistakes with the tenses.

YOU SHOULD: Practise writing sentences with different linking words and tenses.

Question 3: Short story

Here is an example short story question:

> Your English teacher has asked you to write a story.
>
> Your story must begin with this sentence:
>
> *When I got home, I noticed I didn't have my key.*

In this part, you have to show that you can write a short story beginning with a sentence that is included in the question. As this is a story about the past, it is a good idea to make sure you can use past tenses correctly. You should also practise using words like *when, next, after* that show the passing of time. Here is a good answer to the question above:

> *When I got home, I noticed I didn't have my key. It was 3.30 and my mum and dad worked in town, so I couldn't get in until they got home at about 6.00. I didn't want to wait that long, so I walked to the back of the house to see if a window was open. First, I climbed on my dad's shed and then reached up to my bedroom window to see if I could open it. All of a sudden, as I was pushing the glass, my mum appeared at the window! She had decided to come home early and was tidying my room.*

This is a good answer because:
- it uses the opening sentence to tell the story.
- it uses linking words to join ideas (*and, so*).
- it uses words that show when things happened (*First, then, All of a sudden*).
- It uses correct past tenses (e.g. *walked, started, had decided, was tidying*).

COMMON MISTAKES: Writing without clear linking words. / Making mistakes with the tenses.

YOU SHOULD: Prepare for the test by writing sentences using past tenses to tell a story.

Listening Part 1

In this part of the test, there are seven multiple-choice questions. For each question, you see three pictures, A–C. You will hear two people or sometimes just one person talking in an everyday situation and you have to choose the correct picture. Here is an example:

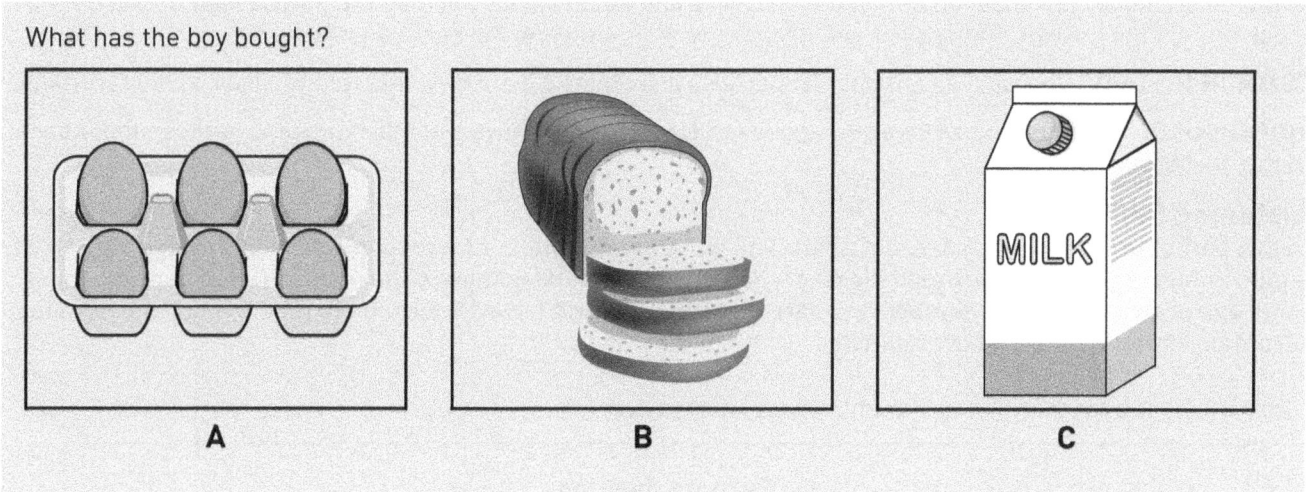

How to prepare for the test

This is the recording for the example above:

Mother:	Did you remember to get the shopping, Michael? I need to make the dinner.
Boy:	Well, I've bought the eggs that you asked for. Here you are, Mum.
Mother:	What about the loaf of bread? Did you get that?
Boy:	I didn't have enough money for that. If you give me some more, I'll go back and get it, and the milk as well.

You will hear the recording twice. Be careful: the people might talk about something you see in a picture, but this might not answer the question. The first time you hear the recording, listen for the answer. Check your answer when you hear the recording a second time.

In the recording for the question above, you hear all the items of food in the pictures, but only A answers the question *What has the boy bought?*

COMMON MISTAKE: Choosing a picture just because you hear words that describe it in the recording.

YOU SHOULD: Look at the pictures carefully and choose the one that answers the question.

Listening Part 2
In this part of the test, there are six multiple-choice questions. You will hear two people talking in an everyday situation and you must choose the correct answer A–C. Here is an example:

You will hear a brother and sister talking about a website. The boy says that

- **A** it is easy to use.
- **B** it is very slow.
- **C** it has some great videos on it.

This is the recording for the example above:

Girl:	That looks like an interesting website. What is it?
Boy:	It's that website I was telling you about. My friend at school is building it and it's nearly finished now.
Girl:	He's the one who makes videos, isn't he?
Boy:	Yes, that's what he wants to do, but there aren't any on here yet. The site's well designed, but it takes ages to go from one page to the next.
Girl:	It looks nice, though. I think that's really important too.
Boy:	Yes, but it's not very easy to use. The links aren't very clear.

You will hear the recording twice. Be careful: you might hear a word or words that appear in one of the choices, but this might not answer the question. The first time you hear the recording, listen for the answer. Check your answer when you hear the recording a second time.

In the recording for the question above, the speakers talk about videos and use the phrase *easy to use*, but these are not the answer. The answer is C because *very slow* means the same as *it takes ages*.

COMMON MISTAKE: Choosing an answer just because it contains a word or words that you hear in the recording.

YOU SHOULD: Read the choices carefully and listen for words that have a similar meaning to those that appear in the question.

Listening Part 3
In this part of the test, there is a set of notes with six gaps. You will hear a person giving information as part of a talk, on the radio or as a recorded message. You must listen and complete the notes. In each gap, you must write **one** or **two words** or a **number** or a **date** or a **time**. You will have 20 seconds to read the notes before the recording starts. Here is a short example:

You will hear a teacher telling students about parents evening.

Parents Evening

Get to school at: (14) ....

How to prepare for the test

This is the recording for the example above:

> Teacher: *OK, as you know it's parents evening next Thursday. We'll contact parents to give them further information. They should arrive at 7.00 p.m. and check the noticeboard.*

This part tests if you can listen for detailed information. You will hear the recording twice. Before you listen the first time, quickly read the notes so you have an idea of the subject. Also try to guess what kind of information is needed in each gap (a time, a date, etc.). The information in the recording is in the same order as the notes. You will hear the missing words and numbers in the recording. If the speaker spells the word, you must spell it correctly or you won't get a mark. Check your answers when you hear the recording a second time.

The correct answer in the example above is *7.00 p.m.* Note that in the notes the words used are *Get to school at* but in the recording the speaker says *arrive at 7.00 p.m.* Listen for synonyms when doing practice tests.

COMMON MISTAKE: Waiting for the recording to start without reading the notes or trying to guess what will go in the gaps.

YOU SHOULD: Practise listening to and writing numbers, times and dates; listen to words being spelled out and practise writing them correctly.

Listening Part 4

In this part of the test, there are six multiple-choice questions. For each question, there are three options, A–C. You will hear an interview and you must choose the correct option. You will have 45 seconds to read the questions before the recording starts. Here is an example:

> You will hear an interview with a woman called Issy Riseborough, who helps students find jobs.
>
> **20** What was the reason Issy decided to do this job?
>
>   **A** The pay was good.
>
>   **B** Her friend worked there.
>
>   **C** She wanted to support students.

This is the recording for the example above:

> Issy: *I didn't know what I wanted to do when I finished my university degree, but before I left I saw an advert for the job on the noticeboard and applied. The pay wasn't great, but my friends said I'd be perfect for the job, and I wanted to help students choose the right career.*

This part tests if you can listen for detailed information. You will hear the recording twice. The questions are in the same order as the recording. Before you listen the first time, read the questions quickly as this will help you to understand what the interview is about. Be careful: don't choose an option just because it uses the same words as the recording. The correct option might use different words. Check your answers when you hear the recording a second time.

The correct answer here is C. You don't hear the word *support*, but you hear *help*, which is another way of saying this. The speaker talks about the pay, but says that it *wasn't great*, so A is wrong. She mentions her friends, but doesn't say that any of them work there, so B is wrong too.

COMMON MISTAKE: Choosing an option just because you read the same words as you hear.

YOU SHOULD: Read the options carefully, listen to the recording, and try to find the answer that has the same meaning. / Listen to English radio, podcasts, TV programmes or films to help you with your listening skills.

Speaking Part 1

You can find examples of good answers for all sections of the speaking test in the **Model answers for Speaking** section at the back of the book.

You will have your speaking test with another student, or sometimes with two other students. In this part of the test, you have to answer questions that the examiner asks you. The examiner will ask you your name, your age and where you are from or where you live. Then he/she will ask you a question about an everyday topic. Here is an example:

How to prepare for the test

Examiner: *Do you do any sport?*

A good answer would be:

Student: *Yes, I play football every Saturday for my school. I enjoy keeping fit and being part of a team makes it more fun.*

A good answer often has two sentences. The second sentence explains or adds details about the information in the first one.

COMMON MISTAKE: Giving a one-word or short one-sentence answer.

YOU SHOULD: Give a two-sentence answer.

Speaking Part 2
In this part of the test, you talk about a photograph on your own for about one minute. You must describe what you can see in the photo. This will give you the chance to show you have the necessary vocabulary to describe the scene and also the ability to organise your talk using signposting expressions such as *on the left*, *in the middle*.

COMMON MISTAKE: Not talking for long enough.

YOU SHOULD: Try to organise your talk. Start with a summary statement: *This photo shows ....* Then describe what you can see: *On the left there's ...* Look for opportunities to give detail. For example, *The woman is wearing ...*

Speaking Part 3
In this part of the test, you have to talk about some pictures with the other student for about three minutes. The examiner will give you both instructions and you must discuss the task with your partner. The pictures allow you to compare things, like different sports or different ways of travelling. You should look at the other student and have a real conversation with them. Listen to what they say, ask for their opinion, and say if you agree or disagree with them, giving reasons for your answers, e.g. *I don't like travelling by bus because ...*

COMMON MISTAKES: Looking only at the examiner and not listening to the other student. / Giving short answers that you don't explain.

YOU SHOULD: Have a real conversation with the other student, smile and show an interest in what they are saying. Before the test, practise language for giving your opinion, for asking for someone's opinion, and for giving reasons.

Speaking Part 4
In this part of the test, the examiner will ask you and your partner questions about the topic you discussed in Part 3. The questions will be about your likes and dislikes, your habits and opinions. This section will last about three minutes. Try to give full answers to the examiner's questions. Remember to give examples to express your opinion or to give more detail.

COMMON MISTAKE: Giving short answers to the examiner's question.

YOU SHOULD: Try to relax and simply give your opinion.

On the day of the test

COMMON MISTAKES:
- Trying to revise at the last minute.
- Not answering all the questions in the test.
- Panicking when you don't understand something.

YOU SHOULD:
- leave plenty of time to get to your test centre early.
- answer every question in the test, even if you have to guess.
- not worry about a difficult question that you couldn't answer, and continue with the next question.
- read all the instructions, questions and options carefully before answering the questions.
- try to guess what the answers will be before you read or listen to something.
- pay attention to the clock and leave some time to check your answers.

Test 1

Test 1 READING

Test 1 READING

Part 1

Questions 1–5

For each question, choose the correct answer.

1.
To: Alison
From: Cristine

Hi Alison

I've caught a cold and don't feel well at all. Can you apologise to your mum for me and tell her as soon as possible that I can't come for dinner?

Cristine

A Alison should apologise to her mum.

B Alison isn't feeling hungry.

C Cristine should speak to her mum quickly.

2.
IT Centre
We will close earlier today at 4.30 to carry out work on the computers.
We will open as usual tomorrow.

A The computers in the IT Centre aren't working.

B The IT Centre usually closes at 4.30.

C Pupils can use the IT Centre tomorrow.

3.

Mum
I left my key at home this morning. Will you be in when I get back from school?
Chris

A Chris wants to know if his mum will be home later.

B Chris wants a lift back from school.

C Chris has lost his door key.

4

> Customers should not bring their own food into the cinema. Refreshments are available opposite the ticket office.

A Food is not allowed in the cinema.

B You can only eat food bought at the cinema.

C Refreshments can be bought at the ticket office.

5

To: John
From: Mark

Hi John

Before you buy that mobile phone you were telling me about, have a look on the school noticeboard. Someone is selling a second-hand one that looks good and isn't as expensive.

Mark

A There's a cheaper phone for sale on the noticeboard.

B John can sell his phone on the school noticeboard.

C The school is selling second-hand mobile phones.

Test 1 READING

Part 2

Questions 6–10

For each question, choose the correct answer.

The young people below all want to buy a present for someone.
On the opposite page there are descriptions of eight places to buy items.
Decide which place would be the most suitable for the people below.

6  Lotte is fourteen and wants to get a present for her grandmother. She wants to buy her something she can wear, and knows she needs new clothes for the summer.

7  Rob is twelve and is looking for a birthday present for his best friend. His friend loves reading science fiction novels, especially stories based on well-known films.

8  Barbara is ten and it's her mum and dad's wedding anniversary in three weeks. She would like to get something she can help to design, and that her parents can share.

9  Stuart is fifteen years old and wants to buy himself a jacket using the money he received for his birthday. He wants something he can wear to watch football when it is raining.

10  Ruth, who is twelve, would like to buy her dance teacher a present to say thank you for her help. Her teacher likes plants and flowers and lives in a flat with a balcony.

22

Present Ideas

A Mayfield Outdoor Stores

We are well known for providing top-quality clothing for people who like spending time outdoors, in any weather. We have a sale this weekend and are offering 50% discount on all our men's and women's jackets – guaranteed to keep you warm and dry on the coldest and wettest of days.

B Street Market

Our popular street market takes place next month, and we're looking for anyone who has any books they would like to give away for our charity stall. We are interested in all different kinds, from science fiction to romance. Sadly, we can't pay you for your donation, but all the money we make will go to a charity.

C St Matthew's Centre

Come along to the St Matthew's Centre this Saturday and see what's on offer. We have a small selection of stalls selling fruit and vegetables. You can also pick up some plants for the garden or buy our new book by a local author on growing flowers in small spaces. Our staff are always available to offer advice.

D Bliss Boutique

Getting old doesn't mean you can't be stylish. In fact, we'll help you look your very best this holiday season. We have a new range of items for the older woman and a new selection for the warmer weather. We also have a range of gift cards available for those who want a present for a friend or relative.

E Mattock Garden Centre

With spring just around the corner, now is the time to start getting ready for the growing season. We have all you need for the garden, including a variety of fruit bushes and young trees to plant out now the cold weather has passed.

F Beech's Books

Come along to Beech's Books this weekend for the widest selection of titles. From bestsellers to historical novels, we cover everything from A–Z, and this Saturday we are promoting the latest book from Andy Harrison, *Countdown*, an exciting adventure set in 2091 and based on the popular movie *Alone in Space*.

G Homefront

Having trouble thinking of what to buy for a friend or relation? Now's your chance to get the perfect present for someone you love. Select one of our beautifully designed vases, pots, bowls or dishes and our artists will add your own personal message to the item you have chosen. Please allow 7 days for the item to be completed.

H CBT Online Tech

To all you science fiction fans out there, don't miss our sale this weekend. All our posters will be at half price. As well as being able to pick up a copy of that special film, you can see our wide range of comics while you're here, featuring all your favourite superheroes.

Part 3

Questions 11–15

For each question, choose the correct answer.

The New School
Tara Knowles tells us about starting a new school in Spain

Three years ago, my father was offered a wonderful job in Spain. My family spent hours discussing whether we should move out to Spain with him or settle for having visits from Dad occasionally, when he had holidays. Although I was worried about having to leave my friends and change schools, the thought of living in a sunny climate was certainly exciting to me, and along with my mum and brother, I voted to move to Spain.

I wasn't looking forward to my first day at school in Madrid. I'd spent a few years learning Spanish at school and could manage in everyday conversations. I'd also met my new teacher on a visit the week before school started, and she'd explained the system in the school and what to expect. But the thought of joining a class full of strangers was enough to give me a stomach ache on the first day.

However, I needn't have worried. The teacher introduced me to my classmates and at the end of the lesson some of them walked with me to the school café and introduced themselves. Choosing what to eat at lunchtime was never going to be a problem as I loved Spanish food, but my new friends were nevertheless keen to explain each dish in detail as they thought I hadn't eaten them before.

The next few weeks were spent getting used to the way of life in a Spanish school and making close friends with a couple of girls, Ana and Sofia. We got on really well and would often spend time together after school. My level of Spanish was OK, though understanding the homework was sometimes a challenge, but they were always eager to help me when I needed it.

We returned to England last year and I really missed my Spanish friends and the Spanish way of life. It wasn't that I wanted to be back in Spain. I returned to my old school and loved catching up with my old friends. But I think the lesson I had learned was that friends are the same wherever you make them, and they can help you deal with big changes in your life and make any challenges you face so much easier.

Reading

11 When Tara first heard about her dad's job in Spain
  A she looked forward to spending holidays there.
  B she agreed with the decision to move.
  C she didn't think it was worth leaving her friends for a sunny climate.
  D she thought about the times they had spent there on holiday.

12 What does Tara say about her first day at a Spanish school?
  A The teacher told her about the school system.
  B She met her teacher for the first time.
  C She joined a Spanish conversation class.
  D She felt nervous about meeting new people.

13 What does Tara say about lunchtime?
  A She saw food she had never eaten before.
  B She asked the Spanish students to help her with the menu.
  C She didn't need help to decide what to eat.
  D The dinner menu was very detailed.

14 During her first few weeks at the school,
  A she found it hard getting used to the Spanish school system.
  B her lack of Spanish meant homework could be difficult.
  C her friends did her homework for her.
  D she was late handing in homework.

15 What would Tara be likely to say?

  A Things are sometimes not as worrying as we imagine.

  B Good friends are hard to find.

  C I don't like doing things against my wishes.

  D It can be difficult to get used to a different education system.

Part 4

Questions 16-20

Five sentences have been removed from the text below.
For each question, choose the correct answer.
There are three extra sentences which you do not need to use.

My Love of Music
Kirsty Sinclair explains why music is so important in her life.

Like most people of my age, I love listening to music. My friends and I are always talking about the latest song we're in love with and which singers or groups we're currently keen on. **16** ☐ I honestly think I'd find it difficult to do many of the things I do without the chance to listen to music.

17 ☐ I try to leave early in case there are traffic jams, but as I sit on the bus, I find myself relaxing and caring very little about what's going on around me. I like listening to the radio at this time. I can listen to music but also catch up with the latest news.

I also find it much more enjoyable to go running when I'm listening to music. **18** ☐ This isn't about relaxing but about helping me to focus on the speed I'm going. I like to create a song list with tracks that help me to run gently or fast. I could do the run without music, but having it on in the background certainly helps.

I spend the evenings during the week doing my homework in my bedroom, away from the TV and my noisy little brother. This is when I like to listen to classical music on my headphones as I work. **19** ☐ I can not only concentrate on what I have to do, but I also think it's good to listen to as wide a range of music as possible.

As you can see, music plays an important role in my life, and I'd find it really difficult to get through the day without it. There is one time, though, when I don't listen to music. **20** ☐ But I always ended up staying awake too long and felt tired in the morning. I now tend to leave my phone downstairs and enjoy my music again the next day.

A I used to watch online music videos before I went to sleep.

B I always have my headphones on during the journey to school.

C On the other hand, I don't like pop music.

D I prefer this to pop music when I'm studying.

E However, it's also a great way to keep fit.

F However, I think I'm even more keen than they are.

G That's when I turn my phone off.

H Music offers a different benefit this time.

Test 1 READING

Part 5

Questions 21–26

For each question, choose the correct answer.

Camels

Camels have been used by people for thousands of years as a form of transport in **(21)** .... of the world where other animals would find it hard to live. They can run as fast as a racehorse and can **(22)** .... between 170–270 kilograms. Camels can live for up to 50 years despite the challenges they face. In fact, they have become very well suited to the hot, dry **(23)** .... of the desert. When they find water, they can drink huge **(24)** .... The hump on their back (two in the case of the less common Bactrian camel) is used to store fat that they need when food is **(25)** .... to find. They have thick lips that allow them to eat plants that other creatures would find impossible. They have extra-thick skin and rows of eyelashes around their eyes, which **(26)** .... them against sandstorms.

21	**A** borders	**B** spaces	**C** parts	**D** distances
22	**A** carry	**B** keep	**C** contain	**D** take
23	**A** heat	**B** degrees	**C** forecast	**D** climate
24	**A** amounts	**B** lots	**C** numbers	**D** totals
25	**A** short	**B** hard	**C** bad	**D** weak
26	**A** hold	**B** stop	**C** protect	**D** save

Part 6

Questions 27–32

For each question, write the correct answer.
Write **one** word for each gap.

Jacket Potatoes
By Helen Aylin

Something I often ate when I lived with a family **(27)** .... the UK was a jacket potato. I'm not sure whether this is where they were invented or if they **(28)** .... eaten anywhere else, but I certainly haven't seen them in my country. They're called 'jacket potatoes' because **(29)** .... potatoes are cooked in their skin. You usually bake them in the oven **(30)** .... quite a long time so the inside is nice and fluffy. However, you can also buy them frozen and can cook them in a microwave in just a few minutes. The people I lived with served them with butter, cheese and beans, but you can also choose chilli, curry and many other things. Apart from **(31)** .... easy to cook, people also say they are healthy. The potato itself certainly is, and if you're careful about **(32)** .... you put on top, it can be good for you.

Test 1 WRITING

Part 1

You **must** answer this question.
Write your answer in about **100 words** on the answer sheet.

Question 1

Read this email from your English-speaking friend Steve and the notes you have made.

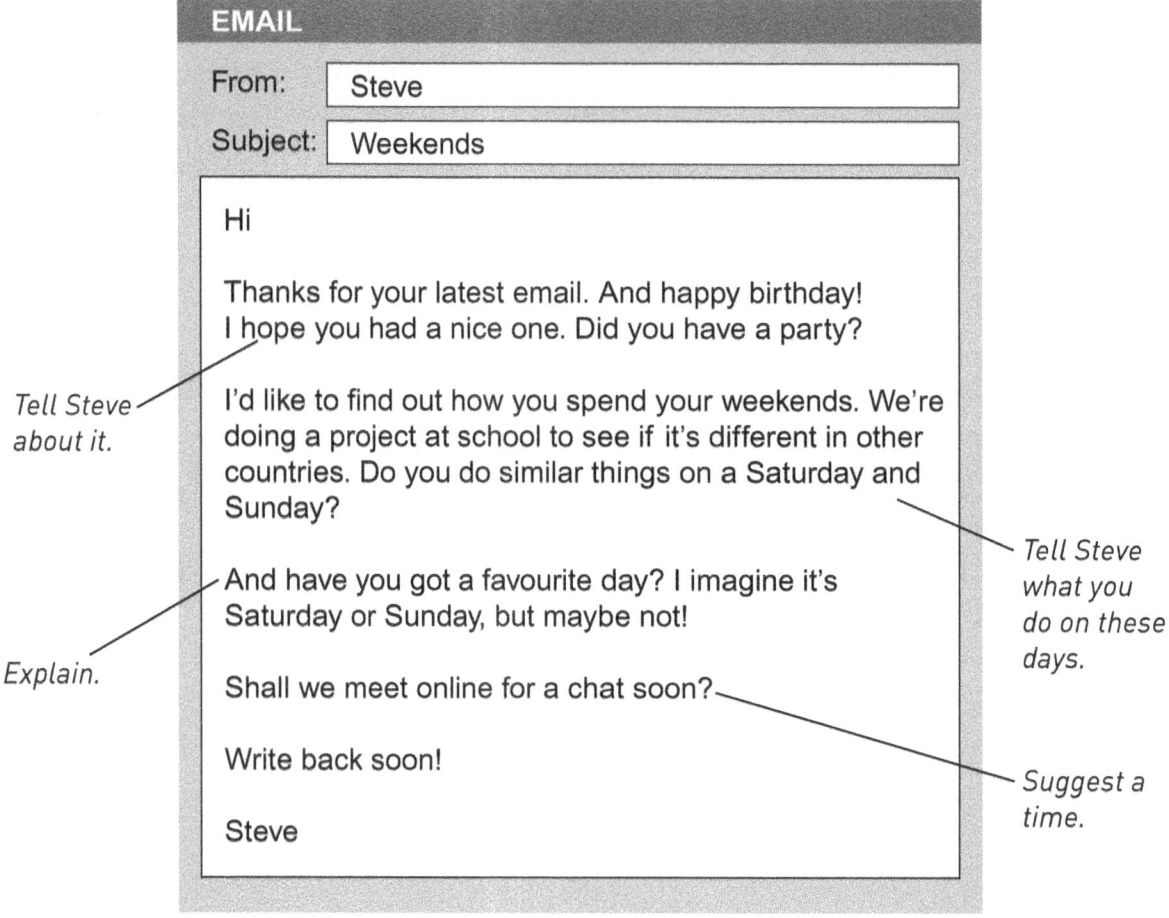

Write your **email** to Steve using **all the notes**.

Part 2

Choose **one** of these questions.
Write your answer in about **100 words** on the answer sheet.

Question 2

You see this notice in an English-language magazine.

Articles wanted!

HAVE YOU GOT A PLACE WHERE YOU FEEL RELAXED?

Do you use this place often?

What is it about this place that helps you to relax?

Write an article answering these questions and we will put it in our magazine.

Write your **article**.

Question 3

Your English teacher has asked you to write a story.

Your story must begin with this sentence.

I was sitting on the bus on the way to school one Monday.

Write your **story**.

Test 1 LISTENING

Test 1 LISTENING

Part 1

Questions 1–7

For each question, choose the correct answer.

1   What was damaged in the fire?

      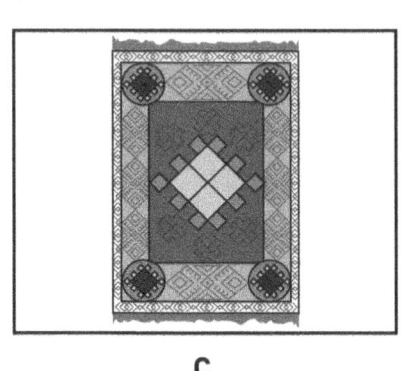

   A   B   C

2   What time does the teacher want the meeting?

   A   B   C

3   How does Katie usually travel home from school?

   A   B   C

Listening

4 What is the weather forecast for Friday?

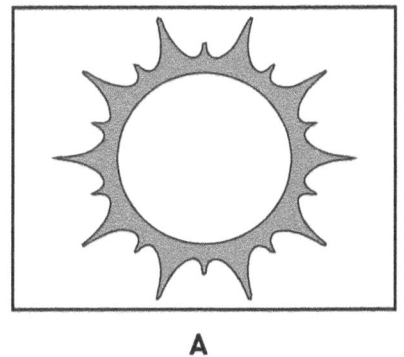
A

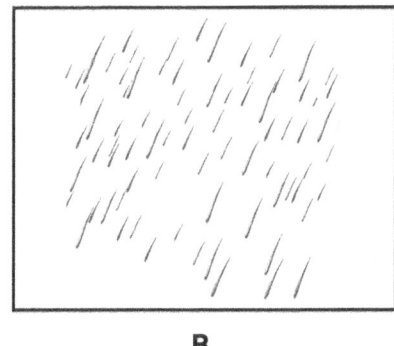
B

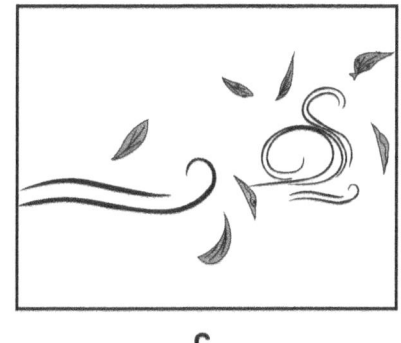
C

5 What colour does the girl think the room should be?

A

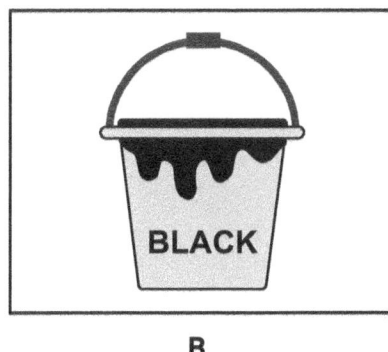
B

C

6 What is Lisa sending back?

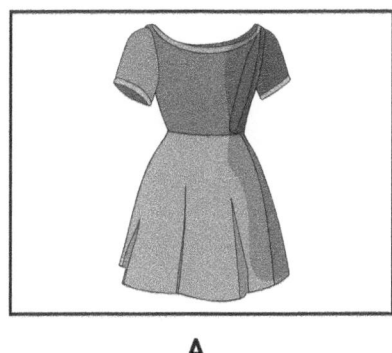
A

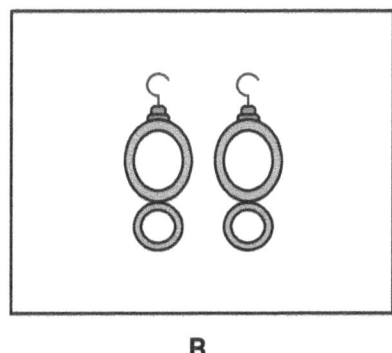
B

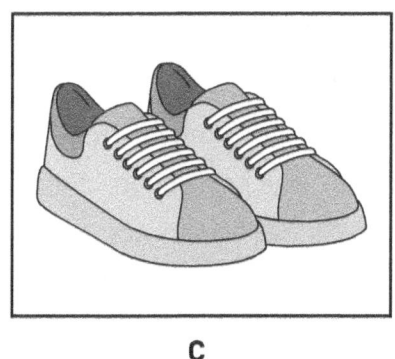
C

7 What might the boy eat less often?

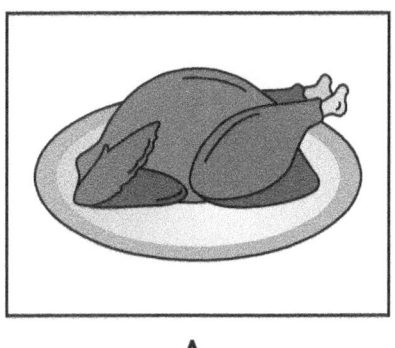
A

B

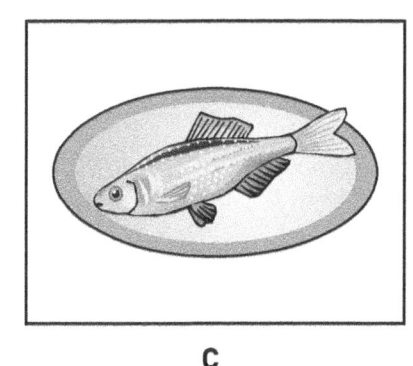
C

Test 1 LISTENING

Part 2

Questions 8–13

For each question, choose the correct answer.

---

8 You will hear two friends talking about a phone.
   What is wrong with it?

   A The camera doesn't work.
   B The screen is broken.
   C It is very slow.

9 You will hear a conversation between a mother and her son.
   Where will the mother be when the boy gets home?

   A having a driving lesson
   B at home
   C at the hairdresser's

10 You will hear two parents talking about their daughter's homework.
   The father says

   A he found it difficult.
   B he helped her finish it.
   C he found the subject interesting.

11 You will hear a brother and sister talking about an email.
   The boy explains that

   A the person has contacted him before.
   B it is from his teacher.
   C he needs to reply quickly.

12 You will hear a girl and her father talking about the environment.
   What does the girl say her father should do?

   A try to recycle more
   B use less paper
   C become a vegetarian

13 You will hear two friends talking about a light one of them has bought.
   What is the boy's opinion of it?

   A It is too bright.
   B It was difficult to find the right position.
   C It was expensive.

Part 3

Questions 14-19

For each question, write the correct answer in the gap. Write **one** or **two words** or a **number** or a **date** or a **time**.

You will hear a recorded message about events at an arts centre.

> ### Slate Art Centre
>
> *Dance Moves for Kids* lasts for **(14)** ………………….. weeks.
>
> The classes are held in the **(15)** ………………….. close to the café.
>
> The exhibition of Jason Perry's **(16)** ………………….. is being held in the main hall.
>
> The cinema is showing the film *To Catch a* **(17)** ………………….. .
>
> You can buy tickets online or at **(18)** ………………….. .
>
> Visit the website for the **(19)** ………………….. of the activities.

Test 1 LISTENING

Part 4

Questions 20–25

For each question, choose the correct answer.

You will hear an interview with a woman called Sarah Mulligan, who advises students about going to university.

20 Sarah says that usually, students
  A haven't lived away from home before.
  B worry about becoming more independent.
  C find it difficult to make decisions when they leave home.

21 Students who leave home to study
  A do not always act in a responsible way.
  B have trouble doing simple jobs like washing clothes.
  C will probably have to change their habits.

22 What does Sarah say is the advantage of living in a university hall?
  A You have more activities to choose from.
  B You gain more knowledge of university life.
  C You have access to better facilities.

23 Sarah says that some students
  A spend all their time focusing on their social life.
  B find it difficult to study at home.
  C see their studies as more important than having a busy social life.

24 What does Sarah say about missing home?
  A Students will feel better if they speak with their parents.
  B The feeling doesn't usually last long.
  C Students need to keep busy to forget about it.

25 Sarah thinks that not having much money
  A helps students manage money in the future.
  B is the reason students have problems finding accommodation.
  C means students find it difficult to buy food.

Test 1 SPEAKING

Speaking

(You are Candidate B. Answer the questions.)

1A

🎧 05–06

1B

Audio scripts on pages 183–216 and Model answers on pages 234–249.

37

Test 1 SPEAKING

07–08

Things parents could buy for their daughter's bedroom

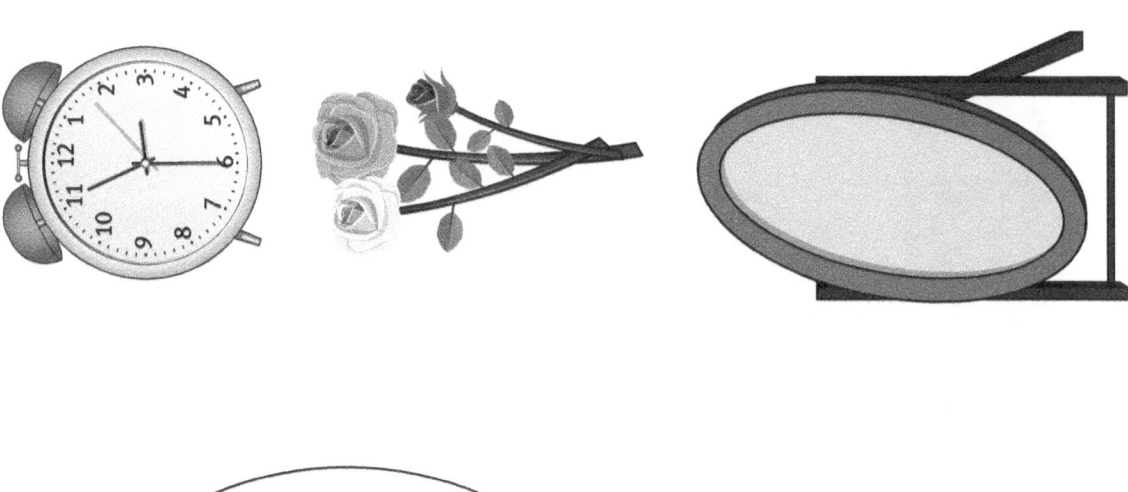

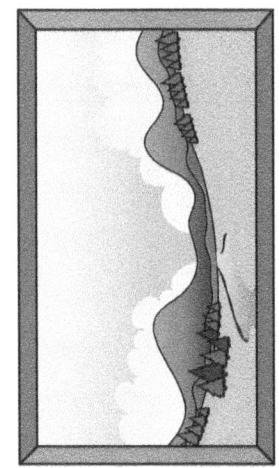
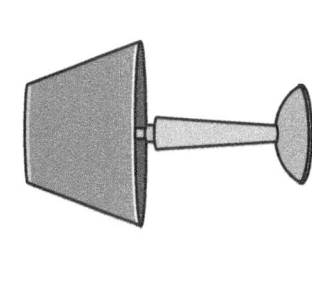
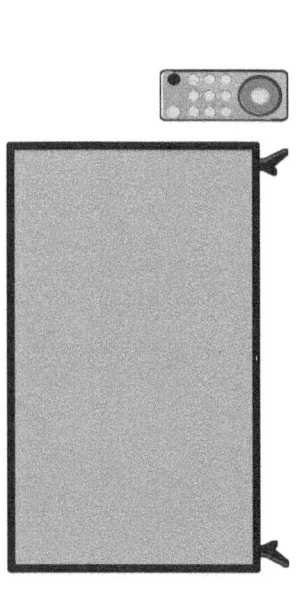

Audio scripts on pages 183–216 and Model answers on pages 234–249.

Test 2

Test 2 READING

Test 2 READING

Part 1

Questions 1–5

For each question, choose the correct answer.

1

> **For Sale**
>
> A boy's bicycle. As good as new. Offers around £75. Will exchange for a laptop in good condition.

A   The bicycle is new.

B   The seller will accept a laptop.

C   A laptop and bicycle are for sale.

2

> **To:** Dad
> **From:** Karen
>
> Hi Dad
>
> Can you pick me up from school later? My dance class starts earlier than usual this evening and I need to go home first to change.
>
> Love you
> Karen

A   Karen's dance class generally starts later.

B   Karen needs a different uniform.

C   Karen wants to change to another dance class.

3

> **From:** Miss Simpson
>
> Hi everyone.
>
> You can now hand your essays in to me one week later (by 19th June). I will be on holiday before then and won't be able to look at them.
>
> Miss Simpson

A   The teacher will only read the essays when she returns from holiday.

B   The teacher is going on holiday on 19th June.

C   The teacher will not mark essays handed in late.

4

Changing room

Do not leave personal items here. Teachers will take anything they find to lost property.

A Speak to a teacher about lost property.

B Please take any items you find to lost property.

C Take all personal items away with you.

5

| To: Tracie |
| From: Rachel |

Looking forward to your party on Saturday. I have classes till late at school, so I won't be there till 8.00 p.m. I won't need any dinner – I'll get a takeaway.

A The party starts at 8.00 p.m.

B Rachel will eat before the party.

C Rachel will be at school till 8.00 p.m.

Part 2

Questions 6–10

For each question, choose the correct answer.

The young people below all want to go somewhere this weekend.
On the opposite page there are descriptions of eight places to visit.
Decide which place would be the most suitable for the people below.

6  Carla wants to find out more about how things are invented. She is doing a project at school about objects we use every day and wants to learn when some of them were first made.

7  Theo enjoys video games and wants to go somewhere where he can play old and new video games on Saturday. He has football training in the morning and would like to go later in the afternoon.

8  David is fifteen years old and looking for somewhere to go with his parents. He is a keen musician and would like to get some advice on how to enter the music business.

9  Thirteen-year-old Rosemarie is working on her school art project and wants to go somewhere where she can be creative. She loves painting and would like to paint something to bring home.

10  Tessa is fourteen and is looking for somewhere to take her five-year-old sister. She is busy on Saturday and can only go on Sunday. She would like to have something to eat while she is there.

Places to Visit

A Children's Museum

Have a fantastic time with a trip to the Children's Museum this weekend. This summer, in addition to our great collection of board games and toys from the past, we also have an exhibition of computer and video games. Come along and play the latest games, and classic ones from the past. Open late Monday to Saturday.

B Museum of Play

Fun from the moment you walk through the door to the time you leave. The Museum of Play will introduce you to some of the favourite games from the past, before the invention of computers and mobile phones. A great day out for the younger and older generations. Open all day Saturday and Sunday.

C Science Centre

Travel back in time and discover how some things we use all the time were invented. Who thought of the idea for a tin opener? What did the first vacuum cleaner look like? And while you're here, visit the café for a quick snack. Open Saturdays from 9.00 a.m. till late.

D Museum of the Railways

Our popular family museum is holding a really special event this weekend. Local artist Pamela Griffith will offer a class for teenagers on how to capture the beauty of old steam trains. All materials are provided free of charge, including paints and paper. Take away something to show your family.

E Museum of Stories

The Museum of Stories explores the world of the imagination. Walk through a forest in the middle of the night as you listen to the story of the fox and the rabbit. Lie down under the stars and let us take you to another world. Children under eight must be accompanied by an adult.

F Gravely Hall

Our latest exhibition includes photos, films and guest speakers looking at some of the great pop artists from the past. From the Beatles to the Rolling Stones, you'll leave with knowledge of how they got started, the important moments in their careers, and perhaps get tips on how to get into the profession.

G Bounders Play Centre

During the school holidays, we are once again running our popular play days for children of all ages. We'll have kids' dance and music activities for the whole family. Open 7 days a week. Hot and cold refreshments available.

H Trescott Art Gallery and Museum

Many famous artists drew sketches before they went on to create their greatest paintings. So, we're very excited to welcome visitors to our new exhibition, where they will be able to see some of these wonderful drawings. They will also have the opportunity to listen to art experts explain how the drawings helped the artist arrive at the final result.

Test 2 READING

Part 3

Questions 11–15

For each question, choose the correct answer.

Kelly David talks about growing vegetables

I have so many happy memories of the times I spent with my grandfather, but one thing above all others which made a big impression on me was helping him grow vegetables in his garden. It was hard work and at first, I wasn't very happy if I came across horrible insects. But going back to his house each week and seeing the progress of the things we had planted was a huge pleasure.

Grandad was a fantastic teacher. He'd guide me very cleverly by asking my advice as we walked round the garden. 'Where should we plant these to get the right amount of sunshine?' 'How are we going to protect these plants from the birds?' As an eight- or nine-year-old, I felt my advice was needed by Grandad, who made sure I always gave the perfect answer, with a little help. And with the arrival of the harvest, he'd always tell me how well I'd done to grow such a wonderful crop of potatoes or such delicious peas and beans.

The experience taught me so much. I gained an understanding of the effect the passing of the seasons has on the growing process, and of where our food comes from. People often say home-grown vegetables taste much better than those bought in supermarkets. I wasn't sure about that at the time, but I certainly had a much wider choice of things I was willing to eat. Most of my friends at the time wouldn't eat anything green on their plate.

I'm delighted to say that my own daughter is now showing signs of getting the same pleasure from growing vegetables as I did. It's clear to me that this is giving her an education about food and eating well, particularly as we have lost our connection with natural ingredients compared to earlier generations. My daughter's teacher persuaded her to bring in a handful of different vegetables and to question the class on how many they recognised. Sadly, most children had no idea what many of them were called, a sad result of our fast-food diet.

11 What does Kelly say about her time with her grandad?
    A She enjoyed seeing how the plants were developing.
    B She didn't like having to work hard in the garden.
    C She stopped being afraid of insects.
    D She didn't see him often.

12 Kelly says her grandad
    A wasn't always sure how to grow some vegetables.
    B made her feel her opinion was important.
    C only grew a few vegetables.
    D sometimes needed help walking.

13 For Kelly, what was the result of growing vegetables?
    A She didn't like eating vegetables from supermarkets.
    B She learned to love the spring and summer.
    C She had more choice of food to eat as a child.
    D She persuaded her friends to eat more vegetables.

14 Kelly says her daughter's classmates
    A didn't know the names of some of the vegetables.
    B tasted the vegetables she had grown.
    C said they preferred eating fast food.
    D asked her lots of questions.

15 What would be the best introduction to this article?

    A Kelly David thinks schools should spend time teaching children how to grow vegetables.

    B Kelly David argues that children should spend more time with the older generation.

    C Kelly David explains how a childhood activity became an important life lesson.

    D In this article, Kelly David explains how to grow your own vegetables.

Part 4

Questions 16–20

Five sentences have been removed from the text below.
For each question, choose the correct answer.
There are three extra sentences which you do not need to use.

Birmingham Canals

I never realised how many miles of canals Birmingham had until I stayed with a friend. **16**   We both love cycling and one day he suggested using his local canal as it was safer there than riding on the roads. I borrowed his brother's bike and soon discovered what an interesting history canals have and what wonderful local leisure facilities they are becoming.

Apparently, there are 35 miles of canals in Birmingham, which some say is more than in Venice. **17**   This was the time of the Industrial Revolution and the canals were needed to transport wool, iron and other goods around the country. During this period, there were over 170 miles of them and they helped make Birmingham one of the major centres of growth. Many people now call it 'England's second city', and one reason for this is the success of the canals.

However, during the twentieth century, for various reasons the canals were used less and less. **18**   Also, once trains and roads started to be used for transporting goods, the canal network became less important to industry. By 1980, canals were no longer used for this purpose. Without any financial investment, many of them were soon in very poor condition.

19   They are now places where local people can escape the city and enjoy a quieter environment. Many of them are now safe, clean and tidy. They are enjoyed by walkers, tourists travelling along them on boats, and cyclists like me and my friend. **20**   In fact, we managed to cycle right into the city centre, avoiding all the heavy traffic. Once in the centre, the canal was surrounded by restaurants, apartments and modern office buildings.

A This is the best place to exit the canal into the central area.

B To start with, the canals were very expensive to look after.

C They were built during the 1700s and 1800s.

D Fortunately, in recent years the local government has spent money on improving them.

E They are also a safe way to get into town.

F He was the local engineer who planned some of the canals.

G He introduced me to them last year during the school holiday.

H This was the first canal to be built.

Part 5

Questions 21–26

For each question, choose the correct answer.

Chess

Chess has been popular for hundreds of years around the world, but it probably began in northern India in the sixth century, when people played a form of the game **(21)** .... chaturanga. Though various other games **(22)** .... before this, experts think chaturanga was **(23)** .... to chess because it had different pieces with different powers, including a king playing a central **(24)** .... Knowledge of the game gradually spread from India to other regions, with the first written records **(25)** .... in stories from Persia at the beginning of the seventh century. There were different ways of playing the game from one country to another. However, in Europe during the fifteenth century, the **(26)** .... were changed to make chess a faster and more exciting game. The powerful queen was introduced and 'checkmate' became a far more common result. These changes were the start of the modern game.

21	**A** called	**B** believed	**C** made	**D** said
22	**A** stood	**B** stayed	**C** existed	**D** lived
23	**A** familiar	**B** similar	**C** same	**D** available
24	**A** action	**B** act	**C** space	**D** role
25	**A** appearing	**B** showing	**C** coming	**D** rising
26	**A** orders	**B** rules	**C** plays	**D** controls

Part 6

Questions 27–32

For each question, write the correct answer.
Write **one** word for each gap.

The Eiffel Tower
By Elaine Styles

During our school trip to Paris, the one place I was really looking forward to seeing **(27)** .... the Eiffel Tower. It's one of the **(28)** .... famous monuments in the world, with over seven million visitors a year, and I was really excited about seeing it with my own eyes. The first thing **(29)** .... surprised me when we arrived was how tall it was. Our teacher told us the tower had actually been the tallest man-made building in the world **(30)** .... many years during the twentieth century. Unfortunately, we didn't have time to go up the tower and visit the three floors. There are restaurants, a shop and even a glass floor! But we managed **(31)** .... see the tower in the evening when it lights up. This happens for five minutes every hour once it gets dark and it makes the tower look even **(32)** .... amazing.

Test 2 WRITING

Part 1

You **must** answer this question.
Write your answer in about **100 words** on the answer sheet.

Question 1

Read this email from your teacher and the notes you have made.

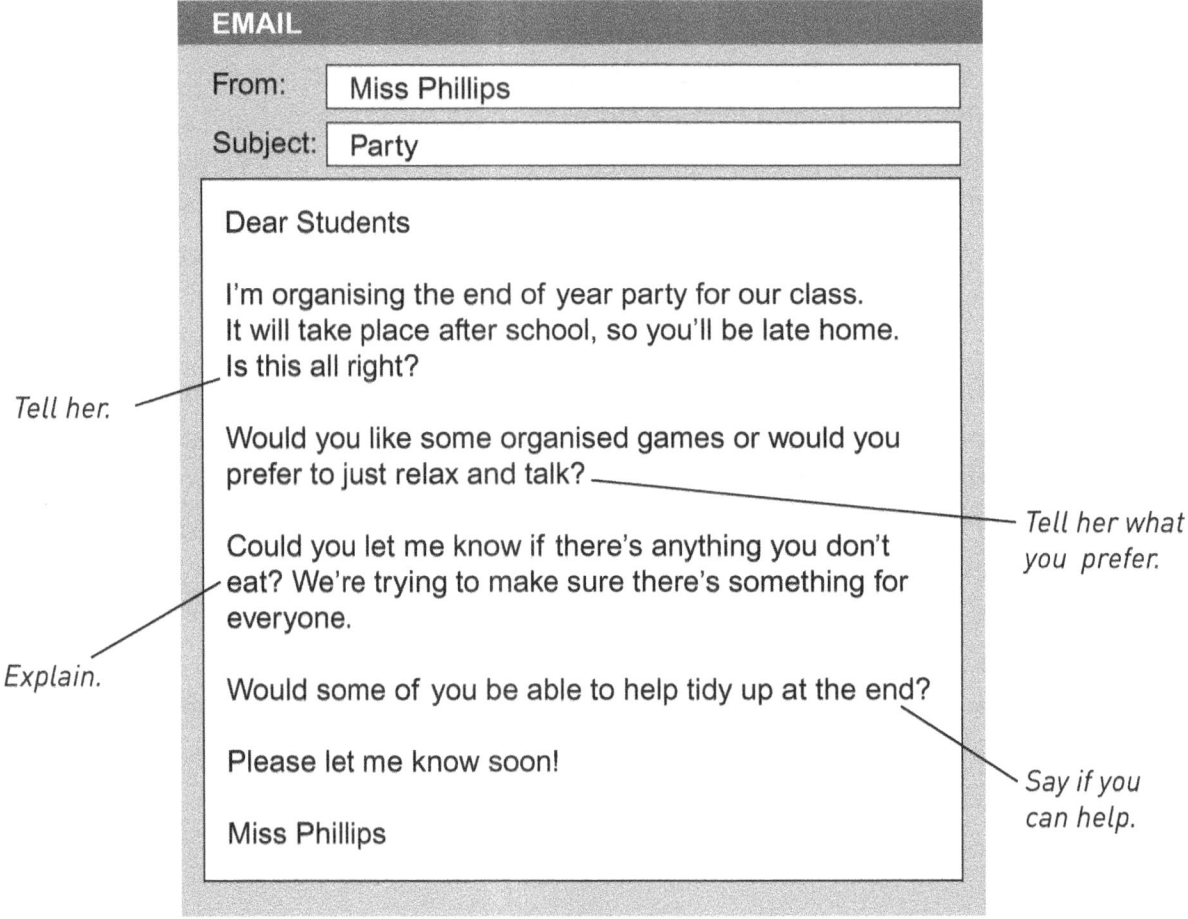

Write your **email** to Miss Phillips using **all the notes**.

Part 2

Choose **one** of these questions.
Write your answer in about **100 words** on the answer sheet.

Question 2

You see this notice in an English-language magazine.

> **Articles wanted!**
>
> **IS THERE A MAGAZINE YOU ENJOY READING?**
>
> What is this magazine about?
>
> Why do you enjoy reading it?
>
> **Write an article answering these questions and we will put it in our magazine.**

Write your **article**.

Question 3

Your English teacher has asked you to write a story.

Your story must begin with this sentence.

I knew what it was before I opened the parcel.

Write your **story**.

Test 2 LISTENING

Test 2 LISTENING

Part 1

Questions 1–7

For each question, choose the correct answer.

1   What does the girl decide to get her mother as a present?

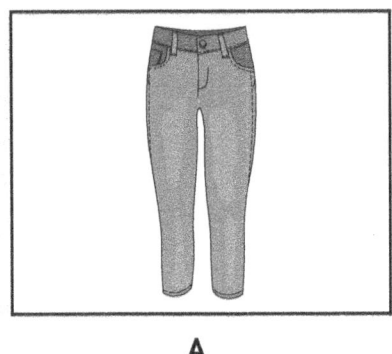 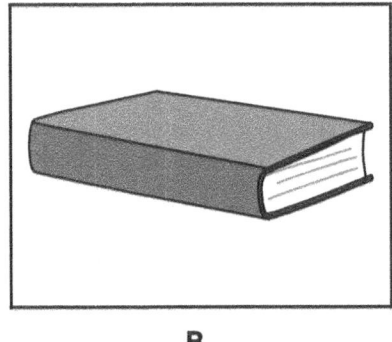 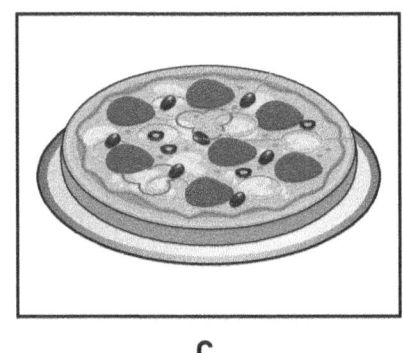

A   B   C

2   How many tickets do they need for the cinema?

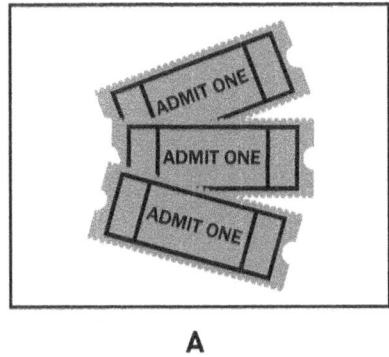 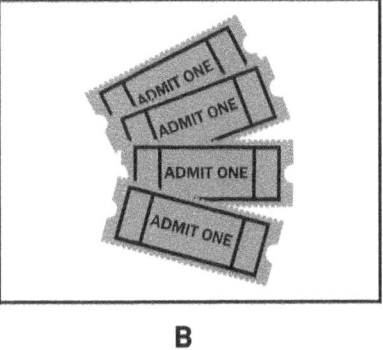 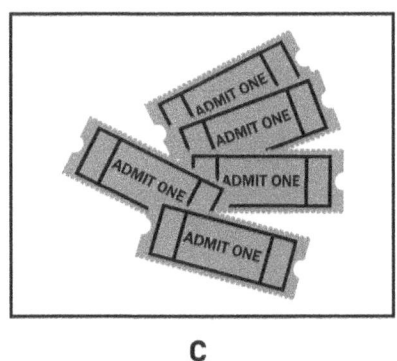

A   B   C

3   Why might the boy decide not to play football?

 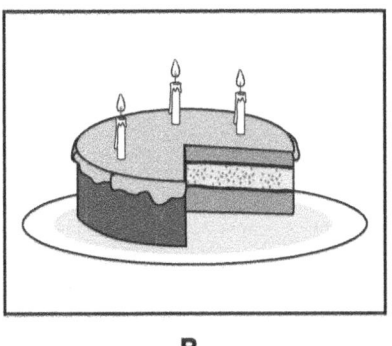 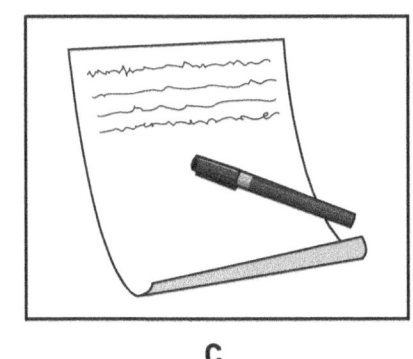

A   B   C

4 What will the next programme be about?

A B C

5 Where did the girl last see her glasses?

 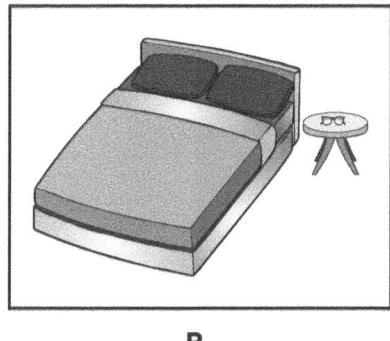 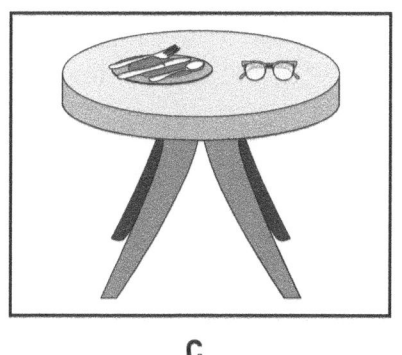
A B C

6 What time is the coach leaving?

A B C

7 What is the boy going to take to the party?

  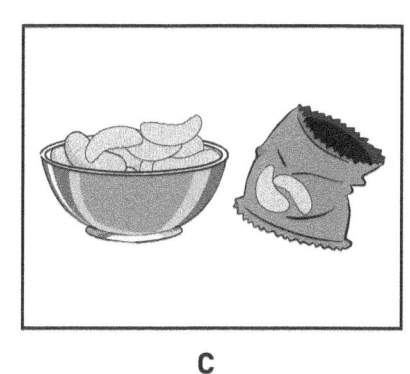
A B C

Test 2 LISTENING

Part 2

Questions 8–13

For each question, choose the correct answer.

---

8   You will hear two friends talking about their plans for the evening.
    What does the girl want to do?

    A   watch TV

    B   finish her homework

    C   get more sleep

9   You will hear a mother and her son talking about a photograph.
    What does the mother say about it?

    A   It was taken a long time ago.

    B   The boy's grandfather took it.

    C   She likes it.

10 You will hear two friends talking about the weather.
    The boy says

    A   it is too cold to go to town.

    B   it will be nicer in the afternoon.

    C   it is going to rain later.

11 You will hear two friends talking about the school football shirt.
    What does the boy think about the old one?

    A   He liked it better than the new one.

    B   He didn't like the colour.

    C   It was uncomfortable.

12 You will hear a girl and her father talking about getting home from school.
    The girl says

    A   she would like her father to drive her home.

    B   she doesn't have the bus fare.

    C   school is finishing early.

13 You will hear a brother and sister talking about a song on the radio.
    Why is the girl listening to it?

    A   She has homework on it.

    B   She wants to be able to think more clearly.

    C   Her classmates like it.

54

Part 3

Questions 14–19

For each question, write the correct answer in the gap. Write **one** or **two words** or a **number** or a **date** or a **time**.

You will hear a student giving a presentation on fast food.

Fast Food Research

I decided that fast food isn't the same thing as a **(14)** ....

I included a **(15)** .... of the interview as well as the questionnaire.

Students generally eat fast food with their family at **(16)** ....

Some students were interested in talking about the school **(17)** ....

I'm interested in finding out what students bring in their **(18)** ....

You'll find more information about my research in my **(19)** ....

Test 2 LISTENING

Part 4

Questions 20–25

For each question, choose the correct answer.

You will hear an interview with a man called Matthew Davies about a person who had a positive influence on him.

20 Matthew thought having a new teacher

    A wouldn't be a problem for him.

    B would make him feel more confident.

    C would affect his studies.

21 What does Matthew say about the first lesson?

    A The teacher wasn't as nervous as the students.

    B The students knew they would enjoy his lessons.

    C The students were made to work hard straightaway.

22 Matthew says Mr Adams

    A talked more than his previous teacher.

    B expected students to do work at home.

    C had interesting opinions about subjects.

23 What did Matthew learn about Mr Adams' way of teaching?

    A He wanted his students to enjoy history.

    B He had taught at university before.

    C He wanted students to be experts in the subject.

24 Matthew says Mr Adams

    A taught him exam skills.

    B answered his emails.

    C organised extra lessons for all the students each week.

25 What does Matthew say about his choice of career?

    A He hopes to teach at university.

    B Mr Adams recommended it to him.

    C He didn't expect to become a teacher.

Test 2 SPEAKING

Speaking

You are Candidate B. Answer the questions.

1A

1B

Audio scripts on pages 183–216 and Model answers on pages 234–249.

Test 2 SPEAKING

🎧 15–16

Things to take to the beach

Test 3

Test 3 READING

Part 1

Questions 1–5

For each question, choose the correct answer.

1

Special Offer

For this week only! Buy two computer games and get another one free.

A   Get three games for the price of two.

B   Computer games are free this week.

C   Buy a computer game and get another for nothing.

2

To: Kevin
From: Paul
Subject: Saturday

Hi

I know I promised to come round on Saturday, but Dad wants me to tidy my room first! If I finish early, I'll call you.

Paul

A   Paul can't come at the time he agreed.

B   Paul's dad said he can't go to Kevin's house.

C   Paul needs to leave Kevin's house earlier than they planned.

3

To all students

No shoes to be worn in the gym. Please change into trainers before entering.

A   Students should leave their shoes with a trainer.

B   Shoes must be taken off before students use the gym.

C   Students should not bring their shoes into the gym.

4

Hi Dad

Your mate Ben called this afternoon. He said he's working late tonight. He will drive straight to football practice, so you don't need to give him a lift.

Keith

A Ben needs a lift.

B Ben will go to football practice from work.

C Ben won't be going to football practice.

5

Please take care of your things. The club is not responsible for any personal items you lose or that get damaged.

A Do not leave your possessions in the club.

B There is a person responsible for lost or damaged items.

C It is not the club's fault if a personal item is lost or damaged.

Test 3 READING

Part 2

Questions 6–10

For each question, choose the correct answer.

The young people below all want to join an art class during their summer holiday.
On the opposite page there are descriptions of eight art courses.
Decide which course would be the most suitable for the people below.

6  Vera is thirteen and is good at painting, but hasn't done many pencil drawings. She is looking for help with her drawing skills. She can only attend classes on Saturdays and would like face-to-face lessons.

7  Matt enjoys painting, but has always had trouble painting people. He wants to follow a course with other students. He doesn't want to use the internet and can take a course on Monday to Friday.

8  Barbara loves drawing cartoon characters and would like to spend some time practising this, as well as meeting other children. She is only free on Saturdays and Sundays and doesn't want to study online.

9  Louis doesn't think he has any ability to draw and paint and never likes what he has created. He wants to take an evening course on Monday or Wednesday, on his own with a teacher.

10  Joe has a lot of artistic talent and wants help from an expert in drawing and painting buildings. He is busy during the week and would prefer to follow a live course on the internet.

Art Courses

A Art Teacher for You

Individual help for the experienced artist as well as those who are less confident! I am a fully qualified art teacher, and I would love to help you develop your creative skills. I can travel to you or offer classes in my own studio. Available Monday to Friday 6.00 p.m.–9.00 p.m.

B Anytime Art

Everyone can draw and paint, and we aim to help young artists of all abilities develop their drawing and painting skills. We cover everything from painting pictures of people to drawing buildings that look really realistic on your paper. Join other young people and your teacher live online as they talk you through each part of the work.

C Art: Step by Step

Learning how to draw cartoons is easy with our online courses. Watch professional artists as they show you how to draw a face. Each video will focus on a different topic, starting with simple shapes, before moving on to the eyes and the rest of the face. All videos are available online for you to follow at a time that suits you.

D The Big Art Club

Starting this Monday until Thursday, from 12.00 p.m.–3.00 p.m. – art classes for the complete beginner. Come along and have lots of fun with other local children and learn how to use a variety of different types of paint and pencils. We have a maximum class size of 10 children, so book your place soon!

E Copy Cats Art Class

Don't spend Sundays lying around with nothing to do. Come and join our lively art classes, make new friends and learn how to copy characters from your favourite comics or films. We'll look at how to draw a range of characters, whether that's cartoon farm animals or the superhero of your choice.

F Independent Art School

Sally Niccols, a talented local artist, will be running classes through the summer holiday for young, experienced artists interested in creating beautiful city landscapes with paint. Learn how to draw famous buildings such as cathedrals, monuments and palaces, as well as street scenes like markets and railway stations. Every Saturday from 9.00 a.m.–12.00 p.m.

G The Art Academy

If you already have a good level of artistic ability and would like to develop your skills in painting people, this course is for you. Bring along some photos of friends or a famous person from a magazine and we'll show you how to paint the eyes, shadows and colours of the human face. Every Tuesday and Thursday from 3.00 p.m–5.00 p.m.

H Weekend Classes

Want to take your art to the next level? Before you can draw, you need to train the eye to see, and our popular small-group Saturday classes at the Arts Centre will help you develop this skill. Bring objects to life with pencil and paper. Due to the level of work, we cannot accept beginners.

Part 3

Questions 11–15

For each question, choose the correct answer.

My Family and the Internet

My mum and dad have always been keen to encourage my brother and me to do our very best, whether that's in our studies or in life generally. Recently, we talked about limiting the time we spend online at home in the evening. We all agreed that we spend too long on our phones and laptops and could be doing other things instead. So, we decided to try an experiment to see what happened.

We couldn't go offline completely as my brother and I both needed to use the internet for our homework. And we didn't want to miss what our friends were chatting about online, so we agreed to set a time in the evening when we could all use the internet, but before and after this time it wasn't allowed. We also agreed to try for one month. A week didn't seem long enough and any longer might be too challenging.

The first few days were really difficult. Every few minutes I'd pick up my phone to see if I had any messages, or whether my social media had any updates. However, I started to read a book that I hadn't looked at since I bought it, and soon got interested in the story and forgot about going online. Dinner time lasted a lot longer as we weren't all eating our food as quickly as we could in order to get back to our phones. This meant we spent more time talking to each other about our day, which was nice.

We didn't quite manage to complete the month, unfortunately. My dad explained that he needed to check his work email in the evening sometimes and wanted to give up. However, it was a real success, I think. This was three months ago, and some of the better habits we started during this time, like spending more time together at the dinner table and talking more, have stayed with us. We're all back on the internet again whenever we want, but we're spending a lot less time online than we used to and I think we're even closer as a family now.

11 The author's parents
   A thought the children weren't working hard enough.
   B wanted the family to do a variety of things in the evening.
   C liked to discuss things online.
   D wanted to stop the children using their phones.

12 What did the family decide to do?
   A stop using the internet for one month
   B avoid chatting with friends online
   C decide on a time they could all go online
   D only use the internet for homework

13 What does the author say about her experience?
   A She decided to buy a book.
   B She ate her dinner quickly.
   C She didn't reply to emails.
   D She found it difficult to ignore her phone.

14 What was the result of the family's experiment?
   A They managed to do what they said they would do.
   B They know they need to get better at talking to each other.
   C They have decided to do it for three more months.
   D They communicate more with each other now.

15 What would a good introduction to this article be?

   A Caroline Stacey argues we are using the internet too often.

   B This is how Caroline Stacey and her family found more time for each other.

   C Caroline Stacey describes a family experiment that went wrong.

   D According to Caroline Stacey, families have forgotten how to communicate.

Part 4

Questions 16–20

Five sentences have been removed from the text below.
For each question, choose the correct answer.
There are three extra sentences which you do not need to use.

Learning how to write a story

A local author recently came into my class to give a talk on how to write stories. She made it really interesting by asking us to think about how our favourite books or films get our attention at the beginning and keep us interested until the end. **16**

We needed an idea, of course. She said this might be based on one of our own experiences or perhaps something we found interesting in a film we'd seen, like a favourite character. **17** This could be the future, the past or the present time. We then thought about whether it was somewhere local or in another country, or even another planet!

18 Obviously, it needs a beginning, middle and end. She explained the importance of having a major problem or challenge in the story that affects the main character. First of all, she got us to think about how this happened in our favourite film or book. We then spent time thinking about what problem our main character might have. Then I had a great idea about two friends who have an argument which causes problems for their friendship.

The author then told us about the need for a 'turning point'. **19** We then had to consider how the problem we'd identified was overcome. Perhaps the main character has to fight a battle or deal with a big challenge in their daily life, and the result of this. I thought about how one of my two characters might help the other after the argument, and how my story could then have a happy ending.

We all really enjoyed the lesson. We're often asked to write short stories at school and I never know where to start. **20** I haven't written my story yet, but I'm looking forward to doing it.

A This is when the main character deals with the challenge.

B So, she then gave us advice on making characters seem real.

C Understanding this would help us to plan our own story.

D But the lesson taught me what to think about before I start writing.

E So, a problem all writers have is how to start.

F Then you have to decide when and where the action takes place.

G As a result, this is something all new writers have to deal with.

H We then had to plan the organisation of the story.

Part 5

Questions 21-26

For each question, choose the correct answer.

Lemons

Lemons have a wide **(21)** .... of uses, from beauty products to cleaning products, and even help to fight disease. However, many of us will be most familiar with their use in food and drink. Like salt, lemon juice improves the flavour of things. The sour taste **(22)** .... our mouth water and this is necessary for our sense of taste. We are all used to seeing a **(23)** .... of lemon next to our fish and chips, and lemon juice is also used with oil on salads. The lemon juice helps to give food a cleaner, fresher taste. When **(24)** .... to boiled vegetables, it helps them **(25)** .... their colour. And finally, the outer part of the skin **(26)** .... the oil of the lemon and is used to improve the flavour of soups and other dishes.

21 **A** space   **B** order   **C** class   **D** range

22 **A** makes   **B** grows   **C** gives   **D** does

23 **A** cut   **B** slice   **C** shape   **D** part

24 **A** joined   **B** mixed   **C** added   **D** collected

25 **A** keep   **B** have   **C** carry   **D** follow

26 **A** connects   **B** compares **C** contains **D** continues

Part 6

Questions 27–32

For each question, write the correct answer.
Write **one** word for each gap.

Early Bicycles
By Grace Sissons

We've just had a talk by someone at our cycling club about early bicycles. I didn't realise **(27)** .... first bicycle was made of wood. It even had wooden wheels! It was invented by Baron Karl von Drais, **(28)** .... rode it in public in 1817. It didn't have any pedals, and he had to move it **(29)** .... pushing his feet along the ground. In fact, pedals didn't appear until the 1860s. Later bicycles were made of metal and designed with a larger front wheel for faster speeds. But they were difficult to keep upright and the rider would often fall over. The next main development was in 1885, **(30)** .... the 'safety bicycle' was introduced. This had two wheels of **(31)** .... same size, a chain that attached to the back rather **(32)** .... the front wheel, and brakes. Air-filled tyres arrived in 1888 and were invented by John Boyd Dunlop.

Test 3 WRITING

Part 1

You **must** answer this question.
Write your answer in about **100 words** on the answer sheet.

Question 1

Read this email from your English-speaking friend Anna and the notes you have made.

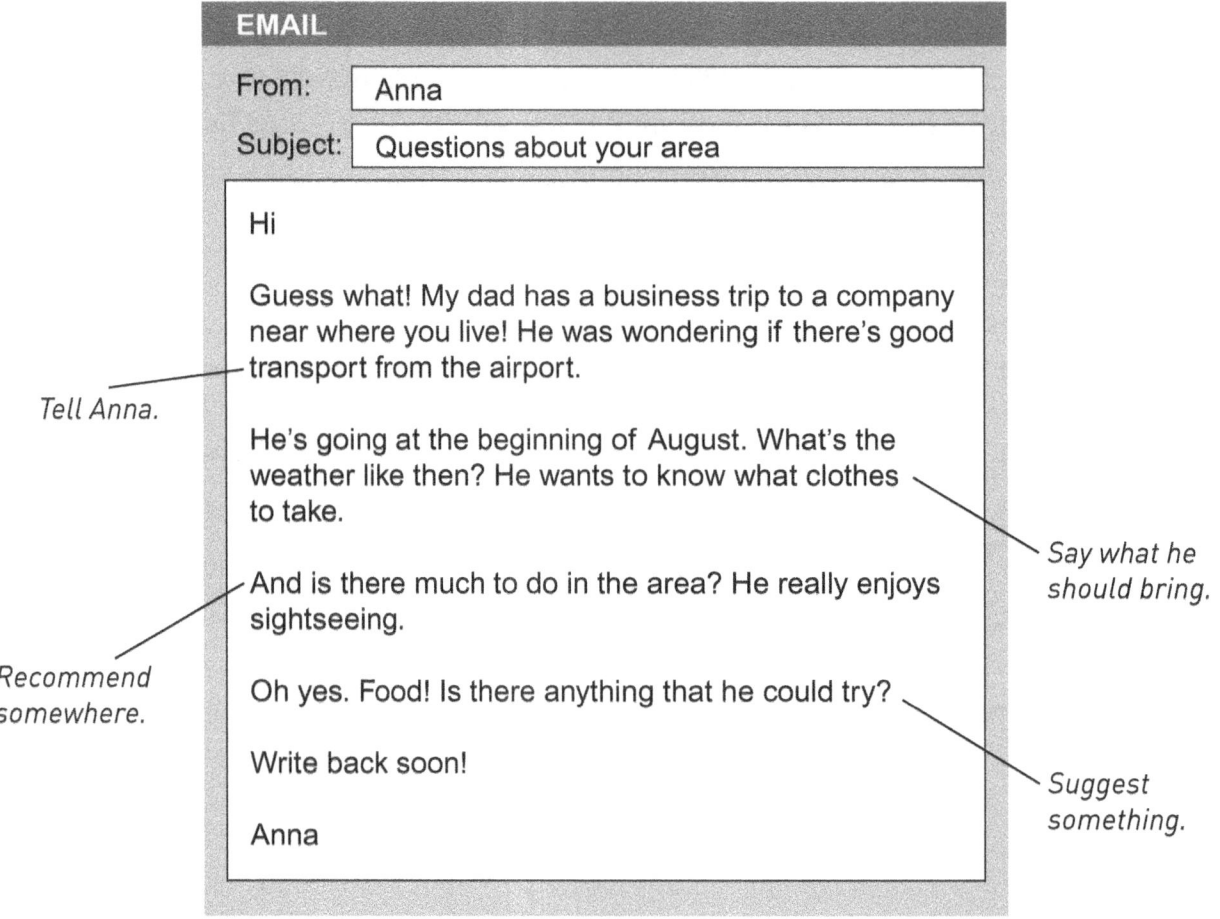

Write your **email** to Anna using **all the notes**.

Part 2

Choose **one** of these questions.
Write your answer in about **100 words** on the answer sheet.

Question 2

You see this notice in an English-language magazine.

> **Articles wanted!**
>
> **WHAT IS YOUR FAVOURITE APP?**
>
> How long have you used it?
>
> Why do you like it so much?
>
> **Write an article answering these questions and we will put it in our magazine.**

Write your **article**.

Question 3

Your English teacher has asked you to write a story.

Your story must begin with this sentence.

I was looking forward to the trip to the coast.

Write your **story**.

Test 3 LISTENING

Test 3 LISTENING

Part 1

Questions 1–7

For each question, choose the correct answer.

---

1 Where will the café be in the future?

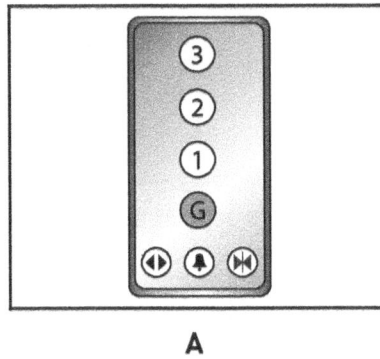

A   B   C

2 When does the boy return to school?

A   B   C

3 How much is the laptop?

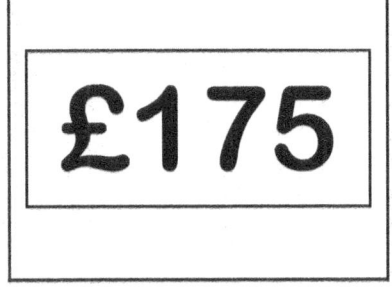

A   B   C

Listening

4 What did the boy do at the weekend?

A

B

C

5 What did the girl forget?

A

B

C

6 Why is the girl going to be late home?

A

B

C

7 How does the boy recommend getting to his house?

A

B

C

Test 3 LISTENING

Part 2

Questions 8–13

For each question, choose the correct answer.

8   You will hear a brother and sister talking about a birthday present for their father.
    What do they decide to do?

    A   take him shopping

    B   ask their mother for advice

    C   get him a surprise

9   You will hear two friends talking about a new teacher.
    What does the girl say about him?

    A   He isn't as frightening as he looks.

    B   He was a little nervous.

    C   He knew some of the students already.

10 You will hear a mother and her son talking about the weather.
    The mother says

    A   it definitely won't rain.

    B   the forecast is usually correct.

    C   it doesn't matter what the weather is like.

11 You will hear two parents talking about dinner.
    What are they going to have that evening?

    A   The man will cook a curry.

    B   They will get a takeaway.

    C   The woman will make a salad.

12 You will hear a girl and her father talking about a journey.
    How are the girl and her friends getting to the festival?

    A   Her father is going to take them.

    B   Her friend's mother is taking them.

    C   They have already arranged something.

13 You will hear two friends talking about selling a bicycle.
    Why is the girl selling it?

    A   She doesn't enjoy cycling.

    B   She needs the money.

    C   There isn't room for it in the house.

Part 3

Questions 14–19

For each question, write the correct answer in the gap. Write **one** or **two words** or a **number** or a **date** or a **time**.

You will hear a teacher talking about a special event at the school.

Mr Hastings

Mr Hastings' final day at school is at end of the
(14) ....

Volunteers are needed to show Mr Hastings' old students around the (15) ....

Students can take part in the (16) .... the school is making for him.

Contact the teacher no later than (17) .... to take part.

Students can write something nice in his (18) ....

He will be given some (19) .... equipment bought by teachers at the school.

Part 4

Questions 20-25

For each question, choose the correct answer.

You will hear an interview with a woman called Christine Peake, who runs football training for girls.

20 What does Christine say about football?
   A Christine's sessions are for both boys and girls.
   B There are as many girls playing football as boys.
   C Girls are taking a greater interest in playing football.

21 Christine thinks more girls have joined the club because
   A the women's national team did well in a competition.
   B women's football is always on TV.
   C the club have been getting good results.

22 Christine says that girls who join her organisation
   A need to have some basic football skills.
   B do activities that are suitable for their age.
   C sometimes come from other clubs.

23 Why is the club for girls only?
   A Older girls want to focus on playing football.
   B Some girls worry they wouldn't be as good as the boys.
   C The younger girls don't like playing against boys.

24 Some of Christine's girls
   A have now joined professional clubs.
   B could play for men's football teams.
   C have now started their own women's team.

25 Why does Christine want parents to contact her?
   A She knows the younger girls will be worried about coming.
   B They might have questions.
   C She wants them to join in the classes.

Test 3 SPEAKING

Speaking

(You are Candidate B. Answer the questions.)

🎧 21–22

1A

1B

Audio scripts on pages 183–216 and Model answers on pages 234–249.

Test 3 SPEAKING

Hobbies a teenage girl could start

Test 4

Test 4 READING

Part 1

Questions 1–5

For each question, choose the correct answer.

1

> Trip to the Cathedral
> Due to the possibility of icy roads, the trip is now planned for Wednesday instead.

A The trip that was planned will not take place.

B The trip was going to be on Wednesday.

C The trip will now take place on a different day.

2

> Hi Greg
>
> I've still got that spare ticket for the football on Saturday. Let me know if you want it by Friday as Tim will buy it if you don't want it.
>
> Luther

A Greg should tell Tim whether he wants the ticket.

B Greg needs to contact Luther.

C Luther knows Greg wants the ticket.

3

> **Delivery**
> Free delivery for goods worth at least £25. For smaller orders, please check charges for delivery carefully.

A There is no charge for delivery if goods cost less than £25.

B Delivery charges will be at least £25.

C Customers may have to pay for items to be delivered.

80

4

> Hi everyone
>
> Just to let you know the lessons will be in Room 27 just for this week while our normal classroom is used for end-of-year exams.
>
> Miss Chandler

This week

A   lessons are in another classroom.

B   lessons are in the usual classroom.

C   exams are taking place in Room 27.

5

> This chicken must be kept in a refrigerator and eaten within two days of opening. After opening, it is not suitable for freezing.

A   Freeze the chicken within two days of opening.

B   Do not eat the chicken more than two days after opening.

C   Keep the chicken in the refrigerator after you have opened it.

Test 4 READING

Part 2

Questions 6–10

For each question, choose the correct answer.

The young people below all want to go to a park.
On the opposite page there are descriptions of eight parks they could visit.
Decide which place would be the most suitable for the people below.

6  Marcus would like to go somewhere to play football with his dad and brother. He would like to get something to eat there, and they need to get there by public transport.

7  Christine is looking for a place where she can go cycling with her friend. They would prefer somewhere with some hills, and they really enjoy beautiful views.

8  Kelly wants to visit a park with her parents this weekend. She likes walking through parks with lovely flower displays, and her mum is interested in seeing work by local artists.

9  Gerald wants to go somewhere where he can get help with his school project on animals. He plans to go with his two younger sisters and wants to avoid spending any money.

10  Mollie and her grandmother are keen on visiting gardens and fancy going somewhere to look at plants. They would like to have a picnic, and would prefer somewhere that isn't too busy and offers easy walks.

Parks

A Canon Bank Park

Canon Bank Park is the perfect place to spend an hour or two in a beautiful place. There are lovely walks in the hills for those who want to be a little more active. Please note that unfortunately, cycling and the playing of ball games are not permitted. The park is easy to get to by public transport.

B Billthorn Park

Our gardeners have been busy this spring making the park look wonderful as usual. Come along and enjoy the result of their work and visit the arts centre for a chance to see an exhibition of paintings by students from local colleges. Leave the car at home if possible as the park can get quite busy!

C Sunnydown Park

Have fun with the family this weekend at Sunnydown. Bring your ball for a quick game with the kids, and enjoy a delicious cake and a hot or cold drink in our café. There are no parking facilities at the park, but we are easy to get to by bus or train.

D Banford Park Animal Centre

Come along and say hello to some new babies at the nature centre, including chickens, rabbits and sheep. Please do not feed the animals with your own snacks, but use food suitable for the animals, which can be bought in the shop at a reasonable price. Tickets can be bought online, or just pay when you arrive.

E Mattock Park

Mattock Park is a great local park situated just outside town. Escape the crowds and enjoy a peaceful time wandering through our colourful park with flowers of all kinds. Our paths are well cared for and offer easy access. Our café is closed at the moment, but you are welcome to bring along your own snacks.

F Broomway Valley

Enjoy a picnic with the family by the lake and watch the world go by at Broomway Valley Park. Why not bring your bike along as we offer an easy, flat cycle path around the lake. We are situated just behind the football stadium, not far from the train station.

G Marston Park

Although we were closed during the winter months, we're pleased to announce the opening of Marston Nature Centre, situated in the heart of the park. Bring the kids along to see the goats and horses, and hold some of our smaller friends in the rabbit house. Free entry for children 15 or younger.

H The Bays Country Park

The Bays Country Park is popular for those who enjoy walking and those who wish to get out on their bikes in challenging but beautiful locations. Your legs may suffer as you climb through forest paths, but the scenery at the top will be well worth the effort.

Part 3

Questions 11–15

For each question, choose the correct answer.

My Magical Hobby
by Robbie Maxwell

My hobby is a little unusual. At least, I don't have any friends with a similar interest. I absolutely love doing magic tricks. I discovered I was keen on them when I was a young boy of about four or five years old. I used to do them in front of my parents, who always looked amazed even though I often got the tricks wrong! They could see magic was something I really enjoyed and have supported me in my interest ever since.

I now study magic quite seriously and am quite good at it, even if I do say so myself. My interest is in close magic, not the big magic tricks you see people performing on stage. Stage magic often requires huge amounts of equipment and I always think the audience knows something else is going on. Close magic uses only my own skill and is also something I can do wherever I am. All I need is a pack of cards, a coin and a few cups to hide something under.

As with anything that requires quite a lot of skill, I have to spend a lot of time practising. There is a huge number of free videos about close magic online and I also attend face-to-face lessons whenever I have the chance. I love these events as they are a chance to see others performing their art and a great way to learn new ideas and techniques. People with more experience are always happy to help those who are getting started in magic.

I don't think magic will ever be anything more than a hobby for me. You can make a career out of it, but there are so many great people doing close magic out there, and the competition is fierce. Anyway, I get plenty of pleasure from showing my tricks to friends and relatives. They always want me to show them how a particular trick works or ask me to do something slowly so they can see for themselves. Of course, I never do, or the magic would die!

Reading

11 When Robbie did a trick as a child, his parents
  A told him if he got it wrong.
  B were surprised he was so good.
  C encouraged him.
  D knew how the tricks worked.

12 Why does Robbie like close magic?
  A It is easy to learn.
  B You need great skill to do it.
  C He likes being on stage.
  D He can do magic tricks using only simple equipment.

13 In order to improve, Robbie
  A demonstrates his videos online.
  B learns from other people doing close magic.
  C goes to magic shows.
  D buys online training videos.

14 What does Robbie say about his future doing magic?
  A He might make it a career.
  B He would like to work with other people doing close magic.
  C He will continue doing what he does now.
  D He hopes to enter competitions.

15 What would Robbie say about doing close magic tricks?

  A It is a great way to entertain friends and relatives.

  B You have to start at a young age.

  C Some people are naturally talented.

  D He enjoys it more if he has a large audience.

85

Part 4

Questions 16–20

Five sentences have been removed from the text below.
For each question, choose the correct answer.
There are three extra sentences which you do not need to use.

School Councils

Stuart Brindley explains what these are and why a school should have one.

Most of us spend years at school and are affected every day by how things are organised. So, it is no surprise that many schools have school councils to give students a chance to share their opinions. **16** But even if pupils can't control certain issues, they can still offer their thoughts to school teachers. In addition, councils provide an opportunity to develop discussion and team skills.

A school council consists of a small number of pupils who, with a teacher, meet on a regular basis. Various issues are discussed. They might be something to do with the school environment, such as untidy rooms or dangerous play areas. Members might also find themselves planning an end-of-year party, or how pupils can help at parents' evenings or other events. **17**

The first thing that happens when forming a council is to have an election to choose members. It is important that the council is representative of the pupils who attend the school, for example by including equal numbers of boys and girls and pupils from different cultural backgrounds. **18** Having too many pupils can make it difficult to manage meetings. However, if possible, there should be someone from each class. All pupils can compete in the election. Children will always be likely to vote for their best friend, but they should also be encouraged to consider someone who has certain qualities. **19**

Once the membership of the council is decided, time needs to be allowed for classes to have weekly or two-weekly meetings to discuss important issues. The class council member can then report the results of the class meeting to the council at the next council meeting. All pupils should be encouraged to participate in class meetings. **20** This will help those who feel nervous about speaking in front of the class.

A   Whatever the subject, pupils can have their views heard.

B   Have small group discussions first.

C   However, this is the most important job.

D   You should also limit the number of people on the council.

E   So, how can pupils be shown how to vote?

F   There are limits to what a council can achieve.

G   It helps pupils become more confident.

H   These include things like being reliable, and being good at listening and communicating.

Test 4 READING

Part 5

Questions 21–26

For each question, choose the correct answer.

Concorde

Concorde was the first supersonic aircraft to be built for passenger flights, and during its service, it flew more than 50,000 times and **(21)** .... 2.5 million people faster than the speed of sound. It was **(22)** .... by France and the UK and made its first test flight on 2 March 1969, and its first passenger flight on 21 January 1976. It had a **(23)** .... speed of 2,179 kilometres per hour, which is more than twice the speed of sound. Flights from London to New York took only three and a half hours compared to the **(24)** .... seven or eight hours taken by an ordinary plane. In 1986 Concorde flew around the world, a **(25)** .... of 45,509 kilometres, in 29 hours and 59 minutes. However, the **(26)** .... of operating Concorde was huge and it never became profitable. Air France stopped passenger flights in May 2003 and British Airways followed in October of the same year.

21	**A** held		**B** went		**C** made		**D** carried
22	**A** developed		**B** grown		**C** raised		**D** worked
23	**A** quick		**B** whole		**C** maximum		**D** big
24	**A** usual		**B** proper		**C** natural		**D** general
25	**A** space		**B** distance		**C** area		**D** length
26	**A** money		**B** value		**C** sum		**D** cost

Part 6

Questions 27–32

For each question, write the correct answer.
Write **one** word for each gap.

Bird Watching
By Natalie Hodges

We recently started a school garden to attract wildlife and find out more about the birds that live in this area. Our school is **(27)** .... the middle of the city, with very little green space, and birds have difficulty finding food there, especially during the winter. We knew that **(28)** .... we provided things for them to eat, we might get more birds in the garden and see them more clearly. We began **(29)** .... placing lots of branches in the corner of the garden. This will attract insects and provide food for the birds. We then purchased a bird table and hung bird feeders outside **(30)** .... of the classrooms. This will be a perfect place to watch the birds **(31)** .... disturbing them. We have a large poster with photos of the kinds of birds that are common in our country and we plan to see how **(32)** .... we recognise.

Test 4 WRITING

Part 1

You **must** answer this question.
Write your answer in about **100 words** on the answer sheet.

Question 1

Read this email from your teacher and the notes you have made.

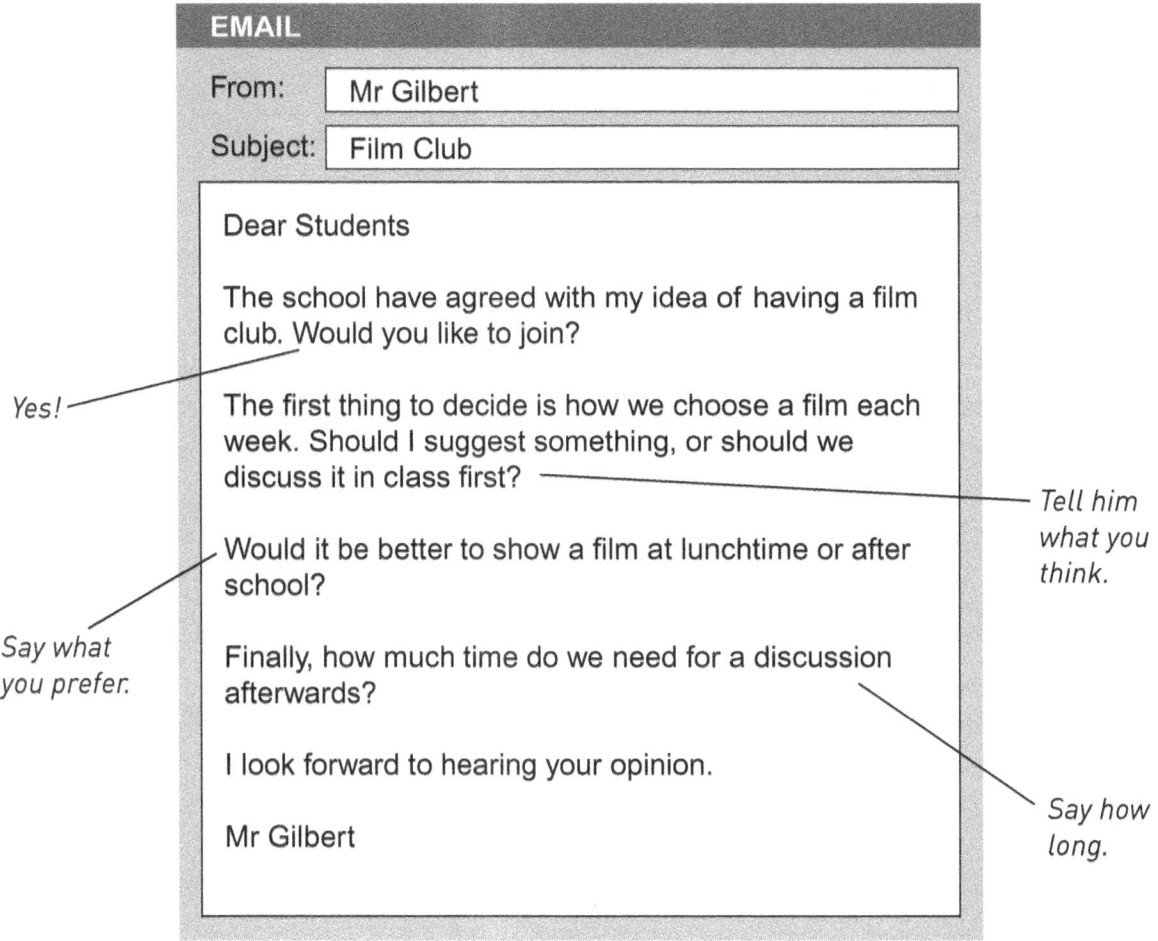

Write your **email** to Mr Gilbert using **all the notes**.

Part 2

Choose **one** of these questions.
Write your answer in about **100 words** on the answer sheet.

Question 2

You see this notice in an English-language magazine.

> **Articles wanted!**
>
> **TELL US ABOUT YOUR BEST FRIEND**
>
> How did you meet this person?
>
> What is it about this person that you like?
>
> **Write an article answering these questions and we will put it in our magazine.**

Write your **article**.

Question 3

Your English teacher has asked you to write a story.

Your story must begin with this sentence.

It was two o'clock and the class was about to start.

Write your **story**.

Test 4 LISTENING

Test 4 LISTENING

Part 1

Questions 1–7

For each question, choose the correct answer.

1 How did the boy find out about the bicycle?

A B C

2 Why should drivers not drive into the city centre?

A B C

3 What did the girl do for the first time?

A B C

Listening

4 Which lesson will be on Monday afternoon?

A

B

C

5 What is the girl going to order?

A

B

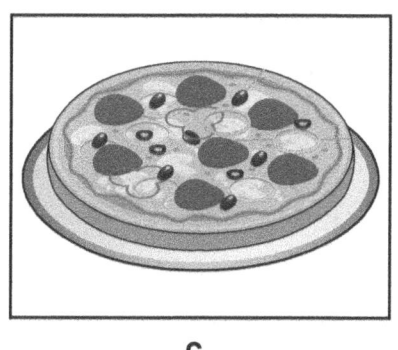
C

6 How should the boy's mother pay for the trip?

A

B

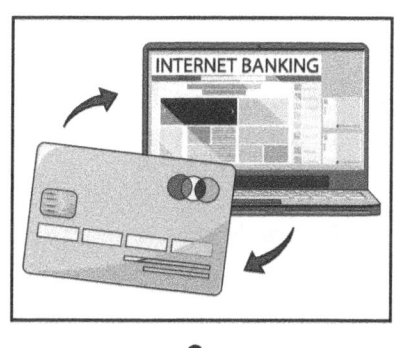
C

7 What does the boy buy?

A

B

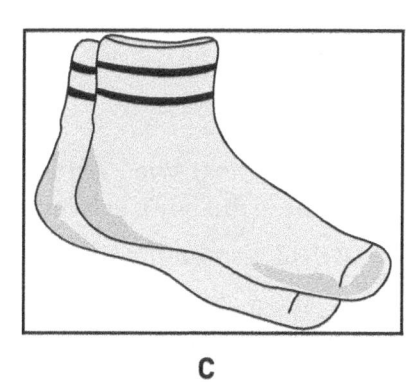
C

Test 4 LISTENING

Part 2

Questions 8–13

For each question, choose the correct answer.

8   You will hear a brother and sister talking on the phone.
    What does the girl say about the ID card?

    A   The boy needs to speak to their mother about it.
    B   She will probably bring it to the college.
    C   Their father will bring it to the college on his way to work.

9   You will hear two friends talking about a friend at school.
    What do they agree is the problem?

    A   He needs to work harder at home.
    B   He has missed some lessons.
    C   He finds the subject difficult.

10 You will hear two friends talking about the school football team.
    The boy says

    A   he can't play in the game.
    B   he will play in a position that isn't familiar.
    C   he will ask the coach if he can change positions.

11 You will hear a mother and her son talking about a new shop.
    The mother wants to go there because

    A   there are special offers this week.
    B   she knows one of the staff.
    C   it is open till late.

12 You will hear two parents talking about a party this Saturday.
    What do they decide to do?

    A   have the party at home
    B   ask people to bring food
    C   invite family members

13 You will hear two friends talking about a school trip.
    What is the boy's opinion of it?

    A   He wanted the trip to be longer.
    B   It was better than the previous trip.
    C   He would like to go again.

Part 3

Questions 14–19

For each question, write the correct answer in the gap. Write **one** or **two words** or a **number** or a **date** or a **time**.

You will hear a news announcer talking about travel problems.

Traffic Report

Parents must not **(14)** ………………….. in front of schools.

The highway is closed due to a **(15)** ………………….. that was hit in an accident.

Follow **(16)** ………………….. for other ways into the town centre.

Drivers must reduce their speed on the ring road until **(17)** ………………….. .

(18) ………………….. mean that buses will be late.

Engineers are carrying out checks to the **(19)** ………………….. that was hit by a bus.

Test 4 LISTENING

Part 4

Questions 20–25

For each question, choose the correct answer.

You will hear an interview with a man called Ian Groves, who helped set up an exciting after-school activity.

20 How did school decide what activity to do?
   A They found the idea on a website.
   B One of the teachers suggested it.
   C They asked the students what they wanted to do.

21 What idea did some students suggest?
   A They wanted to have music lessons.
   B They wanted to learn how to use technology.
   C They wanted to make their own songs.

22 What did the school do to start the activity?
   A They made use of the things they had.
   B They bought some new equipment.
   C They bought some software.

23 What does Ian say about problems starting the activity?
   A Finding a time to do the activity was difficult.
   B Parents weren't happy with the idea.
   C The teachers couldn't please everyone.

24 Apart from the students, who takes part in the activity now?
   A someone from IT support
   B a member of staff
   C professional musicians

25 What does the school hope to do next?
   A start a dance group
   B form a new group to make short films
   C make a documentary about one of the parents

Test 4 SPEAKING

Speaking

You are Candidate B. Answer the questions.

29–30

1A

1B

Audio scripts on pages 183–216 and Model answers on pages 234–249.

Test 4 SPEAKING

Things a family could do together at the weekend

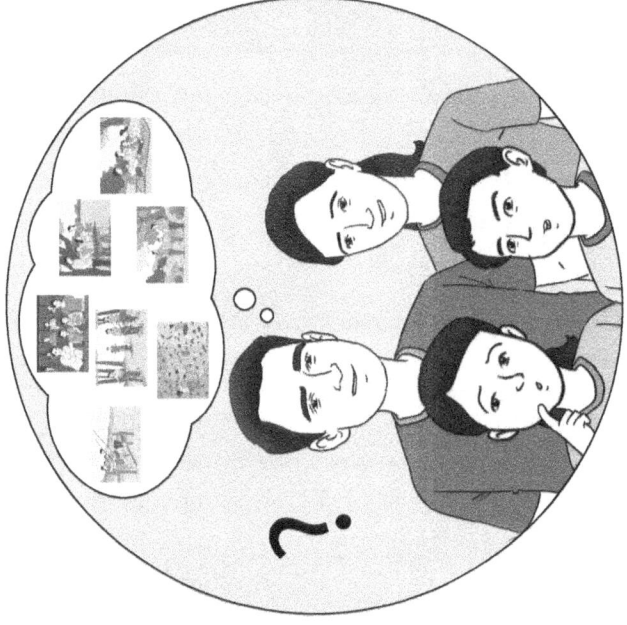

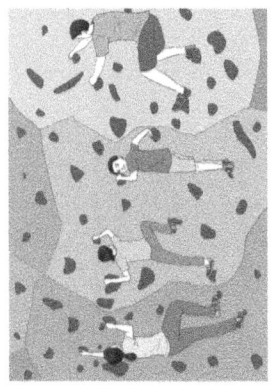

Audio scripts on pages 183–216 and Model answers on pages 234–249.

Test 5

Test 5 READING

Part 1

Questions 1–5

For each question, choose the correct answer.

1

Hi Paul

I've got to go shopping for dinner, so won't be in when you get home. I've left a key at Granny's house if you don't have yours.

Mum

A Mum is going shopping for Paul's grandmother.

B Paul doesn't have a key.

C Paul might need to visit his grandmother.

2

Skateboard for sale.

Hardly used. Safety equipment is also included with sale. I will accept any reasonable offer.

A The skateboard is second-hand.

B Safety equipment costs extra.

C The skateboard is in bad condition.

3

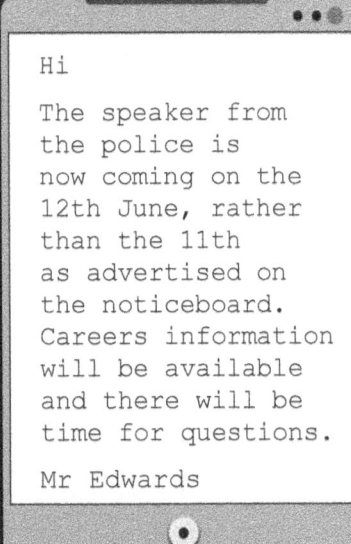

Hi

The speaker from the police is now coming on the 12th June, rather than the 11th as advertised on the noticeboard. Careers information will be available and there will be time for questions.

Mr Edwards

A See the noticeboard for further information.

B Contact Mr Edwards if you have any questions.

C The speaker is coming on a different day.

4

Lost Sports Bag

A bag containing sports equipment was handed in to reception yesterday. See Mrs Graham in room 211.

A Someone has found a sports bag.

B The receptionist has lost her sports bag.

C A bag was found at reception.

5

Hi Grandad

Having a great time on holiday with Mum and Dad. The weather could be better, though. We're looking forward to lying on the beach when the sun finally comes out.

Love
Claire

A The family are spending time on the beach.

B The weather isn't very good.

C They are enjoying sunny weather.

Test 5 READING

Part 2

Questions 6–10

For each question, choose the correct answer.

The young people below all want to watch something to relax.
On the opposite page there are eight advertisements for different kinds of entertainment.
Decide which one would be the most suitable for the people below.

6  Karen wants to see a romantic film with her friends this weekend. The weather is expected to be nice, so she would like to see a film sitting outside.

7  Mark's parents want to book three cinema tickets online to celebrate Mark's excellent exam results. They all like cartoons and they would like somewhere that sells food.

8  Amanda is having some school friends round on Friday. They want to stay up late and download a drama suitable for young people. They like the idea of watching a series from beginning to end.

9  Chloe is going on holiday this Saturday. She has a three-hour journey and wants to watch something on her phone. She likes crime thrillers and hopes to see the whole thing before she arrives.

10  Sean wants to take his younger brother to see a cartoon early on Saturday morning. He wants to pay for everything himself, but doesn't have a lot of money.

Entertainment

A TV Direct
Inviting your friends round this Friday? You supply the food and we'll provide the great entertainment. This week we're showing a film of all the performances from the recent Ashbourne Music Festival, starting at 5.00 p.m. and continuing till early the following morning. You're sure to have a great musical evening.

B Wired Online
Enjoy a film, TV show or documentary wherever you are and at a time that suits you on your phone, laptop or tablet. This week we're pleased to announce that the film you're all waiting for is now available for download. The exciting new thriller *Manhunt* will offer two hours of non-stop excitement!

C Royal Theatre
If you're looking for romance this weekend, the new Royal Theatre should be top of your list of places to visit. We're showing a variety of films from the past and present, love stories that will bring you to tears. With new seats and air conditioning, we can guarantee you a wonderful evening's entertainment.

D Mainstream Media
Nothing on TV this weekend? Wondering what you can watch? Visit our website and plan your evening's fun! You'll find hundreds of well-known films and documentaries, as well as the complete set of many teenage drama series, all ready to download for your entertainment.

E Sandtown
Come along this weekend to Sandtown Park for a lovely summer evening. See your favourite love story on the big screen outdoors under the stars. Order food before the show and we will deliver it to you during the film. Our weekly performances are very popular, so we advise you to book early.

F Mercury Cinema
This weekend we celebrate the wonderful world of cartoons with some of your favourite characters. No need to wait in a queue for tickets. Buy yours from our website before you arrive. Shows start at 7.00 p.m. And don't forget to visit the shop next to the ticket office for a wide range of snacks and drinks.

G Capital Cinemas
This week at Capital Cinemas: Can Detective Wheeler solve the mystery of the stolen jewellery and return it to the museum? We know he's good, but can he defeat these criminals? The best crime thriller you'll see this year. Tickets are available online or at our ticket office. Shows start at 6.00 p.m.

H Weekend Special Offer
We're pleased to announce a repeat of last month's special offer: two tickets for the price of one at our early shows. We're showing a wide range of films this coming week, including crime thrillers, a science fiction film and a couple of new cartoons. Please remember that we don't allow food to be brought into the cinema from outside.

Part 3

Questions 11–15

For each question, choose the correct answer.

Fifteen-year-old Sally McNally's work with older people

I'm so happy I joined my local youth club. It's a great place to hang out with friends and there's always something interesting happening. The youth leaders are also keen to do more than keep young people entertained, and they look for opportunities for us to help people in the area. This has included cleaning up a local river and picking up plastic from the local beach. However, during this last year we've been involved in my favourite activity so far.

It started when we were asked if we'd be interested in coming into the centre once a week to help older people use the internet. Unfortunately, many older people in this area don't have an internet connection and have no idea how to use things like tablets or laptops. We have an IT room with about ten laptops and an internet connection, so all we needed was people willing to help. It didn't surprise me at all when everyone who was present put their hands up to offer their time.

On the first day, I met Pam, a lovely 83-year-old grandmother. She has a daughter and two grandchildren who live in New Zealand. She told me that using the internet was important – although she knew the dangers, she wanted to learn how to shop online. But first of all, I showed her how to use email so she could send and receive photographs. I told her this was easy although I knew she'd also have to learn how to use the laptop and the digital camera. I didn't want to frighten her!

That was three months ago. Since then, she's learned how to work the laptop, search the internet, and how to use her own email address to keep in touch with her daughter. She's also learned to transfer and send photos from the digital camera on her own. And I'll always remember the first time she opened an email with a photo of her grandchildren. We were both in tears! We plan to arrange a video call with her family soon although first we'll also have to solve the problem of the time difference between here and New Zealand.

11 Sally thinks the youth leaders
   A are always looking for more ways to keep young people entertained.
   B ask young people for their ideas for projects.
   C like to encourage members to do work in the local area.
   D no longer do some activities.

12 When young people were asked to help on the project, Sally
   A knew they would want to help.
   B thought older people would not want to use the internet.
   C thought they might need more laptops.
   D was surprised more people didn't want to help.

13 What did Sally learn about Pam?
   A She knew what she wanted to do.
   B She thought shopping online was too dangerous.
   C She already had some basic IT skills.
   D She was frightened at the beginning.

14 Sally says that Pam
   A isn't sure of the time difference between the two countries.
   B has arranged a video call with her daughter.
   C doesn't need help to email photos to her daughter.
   D now has her own digital camera.

15 What might Sally say about this project?

   A The youth club needs more laptops.

   B Older people aren't interested in using new technology.

   C The internet can make a huge difference to someone's life.

   D There are some things younger people can do much better than older people.

105

Part 4

Questions 16-20

Five sentences have been removed from the text below.
For each question, choose the correct answer.
There are three extra sentences which you do not need to use.

How to be kind
by Natasha Hartwell

A few weeks ago, I was walking through a park with my daughter on the way home from school. **16** As we got closer, we realised it was a rock, which had the message 'You are loved' painted on it. I didn't know it at the time, but decorating rocks like this is a popular activity in countries around the world.

17 It seems that it all started in the USA with someone called Megan Murphy. She had the idea of decorating heart-shaped rocks with messages of love and hope and leaving them for someone to find. **18** Because someone has taken the time to decorate the rock, the person who finds it might feel loved. They can then hide the rock themselves and pass it on to someone else or paint one of their own.

It's a lovely, simple idea and it's not surprising that it became very popular. People of all ages started painting their rocks and leaving them for others to find. **19** Others do this as part of a group, sharing the idea with people in their area. Social media is used to attract new painters, but it's also a great way to help find the rocks as people post photos showing where they are hidden. Messages from people who have found a rock show how some rocks have travelled long distances, with some even appearing in other countries.

Both my daughters have now joined the trend. **20** The older one has taken it very seriously and has joined a local group who share photos of their rocks online. We're all hoping that one of our rocks will finally be found thousands of miles away on the other side of the world, just like people who leave a message in a bottle and throw it out to sea.

A The person who discovers the rock hopefully benefits from the message.

B Later, some research on the internet explained the strange rock.

C But she decided to paint one herself.

D There are some rules you should try to remember.

E The younger is happy to decorate them in lovely bright colours.

F Some do this by themselves as a hobby.

G However, it's important to use the right kind of paint.

H Suddenly, she noticed something colourful at the bottom of a tree.

Part 5

Questions 21–26

For each question, choose the correct answer.

Chilli Peppers

Chilli peppers were once eaten only in South America, where they grow **(21)** .... However, today they are popular all over the world, including Asia, where they were **(22)** .... by Portuguese traders hundreds of years ago. It is now estimated that chillies are eaten by a quarter of the world's population each day. There are many varieties of chillies, all with different levels of heat. The hottest one in the world is the Carolina Reaper, which is **(23)** .... to be 600 times hotter than some of the hottest chilli sauces. The substance that gives chillies their hot taste also protects the plant **(24)** .... animals that might otherwise eat them. These animals would damage the seeds with their teeth when they ate the fruits and so **(25)** .... new plants from growing. Unlike most other animals, however, birds do not **(26)** .... the heat of the chilli and eat the seeds whole.

21	A mainly	B naturally	C usually	D finally
22	A introduced	B transferred	C made	D found
23	A presented	B admitted	C imagined	D supposed
24	A along	B among	C against	D about
25	A leave	B stop	C end	D hold
26	A feel	B touch	C catch	D follow

Part 6

Questions 27–32

For each question, write the correct answer.
Write **one** word for each gap.

Collecting Football Programmes
By Ian Buckles

Like lots of other football fans around the world, I've got quite a few football programmes that I've bought when I've been to a match. They're great memories of the game, but I didn't know until recently that **(27)** .... can be very valuable and some people collect them. It helps **(28)** .... they are old and therefore quite rare and from important matches, like a game where a famous player made his last appearance, or the final of **(29)** .... important competition like the World Cup. Very early programmes that **(30)** .... just a few pieces of printed paper can be worth a lot of money. One programme from an English Cup Final that is supposed to be the oldest one **(31)** .... the world sold for £30,000. Another, just one sheet of paper from the 1909 FA Cup Final **(32)** .... Manchester United and Bristol City sold for £23,500.

Test 5 WRITING

Part 1

You **must** answer this question.
Write your answer in about **100 words** on the answer sheet.

Question 1

Read this email from your teacher and the notes you have made.

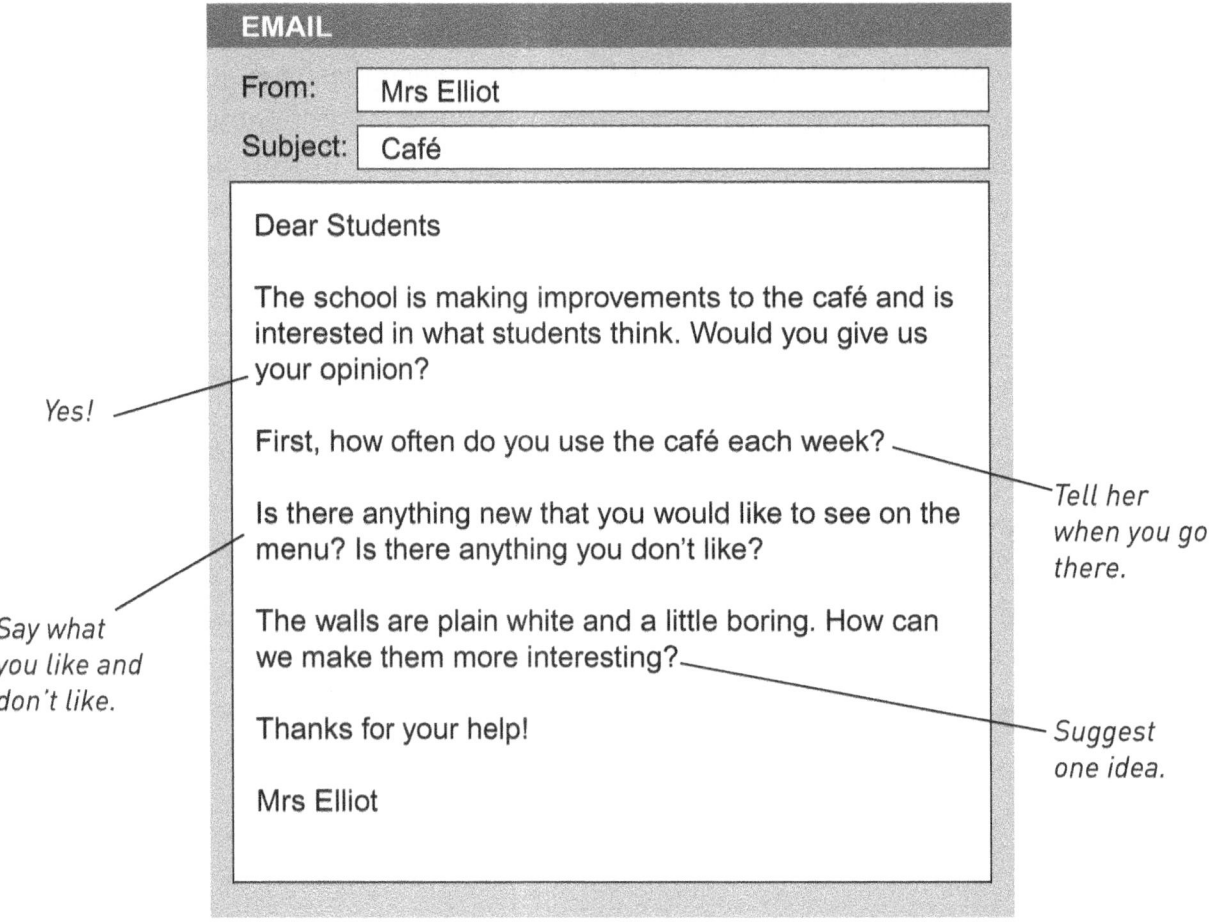

Write your **email** to Mrs Elliot using **all the notes**.

Part 2

Choose **one** of these questions.
Write your answer in about **100 words** on the answer sheet.

Question 2

You see this notice in an English-language magazine.

> **Articles wanted!**
>
> **TELL US ABOUT YOUR FAVOURITE KIND OF WEATHER**
>
> Why do you like it?
>
> What do you do when the weather is like this?
>
> **Write an article answering these questions and we will put it in our magazine.**

Write your **article**.

Question 3

Your English teacher has asked you to write a story.

Your story must begin with this sentence.

I switched on the light, but nothing happened.

Write your **story**.

Test 5 LISTENING

Test 5 LISTENING

Part 1

Questions 1–7

For each question, choose the correct answer.

1   What does the girl want her brother to buy?

A

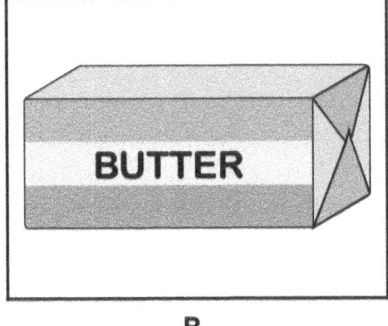
B

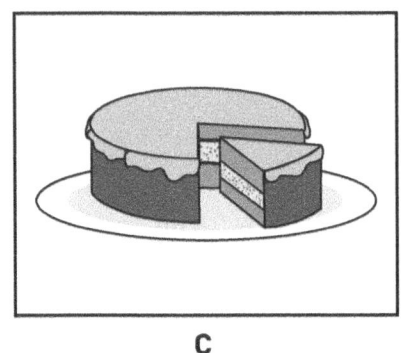
C

2   Where did the boy last see his bag?

A

B

C

3   When does the next train to the city centre leave?

A

B

C

4 How much does the girl want to borrow?

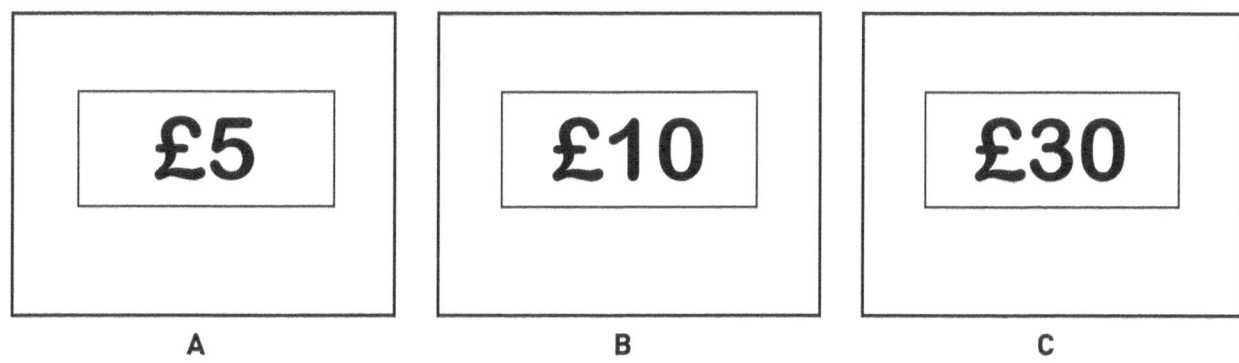

5 What should the children take on the trip?

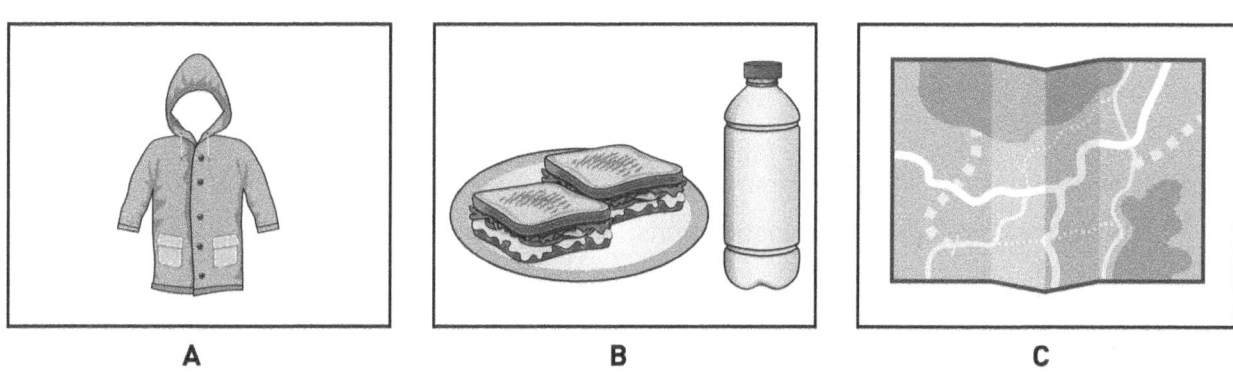

6 What is the boy going to give away to charity?

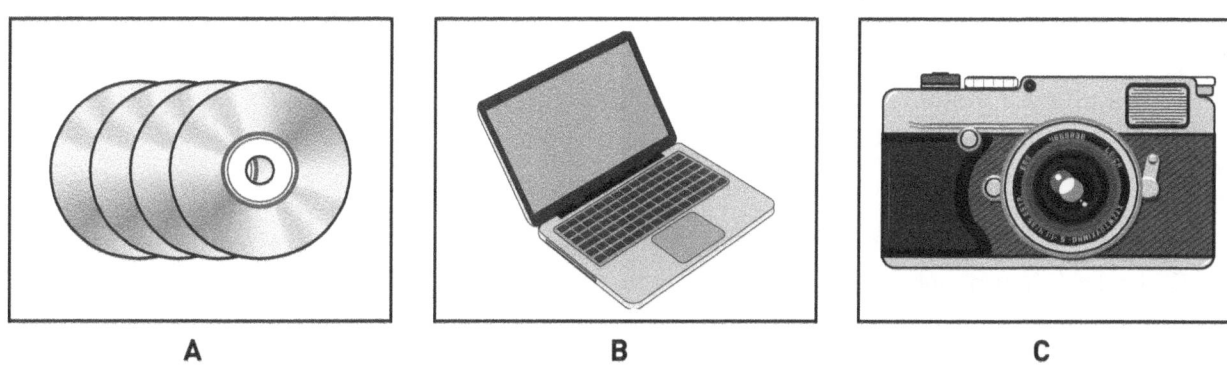

7 Where are the friends going to meet Hollie?

Test 5 LISTENING

Part 2

Questions 8–13

For each question, choose the correct answer.

---

8 You will hear two parents talking about their daughter.
   What does the mother say they should do for her?

   A take her out for a meal
   B buy her a watch
   C give her some money

9 You will hear two friends talking about a vlogger.
   What does the boy say about him?

   A The boy doesn't understand him.
   B The man doesn't know how to make cakes.
   C The man doesn't give clear instructions.

10 You will hear a brother and sister talking about doing housework.
    The girl says

    A they don't do any housework.
    B the boy should talk to their mother.
    C she feels too tired to do housework.

11 You will hear a mother and her son talking about the summer holiday.
    What does the boy plan to do?

    A spend all the time reading for his university course
    B work as a volunteer at the leisure centre
    C find a full-time job

12 You will hear two friends talking about a football match.
    Who does the boy think is mainly to blame for losing?

    A the manager
    B the goalkeeper
    C the whole team

13 You will hear a father and his daughter talking about guitar lessons.
    The girl says she will

    A have lessons at school.
    B just have lessons with a teacher.
    C try to have lessons in the week and at weekends.

Part 3

Questions 14–19

For each question, write the correct answer in the gap. Write **one** or **two words** or a **number** or a **date** or a **time**.

You will hear a recorded message about activities at a skateboard centre.

Marshlands Skateboard Centre

Sessions are taught by **(14)** ………………….. instructors.

Date: 18 June. Time: 6.00 p.m.: 'Skateboarding Safety First' is for **(15)** …………………... .

Date: 23 June. Time: **(16)** ………………….: advanced skateboarding techniques.

(17) ………………….. lessons are available for those who are unable to book a session.

All sessions cost **(18)** £…………………….. per person.

If we have to cancel a session, we will offer another **(19)** …………………. or make a refund.

Test 5 LISTENING

Part 4

Questions 20–25

For each question, choose the correct answer.

You will hear an interview with a man called Chris Thompson, who is a sports teacher.

20 Chris became a sports teacher mainly because
   A he was brilliant at sports himself.
   B his parents wanted him to become a teacher.
   C he enjoyed doing sport at school.

21 Which sport does Chris enjoy most now?
   A running
   B gymnastics
   C football

22 What does Chris like most about being a sports teacher?
   A It is a chance for him to get away from a computer screen.
   B All the students seem to enjoy his classes.
   C His classes give students the opportunity to get some exercise.

23 What does Chris find most challenging about being a sports teacher?
   A encouraging students to do sport when they aren't at school
   B not being able to spend more time with students
   C dealing with students who aren't interested in attending his classes

24 Chris thinks the main reason students should do sport is because
   A it will improve their fitness.
   B it will make them feel more positive.
   C they might achieve success in a particular sport.

25 What does Chris say about a student he had a few years ago?
   A He was in Chris's swimming class.
   B He once swam for his country.
   C He played for the football team.

Test 5 SPEAKING

Speaking

You are Candidate B. Answer the questions.

37–38

1A

1B

Audio scripts on pages 183–216 and Model answers on pages 234–249.

Things to take on the first day at school

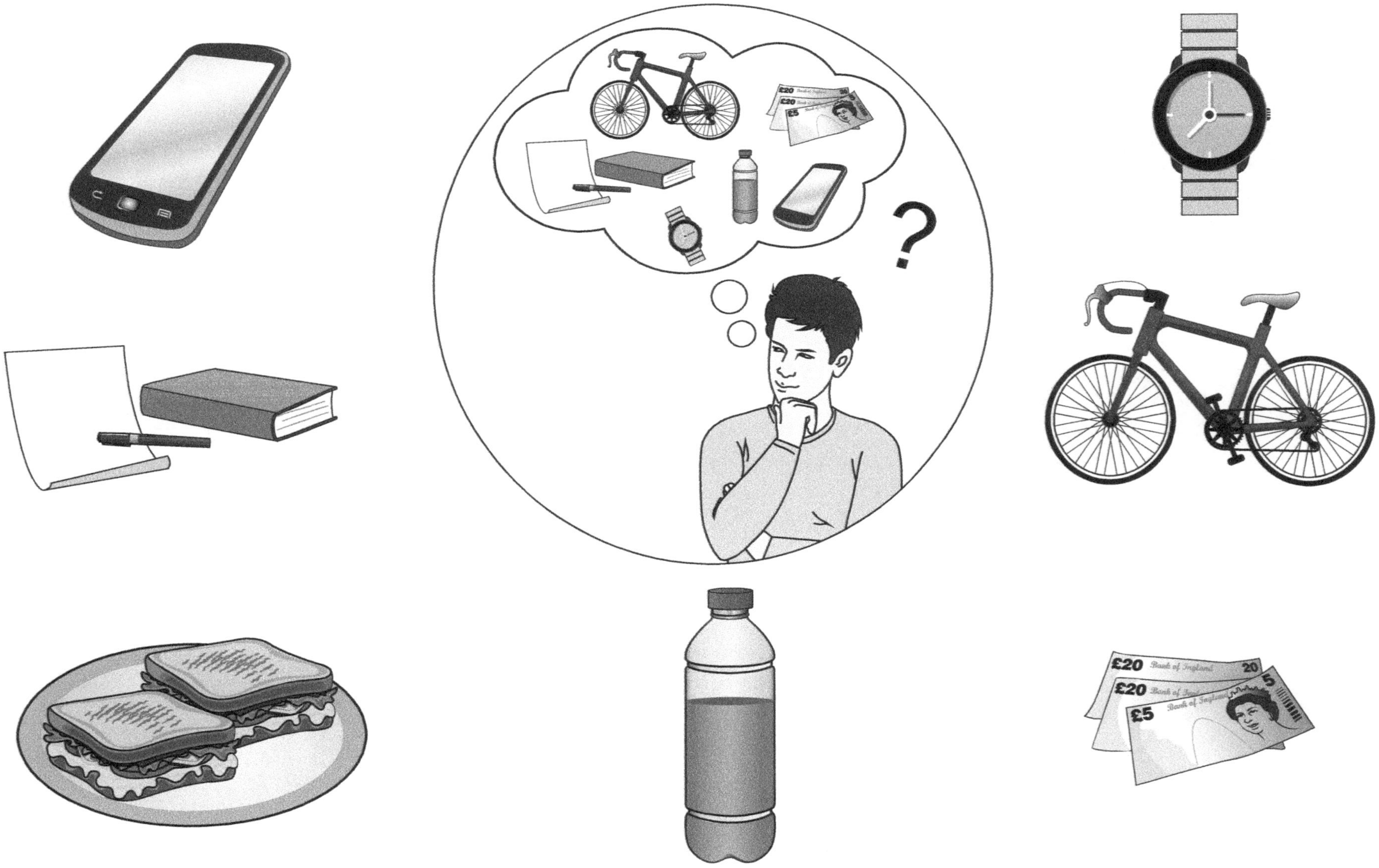

39–40

Audio scripts on pages 183–216 and Model answers on pages 234–249.

Test 6

Test 6 READING

Test 6 READING

Part 1

Questions 1–5

For each question, choose the correct answer.

1.
Warning
Barbecues are not permitted on this site. Please use the area provided for them by the playing fields.

A Barbecues are forbidden.
B Ask permission before having a barbecue.
C Barbecues are allowed in certain places.

2.
Hi all
Remember that exams are taking place on the top floor next week. To keep noise to a minimum, please go straight to your classrooms after breaks.

A Do not make any noise during the exams.
B Return to classrooms quickly.
C Do not use the top floor during exams.

3.
For sale
Child's school desk. The top needs some repair, but it can be used safely. Chair is also included.

A The desk should be repaired before use.
B You can have the chair if you buy the desk.
C Both the desk and chair need to be repaired.

4

Keep this product away from young children. If it gets in contact with skin, wash the area carefully for several minutes.

A This product can be used to wash up.

B Avoid getting this product on your skin.

C Contact the company if you have a problem.

5

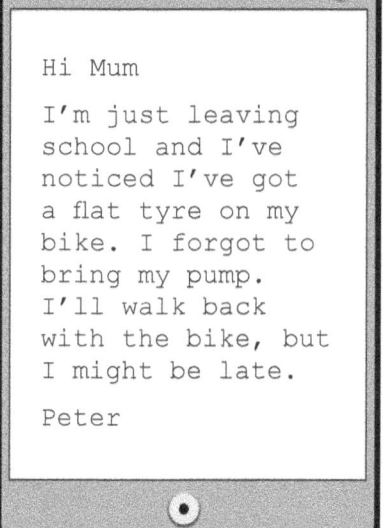

Hi Mum

I'm just leaving school and I've noticed I've got a flat tyre on my bike. I forgot to bring my pump. I'll walk back with the bike, but I might be late.

Peter

A Peter will take longer to get home.

B Peter wants his mum to bring his pump to school.

C It is too far to walk home.

Test 6 READING

Part 2

Questions 6–10

For each question, choose the correct answer.

The young people below all want to buy a magazine.
On the opposite page there are descriptions of eight magazines they could buy.
Decide which one would be the most suitable for the people below.

6  Matt has recently become interested in painting and wants to improve his skills. He doesn't live near any shops and would like to get something delivered regularly.

7  Martina's sister studies fashion at university and Martina would like to buy her something for her birthday. She is thinking of paying to subscribe to a magazine for a year.

8  Neil loves visiting art galleries with his friends. He is thinking of studying art history at university and would like to find out more about artists from the past.

9  Bethany is looking for something to read on the way to school. She likes to keep up to date with fashion and has lots of photographs of pop stars on her bedroom wall.

10  Jasper dreams of being a disc jockey in a club when he leaves school. He enjoys listening to the latest songs and is interested in finding out more about the equipment he will need.

Magazines

A Music Live

Looking for music industry news, reviews of the latest albums and songs, what we think is cool and what's not? We have this, plus news of all the latest technology for those interested in listening to or playing their favourite music for themselves or others at big and small events.

B Music for You

Music lessons can be expensive and difficult to fit into your timetable. If you're keen to develop your skills as a musician and would like help from some of the best teachers available, sign up for our monthly magazine. Easy to follow guides and helpful tips, along with links to useful video lessons.

C Art and Artists

Experience the beauty of art through the years. Find out more about the stories behind some of the world's most famous paintings. Explore the different subjects that artists have returned to again and again. The latest issue looks at some of the best new artists at the moment.

D Rewind

For interviews with important leaders in the music industry. We speak to some of the people who don't just follow the latest fashion, but discover new talent themselves. The magazine is published twice a year and is perfect for anyone who wants to manage musicians.

E Artist Monthly

For those new to the wonderful world of art and painting or those with years of experience. *Artist Monthly* is full of interviews with experts, useful tips on how to improve skills, and information about all the latest products to help you with your hobby. 12 issues per year will be posted to you free of charge.

F This

This magazine is perfect for the teenager who is keen on movies, music and what you should be wearing this summer. Interviews with Hollywood stars, celebrity news, plus our monthly colour poster of your favourite singer, group or film star. All for only £5 per copy.

G Art World

Subscribe to *Art World* for important news of art sales you won't want to miss. In addition to our monthly magazine, which we'll deliver to you for free, we'll send you regular news informing you of any sales that are taking place in your country or around the world.

H Fashion Sense

If you like to be up to date with the latest fashion, this is the magazine for you. Whether it's news of fantastic make-up products, clothing or jewellery, this magazine has everything. Get a copy from your local shop or sign up on the website for a monthly issue delivered to your door.

Part 3

Questions 11–15

For each question, choose the correct answer.

My Five-Second Videos
by Tommy Saunders

I've always kept a daily diary. Ever since I can remember, I ended the day by writing something. It wasn't always very interesting – what I had to eat or what time I got up – that kind of thing. But I found it enjoyable, and I like to think my entries are a little more interesting now. I haven't stopped writing, but recently I discovered a new way of recording my days, this time using technology!

At the beginning of this year, I started to keep a daily video diary using my phone. Each video has to be five seconds long exactly. It gives me the chance to practise video production skills, which will be useful for my school work in the future. But mainly I wanted to record things that would give me pleasure when I look back at them in the future. I knew it wouldn't be difficult. I always have my phone with me, so if I find something interesting, I can film it easily.

It's now May and I've managed to record one video every day so far. I try to record something different each time, so I've filmed lots of different subjects. There are videos of a sunrise, of my dinner, of a bee on a flower, all just five seconds long. It's a big decision deciding what to film because the first video I choose to film is always the one I use. Sometimes something happens later in the day that I think would be even better to film, but I always keep the original video to keep things simple. At the end of each month, I join all the videos together to make one film which lasts about 150 seconds.

The thing I've enjoyed most about doing this is that I notice things around me more than I used to. Before, I used to run around from one place to another and not really pay attention to what was happening in front of my eyes. Now, I'm always looking for a great thing to film. It will be a wonderful record of my daily life when it's finished, but meanwhile, I'm benefitting from it now.

Reading

11 What does Tommy say about the diary he writes?

    A He can't remember some of his entries.

    B He doesn't always remember to write in it.

    C He usually writes about food and what time he gets up.

    D He writes about more things than he used to.

12 Tommy says that keeping a video diary

    A is part of his homework.

    B is mainly so he can learn how to edit videos.

    C is quite simple to do.

    D was something he wanted to do in the future.

13 Tommy explains that

    A he only uses the first video he takes.

    B he makes the films at school.

    C it is difficult to decide which video to use.

    D he prefers to film things later in the day.

14 What does Tommy enjoy about making the videos?

    A He notices things around him more.

    B He always finds great things to film.

    C He goes to different places to take videos.

    D He now records music to add to the film.

15 What would Tommy say about making a video diary?

    A It is more enjoyable than writing a diary.

    B You need a good camera on your phone.

    C It can make your daily life more interesting.

    D It will take you much longer than five seconds a day.

Part 4

Questions 16–20

Five sentences have been removed from the text below.
For each question, choose the correct answer.
There are three extra sentences which you do not need to use.

Holidays by the sea
James Martin explains why he enjoys holidays by the sea.

We usually go somewhere in the countryside for our family holidays so we can go walking and enjoy the natural environment. However, sometimes we go somewhere by the sea, and I always really look forward to going. We live in the city and quite a long way from the coast, and the idea of a week or two on the beach always makes me excited. **16** Wherever it is, I know I'm going to have a great time if the weather is good.

The journey often takes quite a while and there are times when my brother and I get bored or impatient and often start annoying each other. **17** We take a nice lunch, so we either stop for a picnic or eat it in the car. As we get closer to our destination, there's always a competition to be the first person to see the sea in the distance.

We usually stay in a rented apartment as near to the beach as possible. Last year we were lucky enough to find one right opposite the beach, just across the road. **18** Usually it's about which bed we want, but once that's agreed, we go down to the beach as quickly as we can. I love that first moment when I feel the sand between my toes.

The seaside is the perfect destination for all kinds of people. **19** There are young people jogging along by the beach for their daily exercise, and families making castles in the sand or swimming in the sea. All these activities come free and are all part of what a holiday on the coast has to offer. **20** Ice creams, for example! But most of the pleasure simply comes from just being by the sea.

A You see elderly couples on the beach enjoying the fresh air.

B But Mum and Dad do their best to keep us entertained.

C We keep these in the back of the car.

D That's why it's usually too cold to go swimming.

E As we unpack, there's usually another argument between my brother and me.

F However, we're never ready to leave on time.

G I never mind where we go.

H Of course, there's always something to spend your money on.

Test 6 READING

Part 5

Questions 21–26

For each question, choose the correct answer.

Frida Kahlo

Frida Kahlo, who was born in 1907, was a famous artist from Mexico. She experienced a lot of problems during her life. She **(21)** .... polio when she was around six years old, which damaged her right leg and foot. In 1925 she was **(22)** .... in a serious bus accident. As a result of this, she had to have thirty **(23)** .... during her life. It was in the months after this accident that she started to paint.

A lot of Kahlo's art is paintings of herself that show some of the problems and experiences she had in her life. Her later paintings were very colourful and were **(24)** .... on traditional Mexican art. Before her death in 1954, her paintings appeared in **(25)** .... in Paris and Mexico. Kahlo became more famous and popular in the 1970s, when historians and people **(26)** .... in women's rights found out about her work.

21	**A** caught	**B** made	**C** met	**D** hit
22	**A** taken	**B** held	**C** put	**D** involved
23	**A** exercises	**B** operations	**C** actions	**D** services
24	**A** set	**B** based	**C** made	**D** taken
25	**A** views	**B** displays	**C** exhibitions	**D** sights
26	**A** interested	**B** keen	**C** excited	**D** familiar

Part 6

Questions 27–32

For each question, write the correct answer.
Write **one** word for each gap.

Victoria Falls
By Simona Johnson

We're just back from our holiday and I'll never forget seeing the Victoria Falls. This waterfall was such a wonderful sight. **(27)** .... is on the Zambezi River, on the border of Zambia and Zimbabwe. The waterfall is huge, nearly two kilometres wide, with a drop of over 100 metres, and it **(28)** .... described as the greatest 'curtain' of falling water in the world. The amount of water in the waterfall changes, depending **(29)** .... the time of year. At the end of the rainy season in April, on average 500,000,000 litres of water flow over it every minute. You can see spray from the waterfall from a long way away and the noise of the waterfall can be heard 40 kilometres away, **(30)** .... explains why people call it 'the smoke that thunders'. David Livingstone named it after Queen Victoria, the Queen of Great Britain. Livingstone was an explorer and was **(31)** .... first European to cross south-central Africa **(32)** .... east to west.

Test 6 WRITING

Test 6 WRITING

Part 1

You **must** answer this question.
Write your answer in about **100 words** on the answer sheet.

Question 1

Read this email from your English-speaking friend Dominika and the notes you have made.

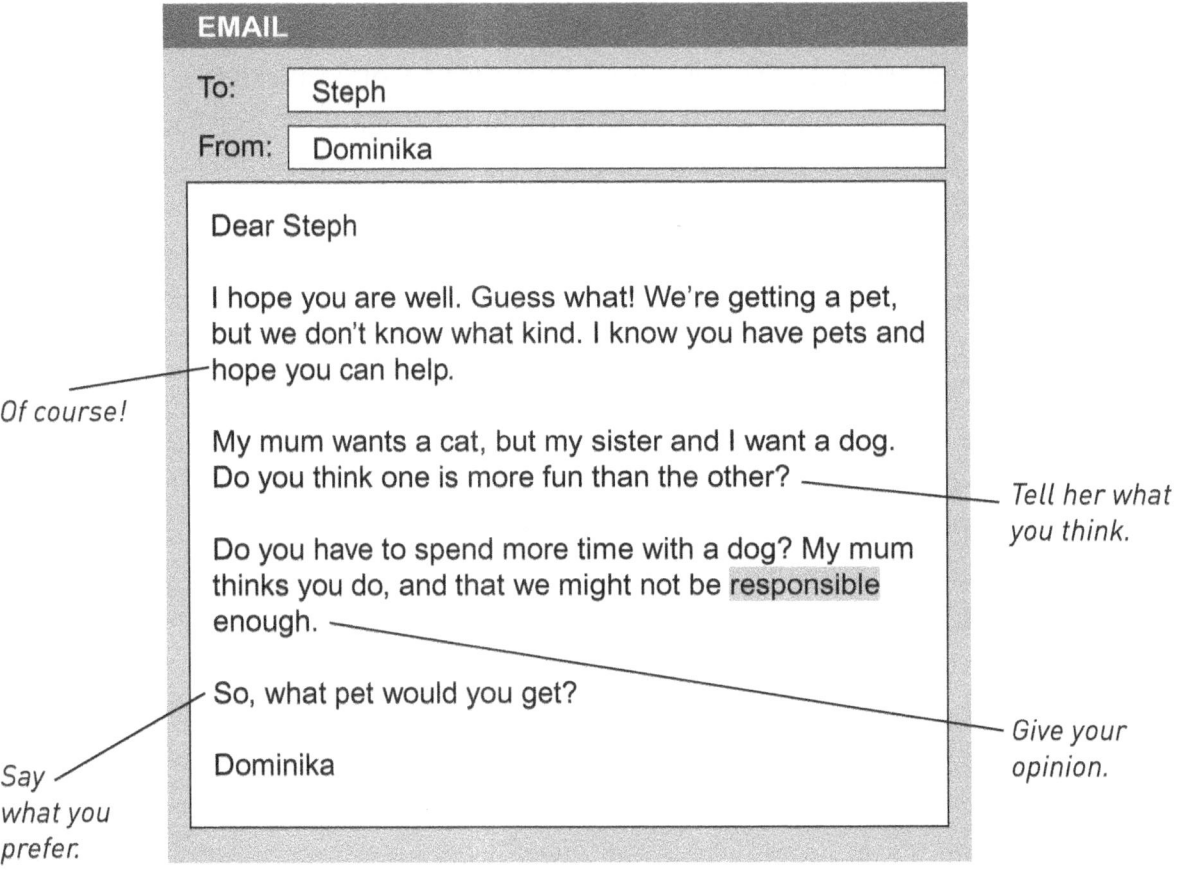

Write your **email** to Dominika using **all the notes**.

Part 2

Choose **one** of these questions.
Write your answer in about **100 words** on the answer sheet.

Question 2

You see this notice in an English-language magazine.

> **Articles wanted!**
>
> **TELL US ABOUT YOUR FAVOURITE PLACE TO EAT**
>
> What kind of food does it have?
>
> What do you like about this place?
>
> **Write an article answering these questions and we will put it in our magazine.**

Write your **article**.

Question 3

Your English teacher has asked you to write a story.

Your story must begin with this sentence.

I woke up early as it was my first day back at school.

Write your **story**.

Test 6 LISTENING

Test 6 LISTENING

Part 1

Questions 1–7

For each question, choose the correct answer.

1 Which activity takes place on a Thursday?

A B C

2 When is Grandad's birthday?

A B C

3 What is the boy doing on Friday?

A B C

Listening

4 What has the girl forgotten to bring with her?

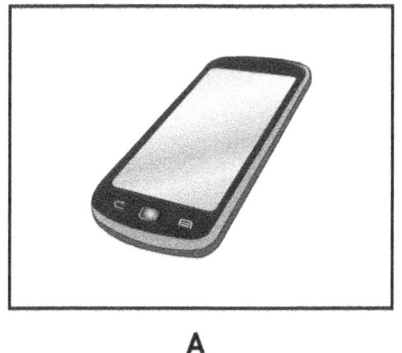
A

B

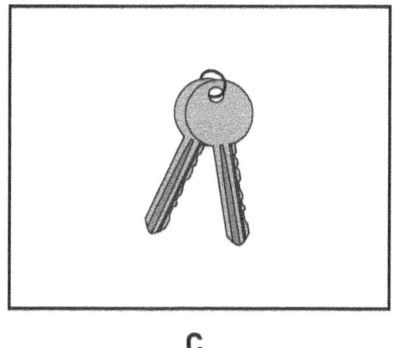
C

5 What did the boy do for the first time today?

A

B

C

6 Where is the boy now?

A

B

C

7 Why has tomorrow's music lesson been cancelled?

A

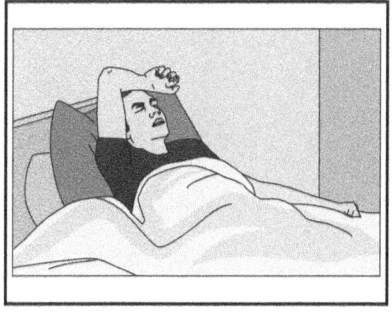
B

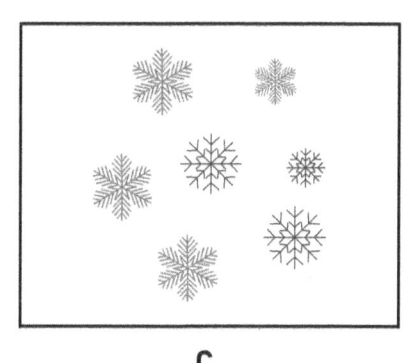
C

Test 6 LISTENING

Part 2

Questions 8–13

For each question, choose the correct answer.

---

8 You will hear two friends talking about a holiday.
   The boy explains that the hotel

   A was difficult to get to.
   B was near the beach.
   C had good views of the sea.

9 You will hear two friends talking about homework.
   What does the girl say?

   A It doesn't usually take her much time to do.
   B She has other homework to finish first.
   C She will finish it next week.

10 You will hear a mother and her son talking about a book.
    The boy says

    A he is a fan of science fiction.
    B the book had a surprise ending.
    C the film was better than the book.

11 You will hear two friends talking about basketball.
    The boy explains that

    A he hasn't played for a few games.
    B he is no longer injured.
    C he felt better than the previous time he played.

12 You will hear two friends talking about a clothes shop.
    The shop

    A is moving to a different area.
    B is opposite the boy's school.
    C has a sale at the moment.

13 You will hear two friends talking about the journey to school.
    What does the girl decide to do?

    A cycle to school
    B use the bus
    C ask her father for a lift

Part 3

Questions 14–19

For each question, write the correct answer in the gap. Write **one** or **two words** or a **number** or a **date** or a **time**.

You will hear a student give a presentation about how she helped her youth club.

Student Presentation

The youth club didn't have enough money to buy
(14) ………………….. equipment.

The speaker made cakes to sell to friends, relatives and to a
(15) ………………….... in the area.

They advertised the event on **(16)** ………………….. .

The speaker and her **(17)** ………………….. made 230 cakes.

The remaining cakes were sold on a **(18)** …………………..
outside her house.

The events managed to make **(19)** £………………….. in total.

Test 6 LISTENING

Part 4

Questions 20–25

For each question, choose the correct answer.

You will hear an interview with a woman called Amanda Wright, who runs a local leisure club.

20 Amanda explains that the leisure club
   A needed repairs before it could be used.
   B is part of the sports centre.
   C has been running for more than 20 years.

21 Which activities does the club organise?
   A drawing and painting classes
   B trips to art galleries
   C dance classes

22 Who attends the club?
   A charity workers
   B older people
   C younger people

23 What can leisure club members learn to make now?
   A items for the garden
   B jewellery
   C safe electrical equipment

24 What does Amanda say about young people?
   A Some have already joined.
   B There is growing interest in learning certain skills.
   C They spend too much time online watching videos.

25 Why does the leisure club need another volunteer?
   A to teach the skill of working with wood or metal
   B to register new members
   C to make food in the kitchen

Test 6 SPEAKING

Speaking

You are Candidate B. Answer the questions.

45–46

1A

1B

Audio scripts on pages 183–216 and Model answers on pages 234–249.

Test 6 SPEAKING

🎧 47–48

Things a girl could buy for her teacher

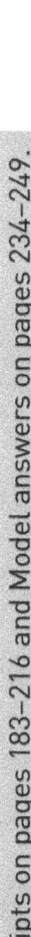

Audio scripts on pages 183–216 and Model answers on pages 234–249.

Test 7

Test 7 READING

Part 1

Questions 1–5

For each question, choose the correct answer.

1.
Notice
Students who are attending the International Day on 19 May must book a place with the secretary by Saturday 12 May.

A The date of the International Day has changed.

B You cannot attend the International Day unless you have told the secretary.

C There will be a place to sell books on the day.

2.
To: Barbara
From: Claire

I'm going away for the weekend tomorrow. I'm back on Sunday. Can we meet up when I get back to do the homework that we've got to do for Tuesday?

A Claire is away until Tuesday.

B Claire wants to meet Barbara on Tuesday.

C They have to hand in the homework on Tuesday.

3.
Library Notice
When you return after the holiday, let us know the books you need for exams by 12 April.

A Books must be returned by 12 April.

B Students need to reserve books by 12 April.

C Exams will take place on 12 April.

4

> Hi Caroline
>
> I'm off to work now. I've hung the washing outside, but just checked the weather forecast, which doesn't look good. Can you bring it in if it looks like it's going to rain?
>
> Mum

A Mum wants Caroline to hang the washing outside.

B Caroline should check the weather forecast.

C Caroline should look out for rain.

5

> **Did you like our food?**
>
> **Ask your waiter for a form and tell us what you think! Suggestions always welcome.**

A Let us know what you think of our restaurant.

B Give the waiter your opinion.

C Our waiters are happy to suggest what to order.

Test 7 READING

Part 2

Questions 6–10

For each question, choose the correct answer.

The young people below all want to work as volunteers during August.
On the opposite page there are descriptions of eight things they could do.
Decide which one would be the most suitable for the people below.

6  Oliver has a younger brother and sister and loves taking care of little children. He would enjoy helping with activities and joining them on day trips. He is not available on Saturdays.

7  Lottie is doing a college course about taking care of elderly people. She would like to spend time chatting with people and doing any small jobs they might need help with. She cannot do weekends.

8  James is interested in growing plants and flowers. He has only just started it and would enjoy leaning from people with more experience. He is only free on Saturdays.

9  Lara's mum and dad want the family to take part in a project to keep the local area looking nice. They would also like to meet up with other families who live nearby.

10  Nancy needs to find some work experience before she goes back to school. She would enjoy working with customers and would like to be part of a team. She is free Monday to Friday.

Volunteer Opportunities

A Village Flower Competition

The village is getting ready to enter the Village Flower Competition after winning Gold in the past two years. We need younger people to join our team of elderly people planting this year's flowers. You'll learn so much from people who have taken part in the competition for years! We meet every Saturday at 9.00 a.m.

B The Chase Garden Centre

Our centre is run by volunteers and we're looking for someone to help with the plant displays and keeping the garden tidy for visitors. If you're interested in plants and gardens, this will be a great opportunity. You can offer as many days as you can manage from Monday to Friday.

C Magnet's Youth Club

We're looking for a young person who can join our team for the whole of August, Monday to Friday, caring for kids from 3-11 years old. Help us plan and organise activities at the club. The person will need to travel with us when we take the children on short trips to local places of interest.

D Coffee Corner Café

Here's your chance to get some work experience at our busy leisure centre. We need someone to help in the café every Saturday, serving older people on our popular coffee mornings. You'll spend time chatting with customers and in return will get to meet some lovely people who will enjoy spending time with the younger generation.

E ABC Charity

We are looking for someone to help in the shop three days a week. This would suit a teenager looking for experience in working with customers. We are a friendly group of volunteers and are looking forward to getting fresh ideas from a younger person on how to attract younger people into the shop.

F Generation Links

Would you like the chance to make someone's life just a little bit easier? We need younger people to help us with our 'Help Out' project from Monday to Friday. If you'd like to spend an hour or two with an older person or going to the shops if they need anything urgently, get in touch.

G Mayfield Shopping Centre

If you have a few hours spare on Saturday, join our small group of volunteers at the Shopping Centre. We offer parents the chance to leave their young children with us while they do their shopping. We offer painting and drawing activities and anything else that can keep the kids happy for an hour or two.

H Litter Champions

Do you have time to spare this Sunday morning? We're looking for young families to help on our latest 'litter pick' as the area can get quite untidy after the Saturday shoppers have left. It's not all work, though. You'll have the chance to get to know some of your neighbours and make new friends.

Test 7 READING

Part 3

Questions 11–15

For each question, choose the correct answer.

The Night Sky
by Christopher Pleat

Enjoying the beauty of the night sky has attracted people for thousands of years. However, in modern times, it has become more and more difficult to see stars in the sky due to the problem of light pollution. This doesn't mean it's impossible to view some of the larger, brighter stars, but too much use of light in towns and cities means that most of the stars and planets are now impossible to see in many places around the world.

We're beginning to understand the effects of light pollution and hopefully, as a result of the need to save energy, we may see it become less of a problem. Meanwhile, for those who want to experience what the night sky was like for people in the past, there are various places around the UK, far away from busy cities, where the skies are dark and the night sky can be seen more fully. It's to these places that many people travel to spend a night watching the stars.

If you're thinking of trying some 'dark sky' stargazing yourself, you'll need to take the right equipment if you don't want a disappointing night. Let's start with the basic things. Make sure you go with the correct clothes. It can get quite cold in the countryside, even in summer, and there's always the chance of rain. Of course, you won't find shops where you'll be, so take some food and refreshments for the night. And although a telescope or pair of binoculars isn't essential, these will obviously help you explore some parts of the night sky more fully.

And finally, there are also some very helpful apps you can take with you as a guide. With the help of GPS, your phone will know where you are, and with an app, it will provide you with a map of the sky wherever you are. This will change as the stars move around the sky. Of course, if you're not interested in technology, you can always take a simple paper map of the sky with you. However, you'll want to take the phone anyway in case of emergencies, so why not try one of the available apps?

Reading

11 Christopher explains that
  A most stars can be seen in cities.
  B we can now see fewer stars in the sky in cities.
  C light pollution has been a problem for hundreds of years.
  D light pollution can be seen from space.

12 What does Christopher say is true?
  A Light pollution affects the whole country.
  B It is still possible to see the sky as people saw it in the past.
  C The stars appear closer in the countryside.
  D Light pollution is becoming less of a problem.

13 If you are planning a trip to see the dark sky,
  A you might be disappointed and not see many stars.
  B it is better to go in summer.
  C you should take something warm to wear.
  D find a shop nearby for food and drink.

14 What does Christopher recommend?
  A Take a paper map with you in case the technology doesn't work.
  B Find someone who can guide you to the correct places.
  C Do not go without your mobile phone.
  D Be ready to move to different areas for the best views.

15 What would Christopher say about seeing the stars?

  A Studying the stars doesn't require much equipment.

  B In the past, people were more interested in the stars.

  C Light pollution only affects some large cities.

  D People have always been interested in the night sky.

Part 4

Questions 16–20

Five sentences have been removed from the text below.
For each question, choose the correct answer.
There are three extra sentences which you do not need to use.

Learning to Swim
Helen Peters tells us about her progress.

I wasn't able to swim until recently and I'm still a beginner. I've always wished I could go to the swimming pool with my friends and I've always felt a bit jealous of others when we went on holiday. **16** People always looked like they were having great fun.

So, last year, on my sixteenth birthday, I decided to take swimming lessons. Unfortunately, our school only had group lessons for the younger children, so I had to find somewhere myself. My friends offered to help me, which was really kind of them, but I wanted to be taught by a professional teacher. **17** I emailed her and arranged our first lesson.

I got to the swimming pool much too early and felt a little embarrassed sitting by the side of the pool on my own. **18** Amelia, my teacher, arrived soon after and we chatted for a while before we started with a few movements. I found the first lesson really difficult and I didn't think I'd ever be able to swim. **19**

I've now had about six lessons and I'm definitely making progress. I can actually swim from one side of the pool to the other now. It takes me a long time, but I can do it. I've booked another four lessons and Amelia thinks I'll be able to swim a length of the pool by the time we finish the classes, and I'll receive my certificate for swimming a length. **20** But I'm sure that as I become stronger, it will be more fun.

A So, I got into the water myself and held on to the side.

B Apart from that, I really enjoyed it.

C It's still very hard work and I can't really say I enjoy it.

D But I told her I didn't like getting water in my eyes.

E Fortunately, I found one with good reviews on the internet.

F Before we started, she told me a little about herself.

G I always sat by the hotel swimming pool and wished I could jump in.

H However, Amelia said I'd done well and I booked another lesson.

Part 5

Questions 21–26

For each question, choose the correct answer.

The First Moon Walk

On 20 July 1969, Neil Armstrong became the first person to walk on the moon during the Apollo 11 moon expedition. 530 million people **(21)** .... the walk on TV, which means almost one in five people around the world saw it. After 20 minutes Buzz Aldrin **(22)** .... Armstrong on the moon, and the two astronauts **(23)** .... photos and collected rocks to bring back to Earth. However, they also left things on the moon to **(24)** .... they had been there. These included items with the names of American and Russian astronauts who had died on space **(25)** .... before. They also left a tiny disk with messages from world leaders. Armstrong **(26)** .... just over two hours on the moon before he returned to the spaceship to begin the journey back home to Earth. In total, the astronauts spent eight days in space and travelled 1.5 million kilometres.

21	A switched	B made	C looked	D watched
22	A joined	B connected	C added	D walked
23	A did	B took	C made	D caught
24	A present	B display	C defend	D show
25	A flights	B tours	C drives	D cruises
26	A filled	B went	C spent	D used

Part 6

Questions 27–32

For each question, write the correct answer.
Write **one** word for each gap.

Dolphins
By Mia Reynolds

I didn't know that the UK is home to a number of dolphins around its coast, from the south of the country up **(27)** .... the north. In fact, dolphins can live easily in different conditions and are found all over the world. Everyone knows **(28)** .... intelligent they are, but I didn't know they can even recognise themselves **(29)** .... a mirror. Only humans and apes can do that too. They live in groups, which can sometimes be as large as 1,000 dolphins. They hunt in a very clever way. They work together to blow bubbles in order to make the fish collect in groups **(30)** .... that they are easier to catch. They also make a variety of sounds to help them find their food. Unfortunately, noise pollution from industry and ships makes this difficult and is **(31)** .... of the problems dolphins have, as well **(32)** .... getting caught in fishing nets.

Test 7 WRITING

Part 1

You **must** answer this question.
Write your answer in about **100 words** on the answer sheet.

Question 1

Read this email from your teacher and the notes you have made.

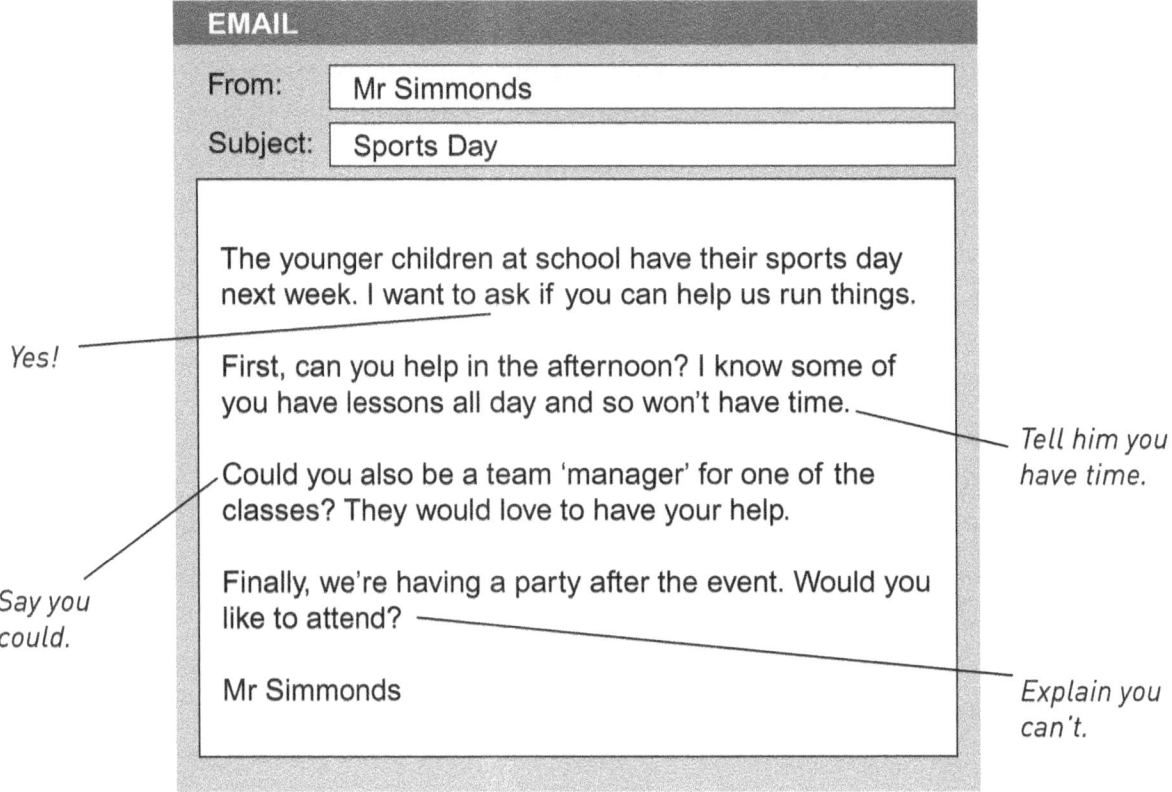

Write your **email** to Mr Simmonds using **all the notes**.

Part 2

Choose **one** of these questions.
Write your answer in about **100 words** on the answer sheet.

Question 2

You see this notice in an English-language magazine.

> **Articles wanted!**
>
> **TELL US ABOUT YOUR FAVOURITE WAY OF TRAVELLING**
>
> How often do you travel this way?
>
> Why do you like travelling this way?
>
> **Write an article answering these questions and we will put it in our magazine.**

Write your **article**.

Question 3

Your English teacher has asked you to write a story.

Your story must begin with this sentence.

As I was getting ready to do my homework, my phone rang.

Write your **story**.

Test 7 LISTENING

Test 7 LISTENING

Part 1

Questions 1–7

For each question, choose the correct answer.

---

1 What is the boy going to buy?

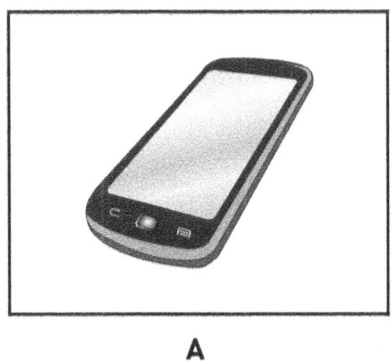
A

B

C

2 When does the Business English course start?

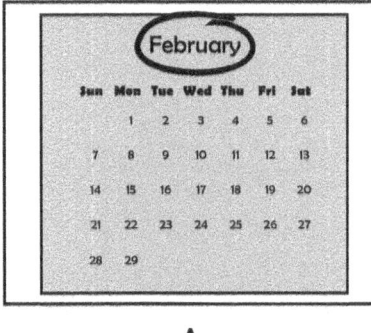
A

B

C

3 Which trip did the boy like best?

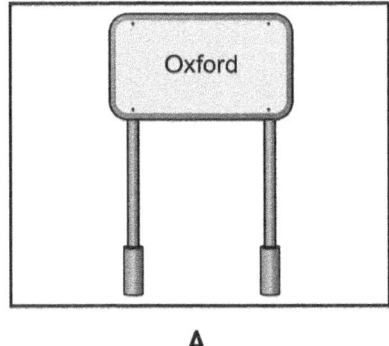
A

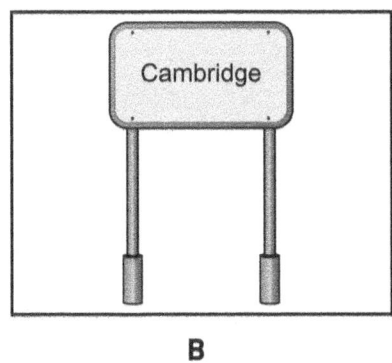
B

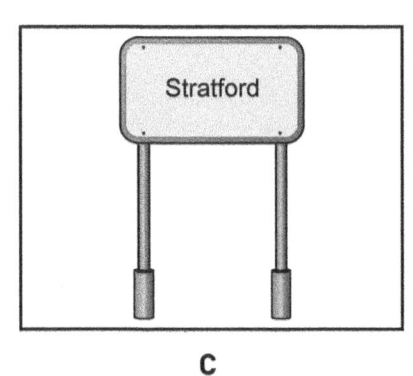
C

Listening

4 What does the girl plan to do when she finishes school?

A

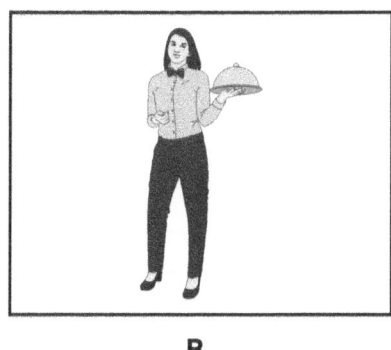
B

C

5 How many students are taking part in the event?

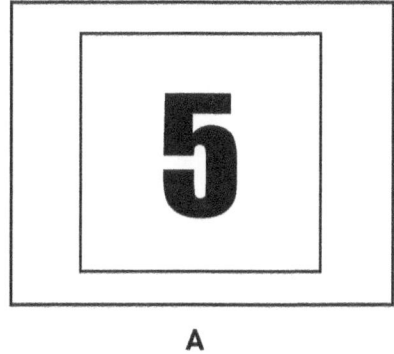
A

B

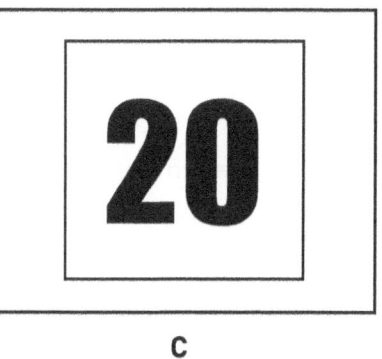
C

6 Which competition is the girl planning to enter?

A

B

C

7 What has the boy forgotten?

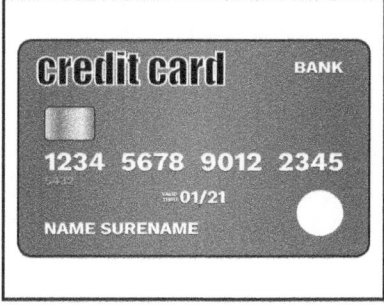
A

B

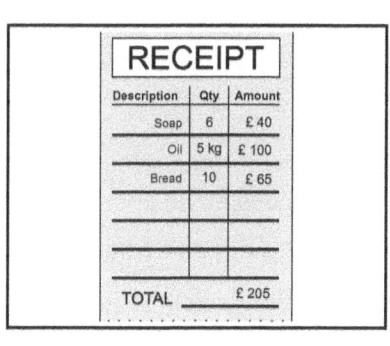
C

Test 7 LISTENING

Part 2

Questions 8–13

For each question, choose the correct answer.

---

8   You will hear a mother and her son talking about ordering a present online.
    What happened when the boy tried to order?

    A   He paid twice.
    B   The computer closed down.
    C   The order page didn't change.

9   You will hear two friends talking about a writing competition.
    Why does the boy think the girl should enter?

    A   It will help her to improve her writing skills.
    B   It is an important competition.
    C   He thinks she will definitely win.

10 You will hear two friends talking about booking a tennis court.
    What does the girl say?

    A   She will phone them in the morning.
    B   She booked it the day before.
    C   She will go there in the afternoon.

11 You will hear two friends talking about a party.
    What does the girl say about it?

    A   The parents have invited their friends.
    B   It is now on a different day.
    C   A lot of people are going to it.

12 You will hear a father and his daughter talking about a TV programme.
    What does the father say about it?

    A   He couldn't watch it as he was working.
    B   It is about world records.
    C   He has seen the programme before.

13 You will hear two friends talking about some apps.
    The boy says

    A   he doesn't find the vocabulary app very useful.
    B   the listening app has examples of American English.
    C   he hasn't downloaded the dictionary app to his phone yet.

Part 3

Questions 14–19

For each question, write the correct answer in the gap. Write **one** or **two words** or a **number** or a **date** or a **time**.

You will hear a radio announcer talking about tours of a new stadium.

Stadium Tour

The first tours start in **(14)** ....

See the athletes' areas, including the **(15)** .... rooms and modern fitness equipment.

(16) .... will be able to give you help with the activities.

You will need your **(17)** .... to get a meal in the café.

Family tickets cost **(18)** £................. .

The ticket office is situated at the **(19)** .... end of the stadium.

Test 7 LISTENING

Part 4

Questions 20–25

For each question, choose the correct answer.

You will hear an interview with a woman called Zoe Staines, who works in student services.

20 Why did Zoe decide to get a job in student services?
   A It was part of her career plan.
   B She had good experiences with a student services team.
   C She studied it at university.

21 Zoe says students who are looking for information about courses
   A don't find the published material very helpful.
   B sometimes don't understand what is in the published material.
   C need to speak to subject experts.

22 What is the main reason students use student services?
   A They are feeling anxious.
   B They need to complain about a course.
   C They have a problem with a teacher.

23 What do student services spend most of their time doing during term time?
   A working with departments to update course information
   B taking telephone calls from students asking about courses
   C dealing with students who aren't attending their course

24 To get a job in student services, Zoe thinks you need to
   A understand how to use their computer system.
   B know a lot about the organisation.
   C be good at dealing with people.

25 Zoe likes working in students services mainly because
   A she has to make important decisions.
   B she finds the job exciting.
   C she likes helping people.

Test 7 SPEAKING

Speaking

You are Candidate B. Answer the questions.

53–54

1A

1B

Audio scripts on pages 183–216 and Model answers on pages 234–249.

Test 7 SPEAKING

Things a family could buy a relative for their garden

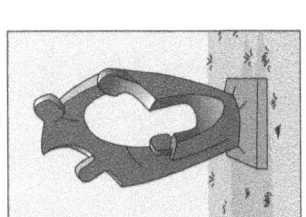
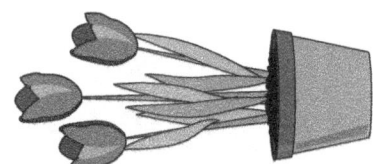
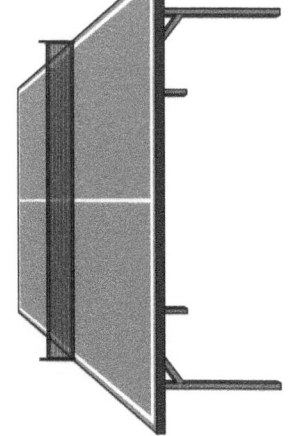

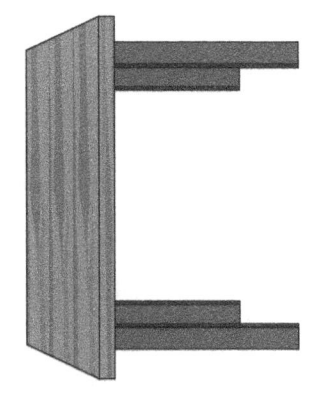
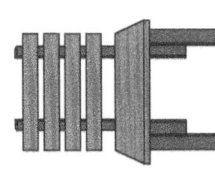
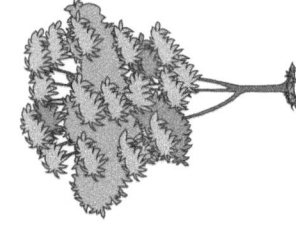

Audio scripts on pages 183–216 and Model answers on pages 234–249.

Test 8

Test 8 READING

Test 8 READING

Part 1

Questions 1–5

For each question, choose the correct answer.

1

> **To:** Emma
> **From:** Sonia
> **Subject:** Saturday
>
> I might not be able to watch you play football on Saturday. If my mum has to work, I'll have to look after my brother. I'll let you know.
>
> Sonia

A Sonia will contact Emma later.

B Sonia can't see Emma on Saturday.

C Emma and Sonia were going to watch a football match.

2

> This printer is for school work. You can make a maximum 10 copies. See an assistant if you need more.

A The printer is only for use by students.

B You must ask for permission to make more than ten copies.

C Speak to an assistant first before using the printer.

3

> **Refunds**
>
> **In addition to receipts, games must be returned in the original box with all parts before refunds are made.**

A A receipt on its own may not be enough to get a refund.

B The shop will only offer a part of the refund if anything is missing.

C If you don't have a receipt, return the game in the original box.

4

To: Students
From: Mr Ealing
Subject: Quiz
The school is organising an end of term quiz and would like a parent to ask the questions. Email me if you know someone who might be interested.

A There will be a quiz for parents at the school.

B The school would like a parent's help for a quiz.

C Parents should contact the school if they have any questions.

5

> Clean headphones after use with the cleaning product provided. Return them to the cupboard before leaving the IT centre.

A Clean the headphones before putting them in the cupboard.

B Do not use the headphones without cleaning them first.

C The cleaning product is kept in the cupboard.

Test 8 READING

Part 2

Questions 6-10

For each question, choose the correct answer.

The young people below are all looking for some games they could plan for the weekend.
On the opposite page there are advertisements for eight things they could do.
Decide which one would be the most suitable for the people below.

6  Amelia has three friends coming round this weekend for her sixteenth birthday. They have all said they would enjoy doing some kind of mystery game in a competition with each other.

7  Jack wants to do something his whole family can join in with this Sunday. They all want to get away from the house, but need to find somewhere local as they don't have a car.

8  Georgia has a family party this Saturday and her parents have asked her to organise some games. She doesn't want everyone sitting around indoors and wants something the whole family can do.

9  Ezme's mum and dad have offered to take her and her brother away for a fun weekend somewhere. Ezme loves solving puzzles and would enjoy doing this with her family.

10  Lucas meets up online with some friends abroad every month. This weekend he would like to add some entertainment to the event. Something they could all do online would be perfect.

Games for the Weekend

A Games Universe

Meeting up with friends or family online? Why not add some entertainment to the event with some of our great online games? Our latest game includes challenges to test your internet search skills. Try searching for the hidden prize. The answers are out there somewhere, but who will be the first to find the prize?

B Greenshall Centre

Looking for somewhere for the children to go this weekend? Greenshall Centre is opening its doors to anyone who wants to take part in team or individual games. We have lots of fun activities for 5- to 11-year-olds to enjoy, including our wide selection of computer games and sports activities.

C Neighbourhood Hunts

With a beautiful weather forecast for this Sunday, there's nothing better than enjoying the sunny days with one of our enjoyable 'search for the prize' challenges. These family-friendly activities can be enjoyed by both adults and children as you find the clues hidden in various areas in your neighbourhood. Follow these until you find the hidden treasure.

D Kids Power

Have you got a party with the children this weekend? Time to relax! Call me in to provide the entertainment. I have games and activities aimed at 5- to 10-year-olds that will keep the children entertained inside or outside, depending on your location and the weather. Available seven days a week.

E Solve It

Our popular board game for two to four players has been updated to include new crimes, with suggestions to guide you and trick you as you do your police work. You'll need a few hours to discover the truth, and will work on your own to find out who the criminal is before anyone else discovers the answer.

F Party Games

Are you having friends round for a party? Get them out in the garden to enjoy some of our games, suitable for family or friends of all ages. Have fun with our badminton equipment, giant water guns, or some gentler activities for the grandparents. We promise your party will be a great success!

G Chess Champions

Join us this Saturday for this year's local chess championships for 12- to 16-year-olds. Sign up online and we'll match you with a suitable partner. Then just come on the day to Colmore Gardens – yes, this year we're taking advantage of the sunny weather and holding the games outside!

H Mystery Weekend

Our popular family mystery weekend starts again this Saturday. Two days of police work in our huge hotel and gardens. Working together as a group, you will read the information and follow the instructions to solve the puzzle we'll set for you. From the moment you arrive, you'll begin your hunt for the bad guy.

Part 3

Questions 11–15

For each question, choose the correct answer.

Becoming a Vegetarian
by Louise Braithwaite

Last year, I decided I wanted to become a vegetarian. Some of my friends had already stopped eating meat, which made me start thinking about doing the same. But the thing that persuaded me in the end was a documentary we watched at school about where our chicken comes from. When I saw all these poor birds kept in small boxes in a factory farm, I made the decision to stop. I wanted to give up eating not just chicken, but anything containing meat.

I'll never forget the looks on my mum and dad's faces when I told them. My mum was always saying she could easily become a vegetarian and she looked very pleased to hear the news. My dad, however, looked a bit worried. He loves eating meat and he was probably thinking that he wouldn't be getting any more on his dinner plate. But he didn't say anything negative and they both promised to do their best to support me.

The first few weeks were easy in some ways and more difficult in others. Eating at home wasn't a problem. Mum, of course, was very happy. She went out and bought lots of books on vegetarian meals and made something nice every night. Going out with friends was often more of a problem. Some of them still like eating meat, so we always had to find somewhere that served both. A lot of the vegetarian meals were disappointing. We ended up going to pizza restaurants as they offered a good selection.

Almost a year has passed since I made the decision and I feel quite relaxed about not eating meat. I don't really miss any meals I used to have when I ate meat, and I actually feel better. I think becoming a vegetarian makes you look carefully at your whole diet and you end up eating and drinking more healthily as a result. Until now, I've continued eating fish and I'm now wondering whether to stop eating that too. I'd probably find that harder than giving up meat as Mum cooks some lovely dishes with fish. Let's wait and see!

11 Louise finally decided to become a vegetarian because
   A her friends were doing the same.
   B she didn't like the meals they served at school.
   C she watched a programme that upset her.
   D she went on a school trip to a factory farm.

12 What happened when Louise told her parents?
   A They said they would help her.
   B Her dad said he didn't want to stop eating meat.
   C They both reacted in the same way.
   D Her mum said she would become a vegetarian as well.

13 What does Louise say about the first few weeks of being a vegetarian?
   A She argued with her friends about where to eat.
   B Vegetarian food in restaurants wasn't always very nice.
   C Her mum did a course on vegetarian cooking.
   D Her friends refused to eat in pizza restaurants.

14 Louise explains that
   A being a vegetarian helps her relax.
   B she would find it more difficult to give up eating fish.
   C there are some meals she still misses.
   D giving up meat has been hard.

15 What would Louise say to someone thinking of becoming a vegetarian?

   A You have to persuade your family to become vegetarians too.
   B You should avoid eating out.
   C It isn't as difficult as you might imagine.
   D It is important to have friends who are also vegetarians.

Part 4

Questions 16–20

Five sentences have been removed from the text below.
For each question, choose the correct answer.
There are three extra sentences which you do not need to use.

My Uncle's Model Railway
Clara Stevens tells us about her uncle's hobby.

One of my uncles, Uncle David, has a really interesting hobby. He is very keen on building model railways. **16** One year Uncle David received a small train set for a birthday present. Dad remembers that David used to play with it all the time, and it was obvious that it was something he enjoyed.

My mum always says that Aunt Stephanie, his wife, must be a very kind person. Uncle David now has a whole room in their house for his model railway. **17** The house has three bedrooms and he uses the largest one for his hobby. Each time I visit them, the model railway seems to get bigger or there is something new for me to see. I am sure he will need another room soon.

The first thing you notice when you walk into the room is the size of the model railway. **18** The model railway is a copy of the real railway in a town in Switzerland that my uncle visited a few years ago. He says it is exactly the same, including the stations, the factories that the trains go past, and the mountains. **19** Just like the large stations you find around the world, his main one has around six different platforms that trains arrive at and leave from at different times.

Whenever we visit, I can't wait to see the latest things he has made. After I have told my aunt about school and anything interesting that is happening in my life, I go with Uncle David to see the model railway. I love making the different trains work and seeing them move around the room. **20** But I really don't need to do this as long as my uncle continues to enjoy the hobby himself.

A This was why he decided to use the large room.

B My dad says it all started when they were both children.

C It fills the whole room.

D I would never be patient enough to build anything similar myself.

E This is why the trains can cost so much.

F So, he downloaded a map of the railway line from the internet.

G It isn't even one of the smaller rooms.

H And there is not just one railway line.

Test 8 READING

Part 5

Questions 21-26

For each question, choose the correct answer.

Parrots

A parrot called Puck holds the world record for the biggest (21) .... of words a parrot can speak – 1,728! Such a high number might be unusual, but parrots are well known for being able to (22) .... the words we say. They are sociable birds that live in groups or 'flocks', and communication is important to them. When they are (23) .... as pets, their group is the people around them. Parrots want to feel part of the group and also (24) .... on us for their food, so they are happy to communicate.

Parrots have a completely different voice box to our own, and don't have lips or teeth to create the sounds we make. However, scientists have (25) .... that parrots are able to use their own voice box to produce noises that are (26) .... to human sounds. They also use their tongue to make sounds, something other birds don't do.

21	A total	B number	C figure	D sum
22	A copy	B do	C take	D make
23	A cared	B saved	C put	D kept
24	A rely	B need	C build	D hope
25	A viewed	B looked	C discovered	D explored
26	A close	B next	C real	D same

Part 6

Questions 27–32

For each question, write the correct answer.
Write **one** word for each gap.

Wall Climbing
By Aiden Mathews

A wall climbing centre opened in our town recently. I went there a few weeks ago for a beginners' session. We learned **(27)** .... two types of climbing. One type was climbing along low walls. You have to get from one end of the wall to the other. There are special parts attached to the wall, and you use **(28)** .... to stand on and hold on to. I tried this and it was great fun. It was like **(29)** .... puzzle as I had to decide **(30)** .... to put my foot or my hand. I didn't fall, but there was a safety mat **(31)** .... case of accidents. The other type of climbing was rope climbing. You are tied to a rope, which another person controls, and the idea **(32)** .... to get to the top of the wall. If I go again, I might try this.

Test 8 WRITING

Part 1

You **must** answer this question.
Write your answer in about **100 words** on the answer sheet.

Question 1

Read this email from your English-speaking friend Camilla and the notes you have made.

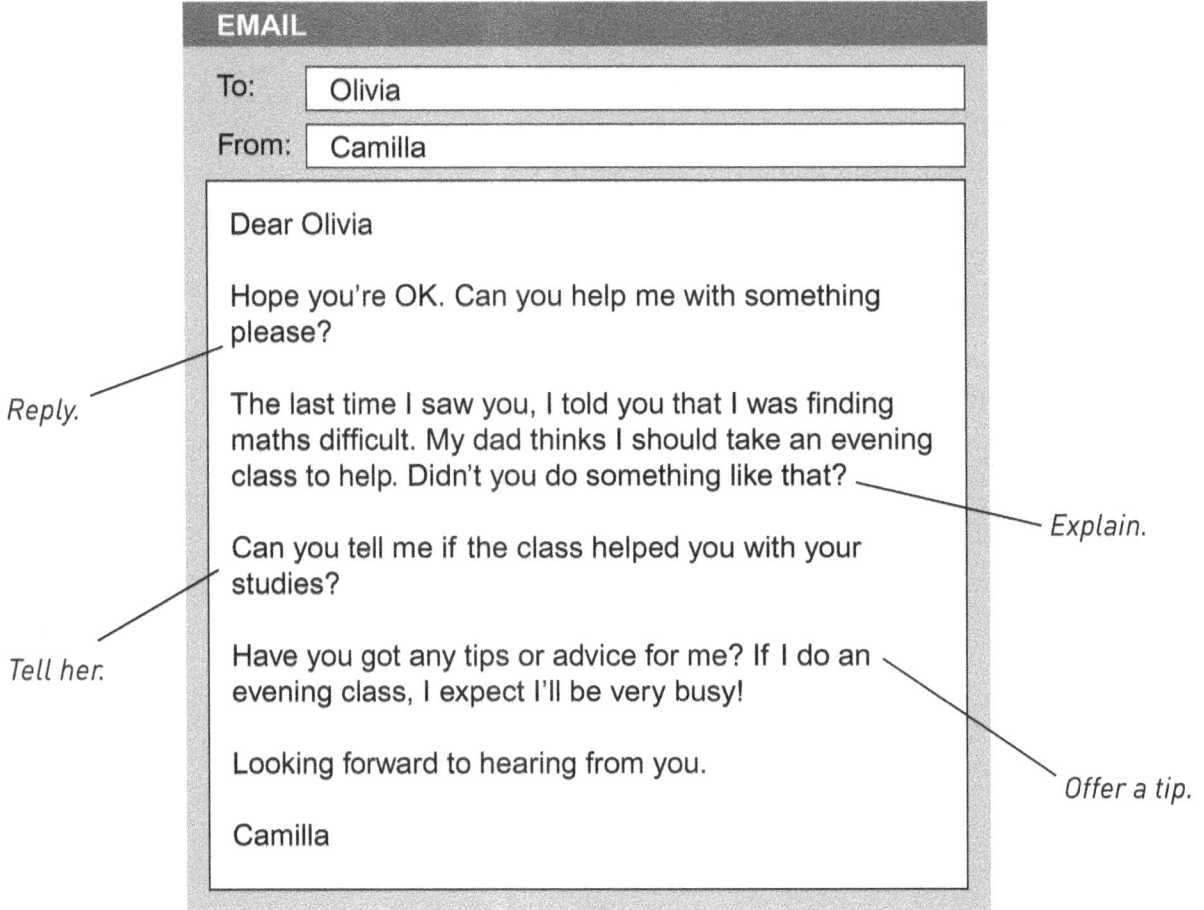

Write your **email** to Camilla using **all the notes**.

Part 2

Choose **one** of these questions.
Write your answer in about **100 words** on the answer sheet.

Question 2

You see this notice in an English-language magazine.

> **Articles wanted!**
>
> **TELL US ABOUT YOUR FAVOURITE WEBSITE**
>
> What kind of things are on the website?
>
> Why do you like it so much?
>
> **Write an article answering these questions and we will put it in our magazine.**

Write your **article**.

Question 3

Your English teacher has asked you to write a story.

Your story must begin with this sentence.

The train was late and we were in a hurry.

Write your **story**.

Test 8 LISTENING

Test 8 LISTENING

Part 1

Questions 1–7

For each question, choose the correct answer.

1 Which exhibition takes place this weekend?

A

B

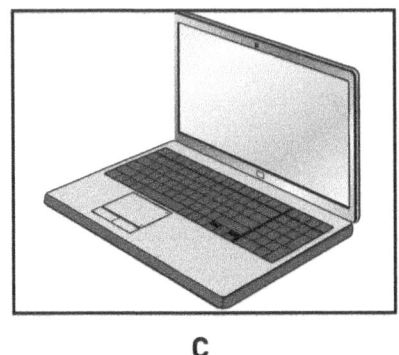
C

2 How much was the skirt previously?

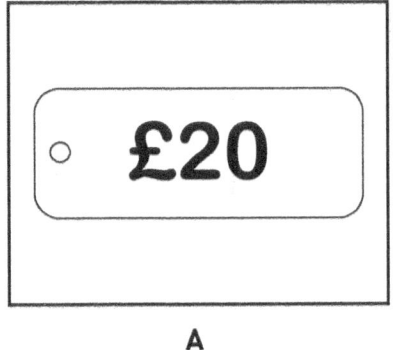
A

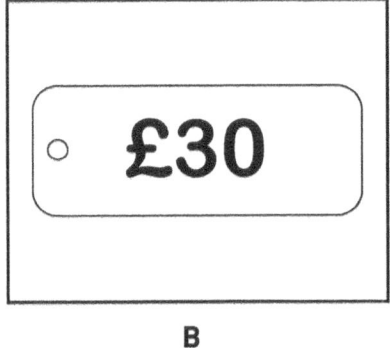
B

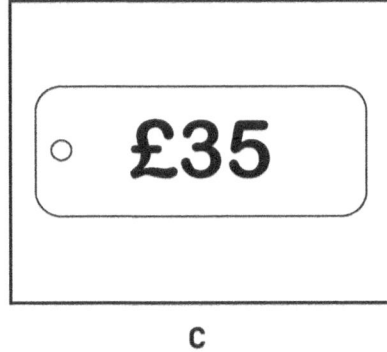
C

3 What does the girl want her brother to collect?

A

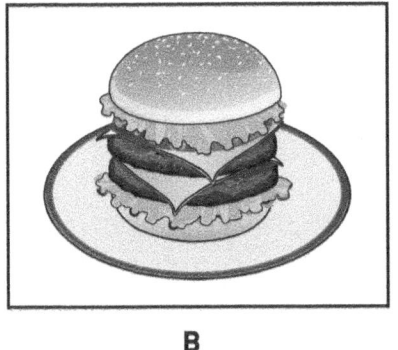
B

C

4 What is the woman afraid of?

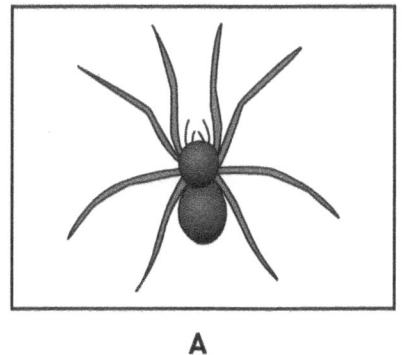
A

B

C

5 What does the dance teacher need?

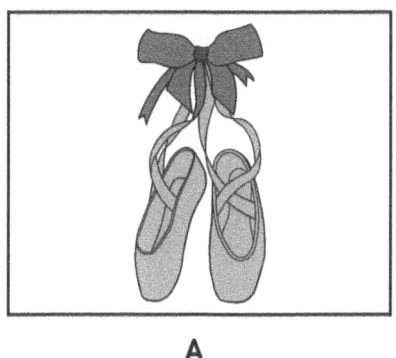
A

B

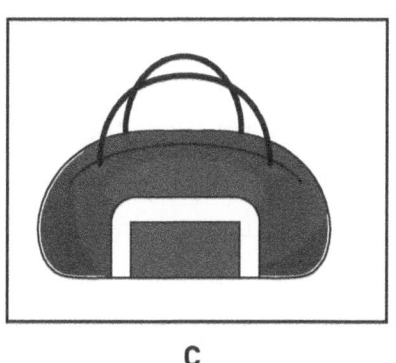
C

6 How is the man getting to work?

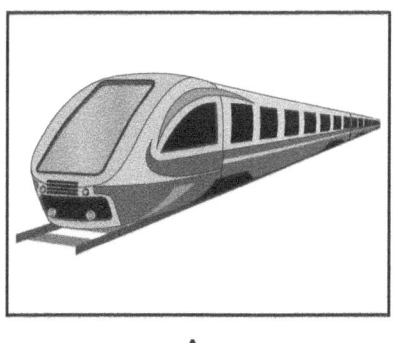
A

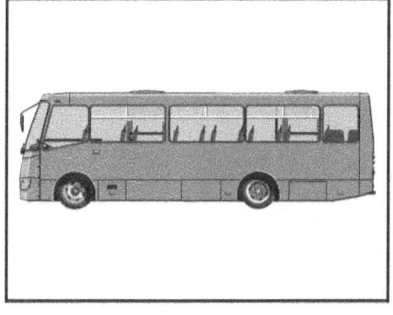
B

C

7 What time does the party start?

A

B

C

Test 8 LISTENING

Part 2

Questions 8–13

For each question, choose the correct answer.

---

8 You will hear two friends talking about eating snacks.
   The girl says

   A she needs to buy a sandwich.

   B people waste too much food.

   C they could save money for the weekend.

9 You will hear a conversation between a father and his daughter about passwords.
   What does the father say?

   A He now uses the same password for different accounts.

   B He was given some advice by a friend.

   C He uses passwords that are easy to remember.

10 You will hear two parents talking about how to travel on holiday.
   The woman thinks going by train

   A would take longer.

   B would be less expensive.

   C would be more relaxing.

11 You will hear two friends talking about cooking a meal.
   What does the boy say about pasta?

   A He likes to make it spicy.

   B His mother thinks he cooks it well.

   C He needs more practice to make it properly.

12 You will hear two friends talking about going swimming.
   The girl says

   A the swimming pool can be busy.

   B you have to book a session.

   C she needs to buy a swimming costume.

13 You will hear two friends talking about using the internet.
   Why doesn't the girl want to go to a café?

   A She will spend too much money.

   B It is not very quiet.

   C She doesn't want people watching her while she is working.

174

Part 3

Questions 14–19

For each question, write the correct answer in the gap. Write **one** or **two words** or a **number** or a **date** or a **time**.

You will hear a teacher talking about the school's 'International Day'.

> ### International Day
>
> The International Day is on **(14)** ………………… .
>
> Students can use the café's **(15)** ……………….. to prepare food.
>
> Speak to your teacher if you need anything **(16)** ……………….. for your presentation.
>
> There will be a disco and Mr James will play the **(17)** ……………….. .
>
> If nobody is collecting you, the school bus will leave at **(18)** ……………….. .
>
> You can practise presentations in the **(19)** ………………… .

Test 8 LISTENING

Part 4

Questions 20–25

For each question, choose the correct answer.

You will hear an interview with a man called Hugh Treadwell, who teaches art.

20 What does Hugh say about creating shadows?
   A It makes the drawing seem more real.
   B It is quite simple to do.
   C It is best to do it when it is light.

21 Hugh says the first thing you should do is
   A draw the shape of a face.
   B make a photocopy of a photograph.
   C draw parts of a face.

22 What type of photograph does Hugh recommend using?
   A one where you can see the side of the face
   B a colour photograph
   C one where the shadows are clearly visible

23 Hugh says that
   A the left side of the face is the same as the right.
   B you can begin by planning where the main parts of the face are.
   C you should pay attention to the lines on someone's face.

24 What does Hugh say about mistakes?
   A It is more difficult to correct a painting.
   B Start again with a new drawing.
   C Don't try to correct small mistakes.

25 What does Hugh say you should do if you are unhappy with your drawing?
   A Tell yourself that there is nothing wrong it.
   B Remember that drawing is supposed to be enjoyable.
   C Try to draw things that are funny.

Test 8 SPEAKING

Speaking

You are Candidate B. Answer the questions.

61–62

1A

1B

Audio scripts on pages 183–16 and Model answers on pages 234–249.

177

Test 8 SPEAKING

People with different occupations invited to give a talk at a school

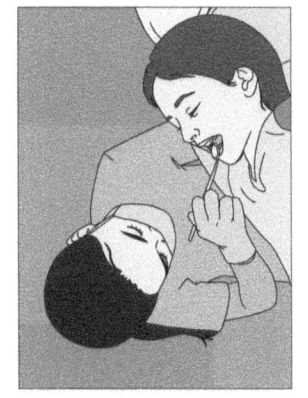

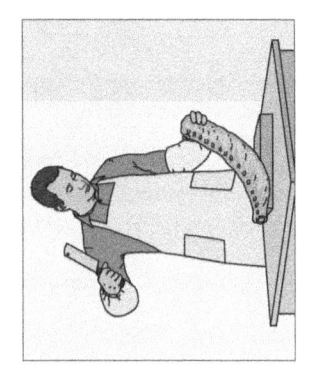
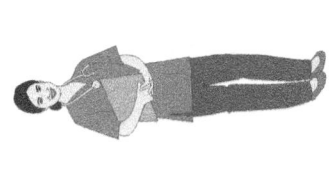
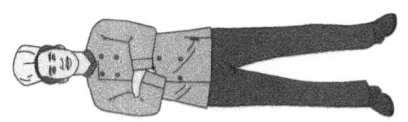

Audio scripts on pages 183–216 and Model answers on pages 234–249.

Mini-dictionary

 Here are some of the more difficult words from the practice tests. Definitions and examples are from *Collins COBUILD Dictionaries*.

TEST 1

apparently /əˈpærəntli/ ADVERB You use **apparently** to talk about something that seems to be the case although it may not be • *The news apparently came as a complete surprise.*

catch up with /kætʃ ˈʌp wɪð/ **(catches up with, catching up with, caught up with)** PHRASAL VERB If you **catch up with** something such as the news, you find out what has happened recently. • *I love nothing more than catching up with the local news.*

currently /ˈkʌrəntli, AM ˈkɜːr-/ ADVERB Something that is happening **currently** is happening, being done, or being used at the present time. • *New guidelines are currently being developed.*

cut down on /kʌt ˈdaʊn ɒn/ **(cuts down on, cutting down on, cut down on)** PHRASAL VERB If you **cut down on** something, you use or do less of it.
• *He cut down on coffee.*

donation /dəʊˈneɪʃən/ **(donations)** NOUN A **donation** is something that you give to a charity or other organisation. • *They requested donations of water, food, medicine, and clothing.*

eager /ˈiːɡə/ ADJECTIVE If you are **eager to do** or have something, you very much want to do it or have it. • *Robert was eager to talk about his new job.*

eyelash /ˈaɪlæʃ/ **(eyelashes)** NOUN Your **eyelashes** are the hairs which grow on the edges of your eyes. • *When I woke up, my eyelashes were stuck together.*

fluffy /ˈflʌfi/ **(fluffier, fluffiest)** ADJECTIVE Food that is **fluffy** is very light because it has a lot of air in it.
• *It goes really well with fluffy mashed potato.*

guarantee /ˌɡærənˈtiː/ **(guarantees, guaranteeing, guaranteed)** VERB If one thing **guarantees** another, the first is certain to cause the second thing to happen. • *Money does not guarantee happiness.*

hump /hʌmp/ **(humps)** NOUN A camel's **hump** is the large lump on its back. • *Some camels have two humps and are covered in fur to protect them from freezing temperatures.*

keep an eye on something /kiːp ən aɪ ɒn/ PHRASE If you **keep an eye on** something or someone, you watch them carefully to see what is going to happen. • *To keep my mind active, I keep an eye on the newspapers.*

nevertheless /ˌnevəðəˈles/ ADVERB You use **nevertheless** when saying something happens in spite of something else. [FORMAL] • *He injured his leg but, nevertheless, he managed to finish the match.*

pop /pɒp/ **(pops, popping, popped)** VERB If you **pop** somewhere, you go there for a short time. [BRIT, INFORMAL] • *He's just popped out to the shops. He won't be long.*

rearrange /ˌriːəˈreɪndʒ/ **(rearranges, rearranging, rearranged)** VERB If you **rearrange** a meeting or an appointment, you arrange for it to take place at a different time from the original meeting.
• *I rearranged the appointment with my doctor.*

remaining /rɪˈmeɪnɪŋ/ ADJECTIVE The **remaining** things out of a group are the things that still exist, are still present, or that you have not dealt with.
• *Pour the remaining ingredients into a bowl.*

responsible /rɪˈspɒnsɪbəl/ ADJECTIVE **Responsible** people behave in a proper and sensible way.
• *He's a very responsible sort of person.*

settle for /ˈsetəl fɔː/ **(settles for, settling for, settled for)** PHRASAL VERB If you **settle for** something, you choose or accept it, especially when it is not what you really want but there is nothing else available. • *The team will have to settle for third or fourth place.*

tend /tend/ **(tends, tending, tended)** VERB If something **tends to** happen, it usually happens or it happens often. • *I tend to forget things.*

track /træk/ **(tracks)** NOUN A **track** is one of the songs or pieces of music on a recording. • *All 10 tracks on the album are love songs.*

TEST 2

apparently /əˈpærəntli/ ADVERB See Test 1

capture /ˈkæptʃə/ **(captures, capturing, captured)** VERB If someone **captures** the atmosphere or quality of something, they show it successfully in pictures, music, or words. • *They took out their cameras to capture the moment.*

checkmate /ˈtʃekmeɪt/ NOUN In chess, **checkmate** is a situation in which you cannot stop your king being taken and so you lose the game. • *The audience was relieved when the checkmate came after 21 moves.*

growth /ɡrəʊθ/ NOUN The **growth** of something such as an industry, organisation, or idea is its development in size, wealth, or importance.

179

Mini-dictionary

• *The country will experience economic growth over the next few years.*

handful /ˈhændfʊl/ (handfuls) NOUN A **handful** of something is the amount of it that you can hold in your hand. • *I ate handfuls of peanuts.*

harvest /ˈhɑːvɪst/ (harvests) NOUN A crop is called a **harvest** when it has been collected. • *The warm summer has led to a big harvest of apples in Scotland.*

impression /ɪmˈpreʃən/ NOUN If someone or something **makes an impression on** someone, they have a strong effect on that person. • *He has already made a good impression on me.*

Industrial Revolution /ɪnˈdʌstriəl ˌrevəˈluːʃən/ NOUN The **Industrial Revolution** was the time in the 18th and 19th centuries when Britain, some European countries and the United States developed many new industries. • *The Industrial Revolution brought thousands of people to the cities.*

investment /ɪnˈvestmənt/ (investments) NOUN **Investment** is the activity of putting money into a business or into a bank. • *They are looking for investment advice.*

process /ˈprəʊses, AM ˈprɑːses/ (processes) NOUN A **process** is a set of actions or events which have a particular result. • *Learning a new language is a long process.*

question /ˈkwestʃən/ (questions, questioning, questioned) VERB If you **question** someone, you ask them questions about something. • *I questioned him on his adventures.*

soaking /ˈsəʊkɪŋ/ ADJECTIVE If something is **soaking** or **soaking wet**, it is very wet. • *My face and raincoat were soaking wet.*

spread /spred/ (spreads, spreading, spread) VERB If you **spread** something such as money or knowledge, you give it out to lots of different people. • *I want to spread the knowledge of how to cook healthily for your child.*

TEST 3

artistic /ɑːˈtɪstɪk/ ADJECTIVE **Artistic** means relating to art or artists. • *This activity develops pupils' artistic talents.*

current /ˈkʌrənt, AM ˈkɜːr-/ ADJECTIVE **Current** means existing, being done, or being used at the present time. • *The competition is open to all current students.*

offline /ˌɒfˈlaɪn, AM ˌɔːf-/ ADVERB If a person or a computer does something **offline**, they do it without being connected to the internet. • *Most software programs allow you to write emails offline.*

overcome /ˌəʊvəˈkʌm/ (overcomes, overcoming, overcame) VERB If you **overcome** a problem or a feeling, you successfully deal with it and control it. • *Molly had overcome her fear of flying.*

pedal /ˈpedəl/ (pedals) NOUN The **pedals** on a bicycle are the two parts that you push with your feet in order to make the bicycle move. • *To help your child learn to ride a bike, remove the pedals.*

safety /ˈseɪfti/ NOUN **Safety** is the state of being safe from danger. • *Most people know that online safety is our own responsibility.*

upright /ˈʌpraɪt/ ADJECTIVE If you stay **upright**, you do not fall down. • *Two riders fell, but I managed to stay upright.*

TEST 4

basis /ˈbeɪsɪs/ (bases) NOUN If something happens or is done **on a** particular **basis**, it happens or is done in that way. • *We're going to meet there on a regular basis.*

bird feeder /ˈbɜːd ˌfiːdə/ (bird feeders) NOUN A **bird feeder** is something that you fill with food for birds. • *Ruth put up bird feeders so that the patients could watch the birds.*

council /ˈkaʊnsəl/ (councils) NOUN A **council** is a specially organised, formal meeting that is attended by a particular group of people. • *In her final year at the school, she was chosen to represent her class in the school council.*

edit /ˈedɪt/ (edits, editing, edited) VERB If you **edit** a film or a television or radio programme, you choose some of what was filmed or recorded and arrange it in a particular order. • *He taught me to edit film.*

fierce /fɪəs/ ADJECTIVE **Fierce** feelings or actions are very strong, or involve a lot of effort. • *Standards are high and competition is fierce.*

independently /ˌɪndɪˈpendəntli/ ADVERB Someone who acts **independently** does not rely on other people. • *This airline will do business independently of others.*

leisure centre /ˈleʒə ˌsentə, AM ˈliːʒ-/ (leisure centres) NOUN A **leisure centre** is a large public building containing different facilities for leisure activities, such as a sports hall, a swimming pool, and rooms for meetings. [BRIT] • *They regularly play football at the local leisure centre.*

magical /ˈmædʒɪkəl/ ADJECTIVE Something that is **magical** seems to use magic or to be able to produce magic. • *He said he had magical talents.*

You can say that something is **magical** when it has a special quality that makes it seem wonderful and exciting. • *Paris is a magical city.*

pack /pæk/ (**packs**) NOUN A **pack** of cards is a complete set of playing cards. [BRIT] • *He pulled out a pack of cards and asked me to pick one.*

patrol /pəˈtrəʊl/ (**patrols, patrolling, patrolled**) VERB When soldiers, police, or guards **patrol** an area or building, they move around it in order to make sure that there is no trouble. • *Two officers are now patrolling the area.*

profitable /ˈprɒfɪtəbəl/ ADJECTIVE A **profitable** activity or organisation makes money. • *Cruises have become one of the most profitable parts of the travel industry.*

representative /ˌreprɪˈzentətɪv/ ADJECTIVE If something is **representative of** a group, it is typical of that group. • *He felt that their views were not representative of Britain as a whole.*

supersonic /ˌsuːpəˈsɒnɪk/ ADJECTIVE **Supersonic** planes travel faster than the speed of sound. • *It is the world's only supersonic passenger jet.*

TEST 5

estimate /ˈestɪmeɪt/ (**estimates, estimating, estimated**) VERB If you **estimate** a quantity or value, you guess approximately what the quantity or value is. • *It's difficult to estimate how much money she has spent.*

guarantee /ˌɡærənˈtiː/ (**guarantees, guaranteeing, guaranteed**) VERB See Test 1

leisure centre /ˈleʒə ˈsentə, AM ˈliːʒ-/ (**leisure centres**) NOUN See Test 4

non-stop /ˌnɒnˈstɒp/ ADJECTIVE Something that is **non-stop** continues without any breaks. • *They played 80 minutes of non-stop music.*

programme /ˈprəʊɡræm/ (**programmes**) NOUN A theatre, concert, or event **programme** is a short book giving information about the play, concert or event. • *As well as playing, he also collected match programmes.*

safety /ˈseɪfti/ NOUN See Test 3

seed /siːd/ (**seeds**) NOUN A **seed** is one of the small hard parts of a plant from which a new plant grows. • *Water newly planted seeds regularly for the first 10 days.*

shaped /ʃeɪpt/ ADJECTIVE Something that is **shaped** like a particular object has the shape of that object. • *This shrub has large heart-shaped leaves.*

subscribe /səbˈskraɪb/ (**subscribes, subscribing, subscribed**) VERB If you **subscribe to** a service or magazine, you pay money regularly to receive the service or magazine. • *I also subscribe to a couple of fashion magazines.*

tablet /ˈtæblət/ (**tablets**) NOUN A **tablet** is a small flat computer that you work by touching the screen. • *App developers have created new software for the tablet.*

trader /ˈtreɪdə/ (**traders**) NOUN A **trader** is someone who buys, sells, or exchanges goods or services. • *They bought the carpet from a trader in the market.*

unlike /ˌʌnˈlaɪk/ PREP You can use **unlike** to compare two people or things and show how they are different. • *Unlike the gym, walking is free and you can do it whenever you want.*

vlogger /ˈvlɒɡə/ (**vloggers**) NOUN A **vlogger** is someone who regularly posts videos on the internet in which they record their thoughts or experiences, or talk about a subject. • *He is a very successful British vlogger.*

waterproof /ˈwɔːtəpruːf/ ADJECTIVE Something that is **waterproof** does not let water pass through it. • *Take waterproof clothing as the Orkney weather is difficult to predict.*

TEST 6

edit /ˈedɪt/ (**edits, editing, edited**) VERB See Test 4

mix up /mɪks ˈʌp/ (**mixes up, mixing up, mixed up**) PHRASAL VERB If you **mix up** two things or people, you think that one of them is the other one. • *When he gets excited, he mixes up his words.*

historian /hɪˈstɔːriən/ (**historians**) NOUN A **historian** is a person who studies and writes about history. • *She is a famous historian who has written many books about the war.*

impatient /ɪmˈpeɪʃənt/ ADJECTIVE If you are **impatient**, you are annoyed because you have had to wait too long for something. • *We've been waiting for hours and we're getting very impatient.*

issue /ˈɪsjuː, ˈɪʃuː/ (**issues**) NOUN An **issue** is the copy of a magazine or newspaper that is published in a particular month or on a particular day • *I read the latest issues of every music magazine available.*

leisure centre /ˈleʒə ˈsentə, AM ˈliːʒ-/ (**leisure centres**) NOUN See Test 4

polio /ˈpəʊliəʊ/ NOUN **Polio** is a serious disease which can make people unable to use their legs. • *He survived polio as a baby.*

remaining /rɪˈmeɪnɪŋ/ ADJECTIVE See Test 1

responsible /rɪˈspɒnsɪbəl/ ADJECTIVE See Test 1

safety /ˈseɪfti/ NOUN See Test 3

spray /spreɪ/ NOUN **Spray** is a lot of small drops of water which are being thrown into the air. • *I could feel the spray from the waterfall.*

subscribe /səbˈskraɪb/ (**subscribes, subscribing, subscribed**) VERB See Test 5

Mini-dictionary

TEST 7

ape /eɪp/ **(apes)** NOUN An **ape** is a type of animal like a monkey that lives among trees in hot countries and has long, strong arms and no tail. • *Like apes, humans have 32 permanent teeth.*

binoculars /bɪˈnɒkjʊləz/ PLURAL NOUN **Binoculars** are special glasses which you look through in order to see things that are a long way away. You can also say **a pair of binoculars**. • *Early on, we spotted three lions through binoculars.*

bubble /ˈbʌbəl/ **(bubbles)** NOUN A **bubble** is a very thin ball of liquid that floats in the air or in water. • *A hippo was blowing bubbles through its nose.*

coffee morning /ˈkɒfi ˈmɔːnɪŋ/ **(coffee mornings)** NOUN A **coffee morning** is an event at which coffee and tea are served. It takes place in the morning, and is often intended to raise money for charity. [BRIT] • *She held a coffee morning for charity and invited all her friends.*

current /ˈkʌrənt, AM ˈkɜːr-/ ADJECTIVE *See Test 3*

GPS /ˌdʒiː piː ˈes/ **(GPSs)** NOUN A **GPS** is a system that uses signals from satellites to find out the position of an object. **GPS** is short for 'Global Positioning System'. • *They used GPS and digital maps to find the missing people.*

leisure centre /ˈleʒə ˈsentə, AM ˈliːʒ-/ **(leisure centres)** NOUN *See Test 4*

marathon /ˈmærəθən, AM -θɒn/ ADJECTIVE A **marathon** task takes a long time to do and is very tiring. • *He won a marathon dance contest in 1932, dancing for 145 days.*

stargazing /ˈstɑːɡeɪzɪŋ/ NOUN **Stargazing** is the activity of studying the stars as a hobby or as part of someone's job. [INFORMAL] • *The campsite is brilliant for stargazing thanks to the lack of light pollution.*

telescope /ˈtelɪskəʊp/ **(telescopes)** NOUN A **telescope** is a piece of equipment shaped like a tube. It has special glass inside it that makes things that are far away seem larger and nearer when you look through it. • *The telescope will allow scientists to see deeper into the universe than ever before.*

TEST 8

factory farm /ˈfæktri fɑːm/ **(factory farms)** NOUN A **factory farm** is a farm in which large numbers of animals are kept in buildings so that food from them can be produced cheaply and quickly. • *The group tries to persuade people not to buy food that comes from factory farms.*

flock /flɒk/ **(flocks)** NOUN A **flock** of birds, sheep, or goats is a group of them. • *They are sociable birds and feed in flocks.*

healthily /ˈhelθɪli/ ADVERB Someone who eats or lives **healthily**, eats and does things that are good for them. • *I want to live healthily for as long as possible.*

model railway /ˈmɒdəl ˈreɪlweɪ/ **(model railways)** NOUN A **model railway** is a very small version of a railway system, often with toy moving trains. • *The singer spoke excitedly about his model railway.*

rub out /rʌb ˈaʊt/ **(rubs out, rubbing out, rubbed out)** PHRASAL VERB If you **rub out** something that you have written, you remove it with a rubber or a cloth. • *She began rubbing out the pencil marks in the margin.*

safety mat /ˈseɪfti mæt/ **(safety mats)** NOUN A **safety mat** is a thick soft mat that is used to to stop people from getting hurt if they fall onto the floor, for example, when doing gymnastics. • *I fell, but landed on the safety mat, so I didn't hurt myself.*

treasure /ˈtreʒə/ NOUN **Treasure** is a collection of valuable old objects in children's stories, such as gold coins and jewellery. • *Find out about pirates and take part in a fun treasure hunt.*

trick /trɪk/ **(tricks, tricking, tricked)** VERB If someone **tricks** you, they make you believe something that is not true, often in order to make you do something. • *Stephen is going to be pretty upset when he finds out how you tricked him.*

voice box /ˈvɔɪs bɒks/ **(voice boxes)** NOUN Your **voice box** is the top part of the tube that leads from your throat to your lungs, which contains your vocal cords. • *Two years ago my dad had his voice box removed.*

Audio scripts

These are the audio scripts for the Listening and Speaking parts of the tests. Listen to the audio online at: www.collins.co.uk/eltresources

TEST 1   LISTENING

Part 1

Track 01

Preliminary English Test for Schools, Listening.
There are four parts to the test. You will hear each piece twice.
We will now stop for a moment.
Please ask any questions now, because you must not speak during the test.
Now look at the instructions for Part 1.
For each question, choose the correct answer.
Look at Question 1.

1 *What was damaged in the fire?*

Boy: Did you hear about the fire in town?
Girl: Yes, I was in my dad's car on the way to school and it came on the radio.
Boy: There were some valuable paintings in that museum. I can't believe none of them were damaged.
Girl: I know. Apparently, the fire didn't pass to the ground floor, so only some rugs were burned. I wonder how it started?

Now listen again.

2 *What time does the teacher want the meeting?*

Teacher: Hello. It's Mrs Sinclair from Jason's school. I'm just calling to ask if it's possible to rearrange the meeting with his mum. I've got the time we agreed in my diary as 2.30. Unfortunately, I've just found out I have a meeting around the same time and won't be able to spend long talking about Jason's progress. I was wondering whether we could make it a little earlier, say 2.15? I'm in school till 5.00 tonight, so could you call me back and let me know?

Now listen again.

3 *How does Katie usually travel home from school?*

Katie: Hi Dad. It's Katie. Are you busy?
Father: I am, actually. Why?
Katie: The bus I catch has been cancelled again. That's the second time this week. I might start getting the train. Anyway, is there any chance you could come and get me from school? And maybe take Kelly home as well? She usually goes home on her bike, but it's being repaired.
Father: OK. Look out for my car. I won't be able to stop long on the main road, so you'll need to get in quickly.

Now listen again.

4 *What is the weather forecast for Friday?*

Teacher: I just wanted to have a word with you all about sports day this Friday. I don't know if you've all been keeping an eye on the forecast, but it's not looking very good. We're usually lucky and have lovely sunny weather and we've never had to cancel before. If we do get the heavy rain they're predicting for Friday, it will be too dangerous to go ahead. Hopefully, it will be OK and the windy weather we've got at the moment will calm down as well.

Now listen again.

5 *What colour does the girl think the room should be?*

Boy: Mum has offered to decorate my room over the holiday, but I don't know what colour to have.
Girl: I don't imagine you'll want to have it done the same as mine. I don't think pink would suit you.
Boy: Jamie at school painted his black. What do you think of that?
Girl: It could work. It would be better than the blue you have at the moment. Yes, try that.

Now listen again.

6 *What is Lisa sending back?*

Lisa: Hi Dominica. It's Lisa. I'm in town and I've just seen the perfect present for Christine's birthday. I've already bought her a dress online, but I'm going to return it as her mum said she probably wouldn't wear it. I've just seen some earrings I think she'll like, so I'm going back to the shop to get them. I was going to buy her that pair of trainers she was talking about, but they're a bit more than we agreed to spend, so I'll leave them.

Now listen again.

7 *What might the boy eat less often?*

Girl: After that lesson in school today, I'm thinking of becoming a vegetarian.
Boy: Really? I can understand why, but I'm not sure I could. We have so many meals with chicken at home. I might cut down on some things, though.
Girl: Like what?
Boy: I'll start by asking Mum and Dad to stop eating so much chicken. I think they'll agree. We don't have red meat anymore and they're always encouraging me to eat more fish. I don't like it much, but I know it's healthy.

Now listen again.

That is the end of Part 1.

Audio scripts

Part 2

Track 02

Now look at Part 2.
For each question, choose the correct answer.

8 *You will hear two friends talking about a phone.*

Boy: I'm going to ask my parents for a new phone for my birthday. I'm tired of this one.
Girl: You've had it a long time, haven't you?
Boy: Quite a while. The camera's not bad, though you can get better ones on phones now. And it's been pretty reliable since I've had it, although I had to have the screen replaced when I dropped it. But it takes ages to start and web pages take a long time to open.
Girl: Well, good luck with your parents! Hopefully, you'll get a new one for your birthday.

Now listen again.

9 *You will hear a conversation between a mother and her son.*

Boy: I'm off to school now, Mum. I'll see you later.
Mother: Don't forget to take your key with you, will you? I won't be in when you get back.
Boy: Why not? Where are you going?
Mother: I told you, I've got my driving test tomorrow afternoon. I'm a bit nervous, so I thought I'd get my hair done to help me relax. I've got an appointment at 3.00 today, so I should be back home by 4.30. I'll call you when I'm done and let you know when I'm on my way home.

Now listen again.

10 *You will hear two parents talking about their daughter's homework.*

Mother: How did Grace get on with her homework tonight? Did she manage to finish it all?
Father: Yes, she didn't need my help, to be honest. She's working hard at the moment and doesn't find the subject too difficult.
Mother: I know she's pleased to have you for support, though. She told me she likes being able to talk to you about it.
Father: She certainly seems to enjoy the subject, which must help a lot. I've discovered a lot about that period of history that I never knew myself – I really enjoyed finding out about the topic.

Now listen again.

11 *You will hear a brother and sister talking about an email.*

Girl: Can I use the laptop after you, please? I want to check my email.
Boy: Yes, I won't be a minute. I'm just reading an email about doing some work as a volunteer with the youth club. They contacted me about it last week, but I forgot to reply, so they've emailed me again.
Girl: Are you going to help?
Boy: I think so, yes. My teacher said it will look good on my CV if I become a volunteer. They're closed for the weekend now, though, so I'll write back on Monday.

Now listen again.

12 *You will hear a girl and her father talking about the environment.*

Girl: We were looking at recycling in school today and how many people don't do it properly. It's a really big problem.
Father: Well, I think I make an effort as far as that's concerned. I think your teacher would be impressed with my recycling.
Girl: You're pretty good, I suppose. I don't expect you to join me and become a vegetarian. I know how much you like eating meat. But I do think you should use the internet to keep up with the news. All those newspapers you buy are bad for the environment.

Now listen again.

13 *You will hear two friends talking about a light one of them has bought.*

Girl: You look much better on the webcam with that new light.
Boy: Thanks. I spent most of the afternoon trying to work out where to put it. There isn't a lot of space in this room and it's easy for things to get knocked over.
Girl: Did it cost a lot?
Boy: I did quite a bit of research. I wanted something that wasn't too bright as I already have one light. It wasn't as much as I was expecting to pay. There were better, more expensive ones, but I couldn't afford them.

Now listen again.

That is the end of Part 2.

Part 3

Track 03

Now look at Part 3.
For each question, write the correct answer in the gap. Write one or two words or a number or a date or a time. Look at Questions 14 to 19 now. You have 20 seconds. You will hear a recorded message about events at an arts centre.

Speaker: Thank you for calling Slate Art Centre. As usual, we have a fun-packed programme of events for all the family this weekend, so we hope you'll come and visit.

Our *Dance Moves for Kids* classes start again this Saturday and run for eleven weeks. These are for children from five to twelve and have always been very popular. The first session this week is free and if your child enjoys it, you can sign up for the remaining ten sessions at the end. The classes now take place in the studio near the café, not in the gym. Bring the kids along. We're sure they'll have a great time.

Why not pop along to see the work of our local artist of the month, Jason Perry. Jason is presenting his photographs of well-known musicians. You never know, you may come across your favourite singer or pop star! The exhibition is being held in the main hall this weekend and until the end of the month.

Finally, the cinema is showing the thriller *To Catch a Thief* on Saturday and Sunday. If you've seen the reviews in the local newspapers, you'll know it's certainly worthwhile taking the time to see it. There are shows in the morning and afternoon, so you should be able to find a time that's convenient. Tickets are available on our website or at reception.

Prices for all our events can also be found on our website. And don't forget there's plenty of free parking in our car park and a café that offers a range of cakes, sandwiches and drinks. We look forward to welcoming you.

Now listen again.

That is the end of Part 3.

Part 4

Track 04

Now look at Part 4.
For each question, choose the correct answer.
Look at Questions 20 to 25 now.
You have 45 seconds.
You will hear an interview with a woman called Sarah Mulligan, who advises students about going to university.

Interviewer: Today I'm talking to Sarah Mulligan, a student advisor, about the advantages and disadvantages of living in a university hall during the first year of university, rather than staying in the family home. What do you think is the best decision, Sarah?

Sarah: It's impossible to say as everyone is different. Certainly, going away from home will give you the chance to become more independent. You'll be able to make your own decisions and be free to live in a way that suits you. This can be wonderful, and for most students it will be the first time they've left home.

Interviewer: But this also means we need to become more responsible, doesn't it?

Sarah: Absolutely. You won't have anyone to wash your clothes, to tidy up after you, to remind you of important appointments, that kind of thing. You'll probably need to become more organised than you were before.

Interviewer: What do you think is the biggest advantage of living in a university hall?

Sarah: Being at university 24 hours a day means you find out more about what's going on. And there's so much going on at university. You'll make lots of use of the facilities, be able to join clubs and take part in activities. This is possible for students living at home too, but I do think you experience more of university life if you live in a hall.

Interviewer: So, that's one good reason for moving out, isn't it?

Sarah: Not necessarily. Some students might not want a busy social life. I know many young people who want to focus on their studies and feel that they'll get more peace and quiet if they stay at home. Having lots of new friends is fantastic, but a very busy social life can cause problems with studies.

Interviewer: OK, I can see what you mean. Any other tips?

Sarah: It's not unusual to miss home during the first few weeks when you're still getting used to your new life and trying to make new friends. This usually gets better as life becomes settled, though. In the end, students are so busy enjoying themselves that they need to be reminded to visit their parents.

Interviewer: And finally, what about money?

Sarah: Yes, money! Young people are used to having their food and accommodation provided free of charge! Obviously, this is no longer the case when you move away and students often have to survive on a limited amount of money. But dealing with that can be a very important skill in later life, so it's a useful experience.

Now listen again.

That is the end of Part 4.

You now have six minutes to write your answers on the answer sheet.

That is the end of the test.

Audio scripts

TEST 1   SPEAKING

Part 1

Track 05

Examiner:	Good afternoon. Can I have your mark sheets, please? I'm Steve Saunders and this is Jenny Wright.
Examiner:	What's your name, Candidate A? How old are you?
Candidate A:	My name's Sara Fernandez and I'm twelve years old.
Examiner:	And what's your name, Candidate B? How old are you?

[PAUSE FOR YOU TO ANSWER]

Examiner:	Candidate B, where do you live?

[PAUSE FOR YOU TO ANSWER]

Examiner:	And Candidate A, where do you live?
Candidate A:	I live in Madrid. I live with my mum, dad and my younger brother. We live in a house just outside the city centre.
Examiner:	Candidate A, what do you like to do at weekends?
Candidate A:	I enjoy going to my friend's house. We play music and watch videos. We both like dancing as well.
Examiner:	Candidate B, what do you do to relax?

[PAUSE FOR YOU TO ANSWER]

Examiner:	Candidate A, tell me what you like about where you live.
Candidate A:	I think I'm lucky. We live near the city, so I can go into town with my friends if I want to. But there's also some lovely countryside nearby, so I sometimes go for long walks with my family there too.
Examiner:	Candidate B, is your area a nice place to live?

[PAUSE FOR YOU TO ANSWER]

Examiner:	Thank you.

Part 2

Track 06

Examiner:	Now I'd like each of you to talk on your own about something. I'm going to give each of you a photograph and I'd like you to talk about it. Candidate A, here is your photograph. It shows somebody buying something. Please tell us what you can see in the photograph. Candidate B, you just listen.
Candidate A:	This photograph was taken in a clothes shop. There are two people, a man and a woman. One of them is buying something and the other person is taking their money. It's difficult to say who is the customer and which person works in the shop, but I think the man is the cashier. He's giving her two bags with the things she has bought, and she's passing her credit card to him. There are some shoes or trainers on the shelves behind the man, and in the background, I can see some clothes on hangers. They both seem to be very happy and are smiling at each other.
Examiner:	Thank you.
Examiner:	Candidate B, here is your photograph. It shows some young people in a classroom. Please tell us what you can see in the photograph. Candidate A, you just listen.

[PAUSE FOR YOU TO ANSWER]

Examiner:	Thank you.

Part 3

Track 07

Examiner:	Now, in this part of the test you are going to talk about something together for about two minutes. I'm going to describe a situation to you. A girl is having her bedroom decorated. Her parents want to buy her something for the room. Here are some things they could buy. Talk together about the different things she could get and say which one would be best. All right? Now, talk together.
Candidate A:	So, we need to decide what the parents could buy for their daughter. I think some of these things are useful. What do you think?

[PAUSE FOR YOU TO ANSWER]

Candidate A:	Yes, that's true. The TV is a lovely present, but it costs a lot of money. What about the picture? I don't think that's a good idea because they might not choose something the girl likes.

[PAUSE FOR YOU TO ANSWER]

Candidate A:	Yes, I agree. So, that leaves the chair, the mirror and the lamp. I think the mirror would be best. It's nice to be able to look at ourselves when we're trying on clothes. That's a nice big one.

[PAUSE FOR YOU TO ANSWER]

Examiner:	Thank you.

Part 4

Track 08

Examiner:	Candidate A, do you like spending time in your bedroom?
Candidate A:	Yes. I usually do my homework in my bedroom. I have a desk and it's quiet. I can concentrate on my work.
Examiner:	And what about you, Candidate B?

[PAUSE FOR YOU TO ANSWER]

Examiner:	Candidate B, what kind of things have you got in your room?

[PAUSE FOR YOU TO ANSWER]

Examiner:	And how about you, Candidate A?
Candidate A:	I told you about my desk. I've also got shelves with my books on them, and there's a lamp on the table that I use for studying. I've also got lots of posters of people on my walls, pop stars and actors.
Examiner:	Candidate B, many people keep their phones, tablets and laptops in their bedrooms. Do you think this is a good thing to do?

[PAUSE FOR YOU TO ANSWER]

Examiner:	And what about you, Candidate A?
Candidate A:	We could leave our laptops and phones downstairs so we can forget about studying or chatting with friends. I think if they're near you at night, they might stop you sleeping.
Examiner:	Thank you. That is the end of the test.

TEST 2 LISTENING

Part 1

Track 09

Preliminary English Test for Schools, Listening.
There are four parts to the test. You will hear each piece twice.
We will now stop for a moment.
Please ask any questions now, because you must not speak during the test.
Now look at the instructions for Part 1.
For each question, choose the correct answer.
Look at Question 1.

1 *What does the girl decide to get her mother as a present?*

Girl:	I can't think what to get Mum for her birthday. Any ideas?
Father:	I know she wanted that book she was talking about. You could get her that.
Girl:	That's not much, though, is it? Anyway, I think she said she was going to buy that online.
Father:	Take her into town and get her something to wear. A pair of jeans, for example. Knowing Mum, she'll get you a pizza while you're out.
Girl:	That's a good idea. I'll do that.

Now listen again.

2 *How many tickets do they need for the cinema?*

Boy:	Hi Leila. My mum's happy to buy the tickets for the cinema online. But how many of us are there?
Girl:	That's kind of her. I know Sally and Chris are coming, so that's four, including me and you. There were five of us, I know, but John can't make it now.
Boy:	It starts at three, so we can meet there and get the tickets from the main office.
Girl:	OK, great. I'll let the others know.

Now listen again.

3 *Why might the boy decide not to play football?*

Boy 1:	Are you still OK for football on Sunday?
Boy 2:	It depends. My leg's still a bit sore after last Sunday's game, but I could probably still play. It's my sister's birthday on Sunday as well, but she won't mind if I'm not around for a few hours. I've told her to save me a slice of cake. I've got an essay to finish by Monday, so it will depend if I can get that done over the weekend. I'll let you know on Saturday.

Now listen again.

4 *What will the next programme be about?*

Announcer:	OK, now before the next song, here's some information about what's on later. Coming next after this show is Matt Gray's look at the animal world. Judging by your messages, you found last week's look at the habits of city wildlife interesting. This week, Matt looks at the issue of how to protect the African elephant. Next, after Matt's show we have a chance to listen to an interview with Angela Killmartin, winner of this year's *Dancing on Ice* competition. You can find out all about her experiences at 9.00.

Now listen again.

5 *Where did the girl last see her glasses?*

Girl:	You haven't seen my glasses, have you? I can't find them anywhere.
Father:	No, sorry. When did you last have them?
Girl:	I remember I took them off after I'd finished working on the laptop. I put them on the table in the dining room and went upstairs to my bedroom to get changed. I know they were there as I remember thinking 'Mum's going to move them'. She keeps putting my things away somewhere. I'll go and see if she knows.

Now listen again.

6 *What time is the coach leaving?*

Teacher:	OK everyone. Can I have your attention? You're now free to go off on your own

Audio scripts

and explore the town. We want to get back to school on time, so the coach will be setting off at 5.30. Wherever you are at 5.00, start getting ready to come back to the coach. Those of you interested in the guided tour should meet me at the museum. I'll be leaving at 2.00, so make sure you're there, or I'll go without you.

Now listen again.

7 What is the boy going to take to the party?

Girl: Have you decided what you're going to take to the party on Saturday? I think we're all supposed to bring something to eat.

Boy: I thought some cakes would be nice. I was thinking of bags of crisps as well, but I'll let someone else take them. Rather than lots of small cakes, I might buy a big one. I'll get a chocolate one. That's my favourite!

Girl: It's not your party! But yes. That's a good idea. Maybe I can get the crisps.

Now listen again.

That is the end of Part 1.

Part 2

Track 10

Now look at Part 2.
For each question, choose the correct answer.

8 You will hear two friends talking about their plans for the evening.

Boy: Some of us are thinking of going to the cinema this evening. If you're free, do you want to come with us?

Girl: Not this time, but thanks for asking.

Boy: Have you still got that homework to do? I haven't done mine yet.

Girl: I should do it as it needs to be handed in on Monday. I'll probably do it over the weekend, though. I'd like to get to bed early, actually. I was watching something on TV last night that went on until late. Anyway, I hope you all enjoy the film.

Now listen again.

9 You will hear a mother and her son talking about a photograph.

Boy: Some of these family photographs are interesting. Look at Dad in this one! It's a great photograph of everyone.

Mother: That's your grandfather there in the background. It was taken when we were on holiday.

Boy: How long ago was that?

Mother: Well, the holiday was only a few years ago, so not that long. Dad looks different with shorter hair, doesn't he? And look at me standing next to him. I don't usually like seeing myself in photographs, but I'm quite fond of this one. That was a lovely holiday. We had such nice weather.

Now listen again.

10 You will hear two friends talking about the weather.

Girl: What time are we meeting in town?

Boy: After school. I'm going home first to get my coat. It's too cold to be walking around without one. I'll meet everyone later.

Girl: That's a good idea. I might do the same.

Boy: Hopefully, this rain will stop. I don't fancy getting soaking wet. The forecast says it's going to be dry after lunch.

Now listen again.

11 You will hear two friends talking about the school football shirt.

Girl: I heard John earlier complaining to the sports teacher about the new football shirt.

Boy: Was he? I know he hates it. It doesn't bother me, really.

Girl: It's better than the kit you wore last year, isn't it?

Boy: Definitely. The shirt really wasn't very comfortable. No, this one's OK. I much prefer wearing a plain shirt compared to the stripes we had before. I really didn't like them.

Now listen again.

12 You will hear a girl and her father talking about getting home from school.

Father: Have a nice day at school today. Have you got many lessons?

Girl: Yes, it's the busiest day of the week. I was hoping to get home early so I could get something to eat before I go to dance class. I hate having to hurry.

Father: You'll have plenty of time, won't you? Your dance class doesn't start till 6.30.

Girl: I'd have much more time if you gave me a lift. The buses are always late, and I could save my bus fare. It would give me an extra half an hour to get ready.

Now listen again.

13 You will hear a brother and sister talking about a song on the radio.

Boy: What's that you're listening to?

Girl: It's classical music. I don't know who wrote it. I like it, though. Do you?

Boy: Yes, it's quite relaxing, isn't it? It makes a change from what we normally listen to.

Girl: The teacher told us it was good to have on in the background when you're doing your homework. I'm hoping it will help me concentrate more. He said it was good for that. None of the kids in my class seem to like it, but I'm not really interested in what they think.

Now listen again.

That is the end of Part 2.

Audio scripts

Part 3

Track 11

Now look at Part 3.
For each question, write the correct answer in the gap.
Write one or two words or a number or a date or a time.
Look at Questions 14 to 19 now. You have 20 seconds.
You will hear a student giving a presentation on fast food.

Student: So, thanks for listening to my talk. I decided to interview students here at school about their attitude towards fast food. Whether they worry about eating too much of it and what kinds of fast food they eat.
To begin with, I had to decide what I meant by fast food. Most people think a takeaway is fast food, but that's not always the case. Some things you buy can be quite healthy. I asked about things like pizza, burgers, chips, food like that.
Then I created my questionnaire. This included questions, for example, to find out how many days a week they eat fast food. I wrote open questions where the student could give a long answer. Questions like 'Why do you like or not like fast food?' I also made a recording of the interviews.
Anyway, the surprising thing is that students at our school are healthier than you'd probably think. Most of the people I spoke to only ate fast food occasionally, often as a family meal at weekends. Most of them said that they knew about the dangers of eating too much fast food and tried to eat a healthy diet.
A lot of students wanted to talk about the food in the school café, but I think I need to write a questionnaire for that particular subject. I'd also like to find out what those who bring their own food to school have in their lunch box. This will be the subject of my next research.
We have to write a report about what we found out, so I'll include more information then. But I must say that it shows young people aren't as unhealthy as the media says. At least, the students at our school aren't.

Now listen again.

That is the end of Part 3.

Part 4

Track 12

Now look at Part 4.
For each question, choose the correct answer.
Look at Questions 20 to 25 now.
You have 45 seconds.
You will hear an interview with a man called Matthew Davies about a person who had a positive influence on him.

Interviewer: On today's show, we're celebrating people who have had a big influence on our lives. I'm talking with Matthew Davies. Who would you like to tell us about, Matthew?
Matthew: A teacher I had at high school, Mr Adams. He was our history teacher in our final year. He didn't join the school until then, so nobody knew anything about him.
Interviewer: How did you feel about having a new teacher?
Matthew: I wanted to go to university to study history, and so having a good final year was important. I felt quite relaxed about it, though, as I was doing quite well in my studies and felt confident.
Interviewer: So, what was your first lesson with him like?
Matthew: We'd had a few new teachers and it usually takes time to get used to their style of teaching. I think we all realised we were going to like him straightaway. He was a little more nervous than us, but that made the students like him even more.
Interviewer: Was he like your previous teacher?
Matthew: No, he was the opposite. She used to talk a lot and never asked for our opinion. Mr Adams always asked us what we thought about an issue. He liked to give us lots of homework, though!
Interviewer: What was it about Mr Adams' style of teaching that you liked?
Matthew: Some teachers know their subject really well, like a professor at university, but they have trouble communicating the subject in a way that's interesting. He obviously knew all about history, but he didn't act like an expert. He was more interested in making you love the subject.
Interviewer: And how did you get on in your exams?
Matthew: Really well. I think I'd have got a good grade with any teacher as I'd worked really hard. But Mr Adams was great at giving us ideas for dealing with exams, and I think he helped me get a high grade. He offered weaker students extra lessons for revision and even replied to emails quickly if you needed to ask him a question, though I avoided doing this.

Audio scripts

Interviewer:	So, have you made any decisions about your career?
Mathew:	Well, I got a place at university and studied history, but I think Mr Adams continued to influence my future. I often thought about his lessons after I'd left school, and I think this was probably one of the reasons for my career choice. I finished my university degree last year and I started a teacher training course. That's something I never imagined doing.

Now listen again.

That is the end of Part 4.

You now have six minutes to write your answers on the answer sheet.

That is the end of the test.

TEST 2   SPEAKING

Part 1

Track 13

Examiner:	Good morning. Can I have your mark sheets, please? I'm Carol Partridge and this is Steve Hilton.
Examiner:	What's your name, Candidate A? How old are you?
Candidate A:	My name's Cristine Garcia and I'm fifteeen years old.
Examiner:	And what's your name, Candidate B? How old are you?

[PAUSE FOR YOU TO ANSWER]

Examiner:	Candidate A, where do you come from?
Candidate A:	I come from Brazil, but I'm living in London at the moment.
Examiner:	And where do you come from, Candidate B?

[PAUSE FOR YOU TO ANSWER]

Examiner:	Candidate B, what food do you like to eat?

[PAUSE FOR YOU TO ANSWER]

Examiner:	And what food do you like, Candidate A?
Candidate A:	I like Italian food too and we eat pasta a lot in my house. I also like chocolate. I probably eat too much.
Examiner:	Candidate A, do you do any sport?
Candidate A:	Yes, I do. I play volleyball for my school. We play every month against other schools near where I live and I also go training once a week.
Examiner:	Candidate B, what about you?

[PAUSE FOR YOU TO ANSWER]

Examiner:	Candidate A, tell us about a lesson you like at school.
Candidate A:	I think my favourite lesson is art. I really enjoy painting and we learn lots about the subject from our teacher. It's also relaxing and feels different to when I'm in a lesson like maths or history.
Examiner:	Candidate B, do you have a favourite lesson?

[PAUSE FOR YOU TO ANSWER]

Examiner:	Thank you.

Part 2

Track 14

Examiner:	Now I'd like each of you to talk on your own about something. I'm going to give each of you a photograph and I'd like you to talk about it. Candidate A. Here is your photograph. It shows people preparing food. Please tell us what you can see in the photograph. Candidate B, you just listen.
Candidate A:	This photograph shows two people working together in the kitchen. There's a man on the left holding a large spoon and he's mixing a salad in a bowl. There's a woman on the right cutting red peppers. There are lots of other vegetables on the table in front of them. I can see a bowl of tomatoes, some carrots and lots of mushrooms. I don't know the word, but they're both wearing something to keep their clothes clean. People wear these in the kitchen when they're preparing food and cooking.
Examiner:	Thank you. Candidate B. Here is your photograph. It shows people looking at a map. Please tell us what you can see in the photograph. Candidate A, you just listen.

[PAUSE FOR YOU TO ANSWER]

Examiner:	Thank you.

Part 3

Track 15

Examiner:	Now, in this part of the test you're going to talk about something together for about two minutes. I'm going to describe a situation to you. A family are going to the beach. They are trying to decide what to take with them. Here are some things they could take. Talk together about the different things they could take and say which one would be best. All right? Now talk together.
Candidate A:	So, the family are going to the beach. What do you think they

	should take? A lot of these things are useful, aren't they?
[PAUSE FOR YOU TO ANSWER]	
Candidate A:	I agree. If they're only going for a little while, they could put the sun cream on before they go out. Then they wouldn't need to take that.
[PAUSE FOR YOU TO ANSWER]	
Candidate A:	Yes, I agree. The towel and the swimsuits go together, really, don't they? If they go swimming, they need both of them. I can't really decide which one of those is most important.
[PAUSE FOR YOU TO ANSWER]	
Candidate A:	Yes, the hats are a good idea. Let's choose them.
Examiner:	Thank you.

Part 4

Track 16

Examiner:	Candidate A, have you been on a holiday recently?
Candidate A:	Yes, I went to a place near where we live with my family a few months ago. The weather was really nice and we spent our time on the beach or swimming.
Examiner:	And what about you, Candidate B?
[PAUSE FOR YOU TO ANSWER]	
Examiner:	Candidate B, is there anywhere you would like to visit?
[PAUSE FOR YOU TO ANSWER]	
Examiner:	And how about you, Candidate A?
Candidate A:	I'd like to go to the USA. I've seen so many places there on TV, but it would be nice to go there and actually see them. It's quite expensive there, though, so I'd need to save up some money first.
Examiner:	Candidate B, what do you like to do when you go on holiday?
[PAUSE FOR YOU TO ANSWER]	
Examiner:	And what about you, Candidate A?
Candidate A:	I'm the same. I really enjoy walking around the shops in a different city. I'm not really interested in visiting old buildings or museums, though. I think I prefer lying on the beach to doing that.
Examiner:	Thank you. That is the end of the test.

TEST 3   LISTENING

Part 1

Track 17

Preliminary English Test for Schools, Listening.
There are four parts to the test. You will hear each piece twice.
We will now stop for a moment.
Please ask any questions now, because you must not speak during the test.

Now look at the instructions for Part 1.
For each question, choose the correct answer.
Look at Question 1.

1 Where will the café be in the future?

Guide:	Thanks for coming along to see the bikes in our museum. We've moved things around recently to give visitors a better experience. The café is still up on the first floor. We plan to move it to the second floor as there's a bit more space. You'll find most of our old motorbikes here on the ground floor, and one or two of the earliest models in the world can be seen on the second floor.

Now listen again.

2 When does the boy return to school?

Mother:	I've just had an email from your school. Do you know when you go back?
Boy:	Yes, I told you. It's next Monday, the 19th.
Mother:	Yes, that's when school starts again. According to the mail, there's a training day on the Monday, and students don't go back until Tuesday the 20th. I've just checked my diary. Don't forget that your bus pass runs out on the 16th. That's this Friday. You'll need that for school, so we'll have to get a new one before it's too late.

Now listen again.

3 How much is the laptop?

Girl:	Can you tell me how much this laptop is?
Shop assistant:	This is one of our second-hand ones. Is that OK?
Girl:	Yes, that's no problem. I saw it last week in the shop and it was £225, but I can see you've now put it up to £275. I was interested before, but that's a bit too expensive for me.
Shop assistant:	I think someone's put the wrong label on this one. We've actually reduced the price to £175. Would you like to try it?

Now listen again.

4 What did the boy do at the weekend?

Girl:	Hi Mark. Did you have a nice weekend?
Boy:	Not really. Some of my friends went over to the park to have a game of football, but I couldn't join them this time.
Girl:	That's not like you. You love playing football.
Boy:	I was supposed to wash my dad's car, but it was raining, so I ended up sitting in front of the TV all afternoon. It was a bit boring, to be honest. My mates said the football was great fun.

Now listen again.

5 What did the girl forget?

Boy:	Did you get everything you wanted?
Girl:	I went into town to buy those books we need for school. I'd forgotten how busy

Audio scripts

it gets on a Saturday. Luckily, they had copies, but I'd left the gift card my mum had given me at home, so I had to pay for them. I didn't stay long in town. As soon as I walked through the door, my mum asked me if I'd remembered to get her face cream. I was pleased to tell her I had.

Now listen again.

6 *Why is the girl going to be late home?*

Girl: Hi Mum. I'm just calling to say I'm going to be late home from school. The teacher has moved that art class I was telling you about. She can't attend next week, so now we're doing it this afternoon. I was planning to go round to Sally's house after school to practise some dance moves, but her mum has visitors, so I'll come home directly from school. I'll catch the later bus, so I should be home about 6.00. See you when I get back.

Now listen again.

7 *How does the boy recommend getting to his house?*

Girl: I'm looking forward to seeing you and your family later. What's the best way to get to your house?

Boy: You're arriving by train, aren't you? There's a slow train from there to my place, but it stops at every station and takes ages. The quickest way would be to get a taxi, but they're not cheap. Why not get the bus? It goes all the way to my street and doesn't cost much. Plus, you'll get to see the town on your way.

Now listen again.

That is the end of Part 1.

Part 2

Track 18

Now look at Part 2.
For each question, choose the correct answer.

8 *You will hear a brother and sister talking about a birthday present for their father.*

Boy: I was thinking about getting Dad a shirt for his birthday. What do you think?

Girl: Well, he definitely needs a few more. We could take him to that new shop in town and get him to choose one if he has the time.

Boy: Yes, though he is a bit busy at the moment.

Girl: That's true. He hates shopping, anyway. I'd be surprised if he agreed. Let's have a chat with Mum and see what she thinks. If you buy him something he doesn't like, he'll probably never wear it.

Now listen again.

9 *You will hear two friends talking about a new teacher.*

Girl: We had our new teacher for the first time today. Mr Johnson. We all enjoyed his lesson.

Boy: Really? I saw him the other day walking up the stairs. He looks quite strict.

Girl: I know what you mean. He does look a bit scary with that bald head and being so tall as well. But he was OK. I always feel sorry for teachers the first time they take a lesson. They must be really nervous standing in front of us all. He was relaxed and friendly, though, and spent time getting to know all the students.

Now listen again.

10 *You will hear a mother and her son talking about the weather.*

Boy: Are you still planning to take us out to the park later, Mum?

Mother: Yes, why not? The weather forecast says it's going to be sunny. We'll have a lovely time.

Boy: You said the same thing the last time we went out and it rained all the time we were there. And it was freezing.

Mother: That's not true. I didn't say that it wouldn't rain. Anyway, you can usually trust the forecast. If it looks like it's going to rain, we can go another day. I don't fancy getting wet again either.

Now listen again.

11 *You will hear two parents talking about dinner.*

Woman: So, what shall we make for dinner this evening? Something the kids will eat! Whose turn is it to cook?

Man: Mine. I could make my delicious curry. They always like that, don't they?

Woman: I know. It's a bit hot today for curry, though. What about a healthy salad? That would be nice. We haven't had one for ages. I'll make a nice big one.

Man: OK, but let's celebrate the weekend tomorrow and get a takeaway, shall we? We could use that new Chinese restaurant that's just opened.

Woman: Yes, let's do that.

Now listen again.

12 *You will hear a girl and her father talking about a journey.*

Father: So, are you ready for your festival weekend?

Girl: Yes, I've packed and I'm ready to go. I'm really excited! Mary's mum was going to take us in her car, but she's got to go into work now, so Mary's bought tickets for the coach. It's not too expensive, actually.

Father: You should have told me. I'd have driven you down.

Girl: I know you would. You're the best dad in the world. But it doesn't matter now. If you could give me a lift to the coach station, that would be great, though.

Now listen again.

Audio scripts

13 *You will hear two friends talking about selling a bicycle.*

Boy: Hi Mia. What are you doing?
Girl: I'm just putting this advert on a website. I'm selling my bike.
Boy: You only bought it recently. What's the matter with it?
Girl: There's nothing wrong with it, to be honest. I always wanted to go cycling to get fit and it seemed like a good idea to get one. But I hardly ever have time to use it and it just sits in the house taking up space and gets in the way. I don't want to give it away because it cost quite a lot of money.

Now listen again.

That is the end of Part 2.

Part 3

Track 19

Now look at Part 3.
For each question, write the correct answer in the gap.
Write one or two words or a number or a date or a time.
Look at Questions 14 to 19 now. You have 20 seconds.
You will hear a teacher talking about a special event at the school.

Teacher: Hello everyone. I hope you're all OK. Before we start the lesson, I need to speak to you about Mr Hastings. As you know, he's leaving the school on the last day of the month. By last September he'd worked here for 35 years, longer than any other teacher in the school. I'm sure you know how loved and respected he is by everyone here. We'd like to show him how much we will miss him.

The teachers have arranged a surprise party for him on his last day. We've invited some of his old students as well. Some of them attended the old school and have never been to this new building. We'd like some of you to give them a tour of the school.

As part of the celebration, we want to make a video for him featuring current and past students as well as the teachers. We just want each person to say something about him, why you like his lessons, what you like about him, that kind of thing. If you think you'd like to take part, email me by Friday and I'll arrange a time for you to be recorded next Monday. And don't forget to write a nice message in the leaving card that we're passing around. I think the other class have it at the moment, but I'll give it to you next lesson. We're going to hold the event in the hall so that everyone can attend. We've collected some money from the staff and bought him some golf equipment, which we'll give him then. We all know how much he likes playing that, don't we?

Now listen again.

That is the end of Part 3.

Part 4

Track 20

Now look at Part 4.
For each question, choose the correct answer.
Look at Questions 20 to 25 now.
You have 45 seconds.
You will hear an interview with a woman called Christine Peake, who runs football training for girls.

Interviewer: I'm with Christine Peake from Gilberstone Football Club. Hi Christine. You've come on today to tell us about how girls can get involved in what is often considered a boy's sport, haven't you?
Christine: Yes, I help run training sessions and organise games for girls who want to play football. There are new clubs for girls opening all over the country – football's become very popular during the past few years. In fact, I don't see it as a boy's sport anymore. There are thousands of girls playing the game now.
Interviewer: And you've been getting lots of new members, I hear?
Christine: Yes, I think it's partly due to the fact that women's football is in the news more these days. It's not on TV as much as I'd like, but our international team recently took part in the World Cup, which was shown on TV, and they did really well. Maybe as a result, lots of girls have joined us over the past year.
Interviewer: What can girls do in your organisation?
Christine: We're open to girls from the ages of five to sixteen. The younger girls come along to run around and play games just for fun, but we teach them basic skills and how they should try to play as a team. The older girls can join one of our many teams, depending on their ability, and play against other clubs.
Interviewer: Is it just girls or can boys also join?
Christine: After speaking with the girls about this, we feel keeping it to girls only is the best option. The younger children probably don't worry too much about playing football with boys, but the teenagers say they can concentrate more on the game if boys aren't around.
Interviewer: Can girls make a career out of football?
Christine: Certainly. Some of our best players have been offered contracts with

Audio scripts

	professional clubs. Most local clubs now have a women's team, and just like with men's football, the chances are there if you have the talent. Things are really changing fast and now is a great time for girls to start playing the game.
Interviewer:	So, if any girls are interested in joining, should they contact you?
Christine:	Definitely. I'd love to hear from anyone who is thinking of joining. Not just older girls either. Parents of younger children can stay during the classes if they're a bit worried about leaving them, and can call me if they have something they want to ask.

Now listen again.

That is the end of Part 4.

You now have six minutes to write your answers on the answer sheet.

That is the end of the test.

TEST 3   SPEAKING

Part 1

Track 21

Examiner:	Good afternoon. Can I have your mark sheets, please? I'm Karen Taylor and this is Martin Brindley.
Examiner:	What's your name, Candidate A? How old are you?
Candidate A:	My name's Vera Bohren and I'm fourteen years old.
Examiner:	And what's your name, Candidate B? How old are you?
[PAUSE FOR YOU TO ANSWER]	
Examiner:	Tell me about what you like to do in your spare time, Candidate B.
[PAUSE FOR YOU TO ANSWER]	
Examiner:	Who do you live with, Candidate B?
[PAUSE FOR YOU TO ANSWER]	
Examiner:	Candidate A, what about you? What do you like doing in your spare time?
Candidate A:	I enjoy listening to music and going to concerts because I really love live music.
Examiner:	Who do you live with, Candidate A?
Candidate A:	I also live with my parents. I don't have any brothers or sisters.
Examiner:	Candidate A, do you enjoy studying English?
Candidate A:	Yes, I do. I enjoy studying all languages. I also speak a little French, and I'd like to learn Chinese in the future.
Examiner:	Candidate B, what about you?
[PAUSE FOR YOU TO ANSWER]	
Examiner:	Can you tell me something about the area where you live, Candidate B?
[PAUSE FOR YOU TO ANSWER]	
Examiner:	Candidate A, what about you?
Candidate A:	We live in the country. My parents are farmers and we live in a small village in the south of Germany. There are one or two shops in the village, but we have to drive into the nearest town when we want to go shopping.
Examiner:	Thank you.

Part 2

Track 22

Examiner:	Now I'd like each of you to talk on your own about something. I'm going to give each of you a photograph and I'd like you to talk about it. Candidate A. Here is your photograph. It shows some people in a gym. Please tell us what you can see in the photograph. Candidate B, you just listen.
Candidate A:	Well, this photograph reminds me of my sports class at school. It shows teenagers playing volleyball. There are two teams, but they're all wearing the same clothes: white vests and blue shorts. I think this must be the sports kit that children wear in the school. They have numbers on the back of the vests, though, so there is some difference. The teams have boys and girls in them. The boy nearest the camera is about to hit the ball and there are boys and girls standing near the net waiting to play. They're all concentrating and want to win.
Examiner:	Thank you.
Examiner:	Candidate B. Here is your photograph. It shows people at an airport. Please tell us what you can see in the photograph. Candidate A, you just listen.
[PAUSE FOR YOU TO ANSWER]	
Examiner:	Thank you.

Part 3

Track 23

Examiner:	Now, in this part of the test you're going to talk about something together for about two minutes. I'm going to describe a situation to you. A girl of sixteen wants to take up a hobby. Her parents have suggested some things she could do. Here are some things they have suggested.

|Candidate A:|Talk together about the different things she could do and say which one would be best. All right? Now talk together.
OK, well these are all popular hobbies, aren't they? Are there any that you think she probably wouldn't like?|
|---|---|
[PAUSE FOR YOU TO ANSWER]
| Candidate A: | I agree. A bicycle would be cheaper and she'd get fit if she started cycling. But she might not be keen on keeping fit. What about photography or dancing? Would these be interesting? |
[PAUSE FOR YOU TO ANSWER]
| Candidate A: | That's a good idea. I can imagine it's something she can do in the evening after she has finished her homework that isn't hard work. |
[PAUSE FOR YOU TO ANSWER]
| Candidate A: | That's true. But I think I prefer your idea of her learning to knit. She probably has art classes at school, so painting wouldn't really be a new hobby. |
[PAUSE FOR YOU TO ANSWER]
| Examiner: | Thank you. |

Part 4

Track 24

Examiner:	Candidate A, is there a hobby or activity you'd like to start doing?
Candidate A:	Actually, I like the idea of learning to knit. My grandmother is very good at it, and every time we visit her, she's making something for someone. I think it would be very relaxing as well.
Examiner:	And what about you, Candidate B?
[PAUSE FOR YOU TO ANSWER]
| Examiner: | Candidate B, are some hobbies better for younger people rather than older people? |
[PAUSE FOR YOU TO ANSWER]
Examiner:	And how about you, Candidate A?
Candidate A:	Yes, I agree. Some things might be dangerous for older people, like mountain climbing, for example. But apart from activities like that, I think younger and older people are able to have the same interests and hobbies.
Examiner:	Candidate B, is it important for people to have a hobby or interest?
[PAUSE FOR YOU TO ANSWER]
Examiner:	And what about you, Candidate A, what do you think?
Candidate A:	I agree. It's also possible to meet new people if you have a hobby. You might have the chance to play football in a team, or join a club to do a hobby like painting, and you might make new friends.
Examiner:	Thank you. That is the end of the test.

TEST 4   LISTENING

Part 1

Track 25

Preliminary English Test for Schools, Listening.
There are four parts to the test. You will hear each piece twice.
We will now stop for a moment.
Please ask any questions now, because you must not speak during the test.
Now look at the instructions for Part 1.
For each question, choose the correct answer.
Look at Question 1.

1 How did the boy find out about the bicycle?

Girl:	Hiya. I saw you yesterday out cycling.
Boy:	Did you? I've only just bought the bike. That was one of the first times I've ridden it.
Girl:	It looks like a good one.
Boy:	It's nothing special. There was one online that someone was selling second-hand. They wanted too much for it, though. Then I was on the phone to a friend and he told me he was selling his. It looked good, and it was less expensive than the ones I'd seen in the bike shop.

Now listen again.

2 Why should drivers not drive into the city centre?

Announcer:	Now on to travel news. The heavy snow that caused traffic problems in many areas is now gone and most traffic is moving. However, an accident in the city centre has caused traffic jams and drivers will need extra time for their journey into town. And don't forget, this week preparations are in progress for the race on Sunday. Several roads will be closed, which is likely to cause traffic problems. As a result, police are asking drivers to avoid the city centre.

Now listen again.

3 What did the girl do for the first time?

Boy:	Hiya Claire. Sorry I couldn't make it on Saturday. Did you enjoy the swimming class?
Girl:	Yes, I did. I'm definitely getting better and it was easier than last week. I'm enjoying all this exercise. Mum and Dad got me a bicycle for my birthday. I went out cycling with them on Sunday. We've never done that before. It was lovely.
Boy:	It's a pity I can't persuade you to play tennis!
Girl:	There's a first time for everything. I might join you for a game soon.

Now listen again.

Audio scripts

4 *Which lesson will be on Monday afternoon?*

Teacher: OK everyone. Before you go home, I've got some timetable changes to tell you about for next Monday. Mrs Jones is off sick, and Mr Edwards will take her English lesson on Monday. He already has lessons in the afternoon, so we're moving your afternoon class to the morning. You'll have French as usual after lunch at 1.30. And don't forget my maths homework. Please leave it at my office on Monday afternoon.

Now listen again.

5 *What is the girl going to order?*

Boy: What are you going to order?
Girl: I can't decide. What about you? Are you having a burger?
Boy: How did you know?
Girl: Because you always do!
Boy: I suppose I do! So, what about you?
Girl: I'm thinking of a pizza. I had a burger for dinner last night.
Boy: You said the last pizza from here was cold and you left most of it.
Girl: That's true. I might just get some chips. I'll make a pizza when I get home.

Now listen again.

6 *How should the boy's mother pay for the trip?*

Boy: Hiya Mum. I'm phoning from school. I need to pay for the school trip by tomorrow or I might not be able to go. There's only one coach booked and it's nearly full. They said I can pay in cash tomorrow, or you can phone the school and pay with your card. It's probably best to do that in case anyone else signs up and takes the last places. You can also transfer money from your bank to the school's bank, but I don't know their details.

Now listen again.

7 *What does the boy buy?*

Audio scripts

	week with some great special offers. I'm not sure if it's still on, though.
Boy:	We don't have to go immediately. They open late today, don't they?
Mother:	No, that's tomorrow. Anyway, I need to get back to cook dinner, so if we're going, we need to go soon.

Now listen again.

12 *You will hear two parents talking about a party this Saturday.*

Man:	Have we agreed what we're doing about Sam's birthday party this Saturday?
Woman:	I think so. He doesn't want to hire the hall in the leisure centre now. He just wants a few friends here at home.
Man:	It would be nice to have the family as well. What do you think?
Woman:	Sam said he'd prefer to have it just with his friends.
Man:	OK. We can always have the family round on Sunday and keep Saturday for his friends. We need to go shopping for food soon. Let's not leave it too late.

Now listen again.

13 *You will hear two friends talking about a school trip.*

Girl:	I enjoyed that trip yesterday. Did you?
Boy:	It was fantastic, wasn't it? It was a long way to go, though. They should choose places that are nearer.
Girl:	I know, but it was a really lively town with some great shops. I enjoyed it.
Boy:	Yes, I'm glad I've been there and seen it. It was definitely more interesting than the place we went to before. I was telling Mum and Dad about it, and they said they'd like to go there. I'm not sure I'd fancy going again, though.

Now listen again.

That is the end of Part 2.

Part 3

Track 27

Now look at Part 3.
For each question, write the correct answer in the gap.
Write one or two words or a number or a date or a time.
Look at Questions 14 to 19 now. You have 20 seconds.
You will hear a news announcer talking about travel problems.

Announcer: That's all from the news desk. Now on to this morning's travel report. Most roads seem to be quiet despite the return to work this Monday morning. However, there are reports of one or two problems.

This is the first day back at school after the holidays and the police are reminding parents not to park outside schools as this could be a danger to children. The police are patrolling some of the schools in the area and will give out fines if necessary.

It's important to note that there's a problem on the highway because of a tree that fell down following an accident and is now blocking the road. Workers are dealing with the problem, but the road remains closed. Please look out for signs providing drivers with other routes into the town centre.

Next, the new 20 mile-per-hour speed limits on the ring road. These have been there since March and will continue until May due to repair work being carried out on the road. There are likely to be delays as a result.

Now on to the buses. Buses from Beechwood to Summerhill will be late due to strong winds. This is likely to be a problem for the rest of the day, so be prepared to find other ways of travelling if necessary.

And on the subject of buses, you probably saw the news about the one that drove into a bridge on the Hollwood Road at the weekend. Well, the damage has now been cleared, but buses aren't using the bridge while checks are carried out by engineers.

That's all for now. I'll be back with you at 8.00 a.m. for any further updates.

Now listen again.

That is the end of Part 3.

Part 4

Track 28

Now look at Part 4.
For each question, choose the correct answer.
Look at Questions 20 to 25 now.
You have 45 seconds.
You will hear an interview with a man called Ian Groves, who helped set up an exciting after-school activity.

Interviewer:	Hello. Today I'm meeting Ian Groves, a teacher at Eastleigh School, to talk about one of the new after-school activities they've set up. Hi Ian. There are so many things you could offer. How did you decide what to do?
Ian:	The teachers had discussed various ideas, but we wanted to make sure we got it right, so we created an online form on our website and asked students to complete it. They didn't have to give their name, so we hoped we'd get honest suggestions.
Interviewer:	And what did you find out?
Ian:	We expected there would be an interest in technology – and there was. Some students were interested

Audio scripts

	in working with music, recording their own songs, some wanted to make videos. Not really lessons on how to use the technology as they know more about that than some of the teachers. They mainly wanted access to the equipment we have as they don't have any themselves.
Interviewer:	So, how did you get started?
Ian:	We decided to go with what was immediately possible. There was a lot of interest in video editing, but we didn't have the necessary cameras or software. But we did have plenty of computers, and there's free software you can download from the internet to make recordings. The students had instruments of their own and we were able to use some from the music department.
Interviewer:	What was the main problem getting started?
Ian:	We had trouble fitting the sessions into the timetable to begin with. But we managed to find times in the week which were convenient for everyone. We knew some parents needed their kids back home for particular reasons, and some students were doing other after-school activities.
Interviewer:	Do you have many adults helping them now?
Ian:	Actually, the group are working quite independently already. There's a music teacher, of course, and we started with someone from IT who knew the software, but he's no longer needed. It's fantastic to see the students managing themselves and actually becoming musicians, and perhaps one day, professional musicians.
Interviewer:	Have you got any other projects planned?
Ian:	We'd like to get more students to take part. The school has promised to give us some money for video equipment and if that arrives, we'll set up another group to do video production. The students have already talked about having different groups work together. We have a successful dance group, and they want to create a documentary about the dancers for parents to see.

Now listen again.

That is the end of Part 4.

You now have six minutes to write your answers on the answer sheet.

That is the end of the test.

TEST 4   SPEAKING

Part 1

Track 29

Examiner:	Good morning. Can I have your mark sheets, please? I'm Marcus Holliday and this is Sarah Davidson.
Examiner:	What's your name, Candidate A? How old are you?
Candidate A:	My name's Daniel Bassot and I'm fifteen years old.
Examiner:	And what's your name, Candidate B? How old are you?
[PAUSE FOR YOU TO ANSWER]	
Examiner:	Candidate B, where do you live?
[PAUSE FOR YOU TO ANSWER]	
Examiner:	And where do you live, Candidate A?
Candidate A:	I live in Marseille with my mother, father and my sister.
Examiner:	Candidate A, did you do anything interesting last weekend?
Candidate A:	Not really. The weather wasn't very good, so I stayed indoors and watched football on TV. My grandparents visited us on Sunday, so that was good fun.
Examiner:	And Candidate B, did you do anything interesting at the weekend?
[PAUSE FOR YOU TO ANSWER]	
Examiner:	Candidate A, what is your favourite time of year?
Candidate A:	I definitely like spring best. I love seeing the trees turning green and flowers appearing in people's gardens. I think people start to feel happier when the weather gets warmer.
Examiner:	Candidate B, what about you?
[PAUSE FOR YOU TO ANSWER]	
Examiner:	Candidate B, do you prefer to eat at home or to go to a restaurant?
[PAUSE FOR YOU TO ANSWER]	
Examiner:	And Candidate A, what about you?
Candidate A:	I like any kind of food, so it doesn't matter if I eat it at home or in a restaurant. I love Italian food, so I always feel excited if my parents take me to an Italian restaurant.
Examiner:	Thank you.

Part 2

Track 30

Examiner:	Now I'd like each of you to talk on your own about something. I'm going to give each of you a photograph and I'd like you to talk about it.

198

Audio scripts

	Candidate A. Here is your photograph. It shows people selling things. Please tell us what you can see in the photograph. Candidate B, you just listen.
Candidate A:	In this photograph, I can see a man and a woman and two children. I think the woman and her kids are having a garage sale. They're selling some of the things they don't want anymore. I imagine that the man is passing the house and is looking to see if there's anything he wants to buy. In the photo, he's looking at a book. There are quite a lot of things for sale. There are some suitcases and a guitar on the ground in front of the table, some clothes just behind the man and a barbecue. There are also some chairs on the right of the photo, but I don't know if these are for sale or if the family are using them to sit on.
Examiner:	Thank you.
Examiner:	Candidate B. Here is your photograph. It shows some people with an animal. Please tell us what you can see in the photograph. Candidate A, you just listen.
[PAUSE FOR YOU TO ANSWER]	
Examiner:	Thank you.

Part 3

Track 31

Examiner:	Now, in this part of the test you are going to talk about something together for about two minutes. I'm going to describe a situation to you. A family want to do something together with their young children this weekend. Here are some things they could do together. Talk together about the different things they could do and say which one would be best. All right? Now talk together.
Candidate A:	OK, would you like to start?
[PAUSE FOR YOU TO ANSWER]	
Candidate A:	No, even the parents might not want to do something that difficult. Going for a walk can be good fun, but sometimes young children get tired and start to complain.
[PAUSE FOR YOU TO ANSWER]	
Candidate A:	I'm not sure about that. It's not very special, is it? Everyone likes food, so a barbecue or a picnic would be a good idea. I'm sure the children would enjoy that.

[PAUSE FOR YOU TO ANSWER]	
Candidate A:	OK, let's say the picnic. They can do that in a local park, can't they? Or even in the garden if they have one.
Examiner:	Thank you.

Part 4

Track 32

Examiner:	Candidate A, what do you like to do for a special occasion?
Candidate A:	I said before that I like going to a restaurant. I always feel excited before I go and look forward to eating something I haven't tried before, or a meal that I've had before and loved.
Examiner:	And what about you, Candidate B?
[PAUSE FOR YOU TO ANSWER]	
Examiner:	Candidate B, does the weather affect what we can do for a special occasion?
[PAUSE FOR YOU TO ANSWER]	
Examiner:	And how about you, Candidate A?
Candidate A:	I agree. I think the best activities are often outside, so the weather is really important. Unfortunately, there are lots of rainy days where I live, so we have to be careful when we want to do something outside.
Examiner:	Candidate B, if you could do any activity at all this weekend, what would it be?
[PAUSE FOR YOU TO ANSWER]	
Examiner:	And what about you, Candidate A?
Candidate A:	I think I'd like to get some tickets for me and my friends to see a football match. I'd like to see a game between two of our best teams and get really good seats in the stadium.
Examiner:	Thank you. That is the end of the test.

TEST 5 LISTENING

Part 1

Track 33

Preliminary English Test for Schools, Listening.
There are four parts to the test. You will hear each piece twice.
We will now stop for a moment.
Please ask any questions now, because you must not speak during the test.
Now look at the instructions for Part 1.
For each question, choose the correct answer.
Look at Question 1.

1 What does the girl want her brother to buy?

Girl:	Are you busy, Jack? Can you go to the shop for me again?
Boy:	Again? I went earlier to get you some biscuits. Why can't you remember what you need?

Audio scripts

Girl: I know, sorry. I thought we had some butter in the fridge for those cakes I said I'd make, but there's hardly any left. Could you be a lovely brother and go and get me some?
Boy: OK. I'll just finish what I'm doing.
Now listen again.

2 *Where did the boy last see his bag?*
Library staff: Hello, can I help you?
Boy: I hope so. I've lost my bag. I was on the bus home when I realised I didn't have it with me.
Library staff: Where were you sitting?
Boy: Over there by the window. I remember picking the bag up and putting it on the chair as I was leaving. I think that was the last time I saw it. I came over to reserve some books. Perhaps I left it on the floor by your desk – I can't remember.

Now listen again.

3 *When does the next train to the city centre leave?*
Announcer: That's all the problems on the roads. Now on to the trains. Due to an electrical problem, the 9.30 train from Bordesley to the city centre is cancelled. Unfortunately, there won't be another one until 10.30. For those of you in a hurry, they have organised an emergency bus service that leaves from the station. This will leave at 9.45. You can get a ticket for the bus at the ticket office. That's all the travel news for you this morning.

Now listen again.

4 *How much does the girl want to borrow?*
Girl: Mum, can you lend me some money until the weekend?
Mother: I gave you £10 yesterday. You said you wanted to buy a T-shirt. What do you want money for now?
Girl: I know. I've still got the £10. But I've seen a different one I really like. It's a bit more expensive. I need another £5. I can give it back to you. I get paid £30 on Saturday for my weekend job.
Mother: OK, but don't forget to pay me back.
Now listen again.

5 *What should the children take on the trip?*
Teacher: Hello. This is Mrs Sandwell from the school. I gave the students a message for parents, but it seems a lot of them have forgotten. It's about the trip on Friday. It's quite a long journey, so could your child bring some lunch – sandwiches and a drink? Something like that. It looks like it's going to rain quite a lot, but the centre have waterproof clothing. The teacher will give out maps of the walk that the students can use to find their way around.

Now listen again.

6 *What is the boy going to give away to charity?*
Boy: I've got so many things in my bedroom I don't need anymore. I might take something to the charity shop.
Mother: That's a good idea.
Boy: There's that camera I got a few years ago that I never use now I have my phone. I'll take that.
Mother: What about all those CDs you have in that box? You don't play them now.
Boy: I might do that, but I need to make a list of them on my laptop first. That's old now. I hope there's enough space to store all the information.

Now listen again.

7 *Where are the friends going to meet Hollie?*
Girl: Hi Hollie. I'm just calling about the cinema on Friday. I know you're eating at home and arriving later. The rest of us are meeting at the pizza restaurant just next door to the train station. We decided to get something to eat first. The film starts at 7.00 p.m. We'll wait for you at the ticket office. I'll get your ticket, so you don't need to worry about that.

Now listen again.

That is the end of Part 1.

Part 2

Track 34

Now look at Part 2.
For each question, choose the correct answer.

8 *You will hear two parents talking about their daughter.*
Woman: I am so proud of Karina and how hard she's worked at school.
Man: Me too. I'd like to show her how pleased we are with her. Maybe give her some money.
Woman: She'd like some extra money. I know she's saving up. But I think a present would be better. I know she needs a new watch for when she's out running, but I don't know which one she wants. I was thinking of booking a table in that Italian restaurant she likes. What do you think?
Man: Great idea. Let's do that.
Now listen again.

9 *You will hear two friends talking about a vlogger.*
Boy: Did you watch any of the videos by that vlogger I was telling you about? The one who makes cookery videos?

Girl: Yes, I watched a couple last night. I really liked them.
Boy: I can understand why girls like him. He's very good-looking. I don't think I'll bother watching him again, though.
Girl: Why? Some of the cakes he made look delicious.
Boy: Well, maybe they are. But he doesn't tell you enough about what to do. Each video ends with a lovely cake, but I don't know how to make it.

Now listen again.

10 *You will hear a brother and sister talking about doing housework.*

Boy: Mum has asked me to tidy the bathroom. She said I keep leaving it in a mess.
Girl: She wants both of us to do more around the house. I think she feels tired when she gets home from work. We should try to help her more. We don't do much housework.
Boy: Yes, you're right. I'll offer to do the bathroom every day.
Girl: I don't think it needs doing that often. Speak to Mum and see what she says. I'll have a chat with her to see how I can help.

Now listen again.

11 *You will hear a mother and her son talking about the summer holiday.*

Mother: What are your plans for the summer holiday? You have a few weeks off before you go to university.
Boy: Well, I've already got a reading list for my first year, so I could start working through that. I'd like to get out of the house and do something else, though. I was going to help at the leisure centre. I won't get paid, but it will be fun.
Mother: Why don't you look for a temporary job?
Boy: I've had a look to see what's available, but most of the jobs were full-time.

Now listen again.

12 *You will hear two friends talking about a football match.*

Boy: I watched the game on TV last night. Did you see it?
Girl: Yes, our team didn't play well at all. The newspapers are blaming the goalkeeper. What do you think?
Boy: Well, they did score five goals, so I don't suppose the goalkeeper is feeling very happy this morning. But some other players were terrible, so they shouldn't just blame him.
Girl: That's true. Some of them didn't seem very interested in playing.
Boy: I think the manager is the real problem. He keeps picking the same players although some of them are playing really badly.

Now listen again.

13 *You will hear a father and his daughter talking about guitar lessons.*

Father: Do you still want me to give you guitar lessons?
Girl: I'd love you to. I was going to ask my teacher at school, but she only teaches groups and I'd prefer to learn on my own.
Father: Well, I'm happy to help you, but I can only do it at weekends. I'm rather busy in the week.
Girl: OK. If I enjoy it, I might look for a teacher during the week as well. Mum said she'd help me pay for lessons. I'll still carry on with you at the weekend, of course.

Now listen again.

That is the end of Part 2.

Part 3

Track 35

Now look at Part 3.
For each question, write the correct answer in the gap. Write one or two words or a number or a date or a time. Look at Questions 14 to 19 now. You have 20 seconds. You will hear a recorded message about activities at a skateboard centre.

Speaker: Thanks for calling Marshlands Skateboard Centre. Building work at the centre is now complete and we are pleased to announce that we will be open again on Sunday 17 June with a full timetable of classes with our qualified teachers.

We have a new session for beginners starting on Monday 18 June at 6.00 p.m. These sessions, called 'Skateboarding Safety First' are very popular, and are a great introduction to this exciting sport. We can supply skateboards for anyone who doesn't yet have their own, as well as safety equipment.

On Saturday 23 June at 9.00 a.m. our top instructor, Gareth Jones, will be holding a two-hour class looking at some of the more advanced techniques you can add to your set of skills. These sessions are for those with experience in skateboarding.

Places are limited, so for those who don't manage to book one, you can also subscribe to our video lessons. These are for people new to skateboarding and will show you some of our top tips. You can find out more information about them on our website.

All classes must be paid for in advance using our online booking form. All sessions cost £13.00 per person. When booking, please make sure you tick the correct box to let us know whether you will bring your own skateboard or not.

Audio scripts

We would also be grateful if you could use the form to tell us how you found out about the centre.

Please note that all classes are held outside. If the weather is bad, we may need to cancel for reasons of safety.

If this is the case, we can arrange a different date or a refund.

Now listen again.

That is the end of Part 3.

Part 4

Track 36

Now look at Part 4.
For each question, choose the correct answer.
Look at Questions 20 to 25 now.
You have 45 seconds.
You will hear an interview with a man called Chris Thompson, who is a sports teacher.

Interviewer:	Today I'm talking to Chris Thompson, a sports teacher from one of our local schools. Hi Chris. Can you tell me what made you become a sports teacher?
Chris:	Well, it's funny, really. I wasn't brilliant at any particular sport at school. I played for the football team and enjoyed the gymnastics lessons and I suppose I was quite ordinary. But it was definitely my favourite lesson of the week. I think that was the main reason. My mum and dad were teachers, but they never tried to influence me.
Interviewer:	Do you now have a favourite sport that you enjoy most?
Chris:	Well, as I said, I used to enjoy gymnastics a lot. That was probably my favourite activity at school. But I injured my shoulder a few years ago and can't do that anymore. I still play football, but I suppose my favourite activity now is running. I do that regularly each week.
Interviewer:	What do you like most about being a sports teacher?
Chris:	The kids work so hard all day and spend all their time sitting at computer screens or at their desks. I love seeing them getting the chance to be active in my classes. They don't all like the sports lessons, but those that do make it all worth it.
Interviewer:	And what's the most challenging thing about being a sports teacher?
Chris:	I think it's persuading teenagers to take up sport outside school. Those that are really good at a particular sport often spend their free time doing it on their own. But most of them often never bother doing any exercise outside school. I always wish I could get more of them to be more active.
Interviewer:	What's the main reason you think people should do regular exercise?
Chris:	Most people would say doing a sport offers you physical benefits. It's certainly good for your fitness and you might make new friends. But I prefer to talk about the benefits doing sport has for our mind. You just feel good when you're taking part in something and have a sense of achievement after.
Interviewer:	Have any of your students gone on to achieve something special in sport?
Chris:	There was a student at the school a few years ago who is now a top swimmer. He might even be picked to swim for the country. To be honest, it wasn't me that helped him, though. I'm not a great swimmer. I worked with him on the school football team.

Now listen again.

That is the end of Part 4.

You now have six minutes to write your answers on the answer sheet.

That is the end of the test.

TEST 5 SPEAKING

Part 1

Track 37

Examiner:	Good morning. Can I have your mark sheets, please? I'm James Huntley and this is Jayne Mathiewson.
Examiner:	What's your name, Candidate A? How old are you?
Candidate A:	My name's Ingrid and I'm fifteen years old.
Examiner:	And what's your name, Candidate B? How old are you?

[PAUSE FOR YOU TO ANSWER]

Examiner:	Candidate B, where do you come from?

[PAUSE FOR YOU TO ANSWER]

Examiner:	And where do you come from, Candidate A?
Candidate A:	I'm from Zurich in Switzerland.
Examiner:	Candidate A, when did you start learning English?
Candidate A:	We had English lessons in my primary school. I think I was about six when I had my first lesson. My

Audio scripts

	mum speaks good English, so she also taught me some words when I was little.
Examiner:	And Candidate B, when did you start learning English?

[PAUSE FOR YOU TO ANSWER]

Examiner:	Candidate A, what do you like to do when you're on holiday?
Candidate A:	I enjoy walking around the shops, especially if they're different from the ones we have at home. I don't think I'd like a holiday in the countryside because I wouldn't be able to do that.
Examiner:	Candidate B, what about you?

[PAUSE FOR YOU TO ANSWER]

Examiner:	Candidate B, in class, do you prefer to work on your own or in a group of other students?

[PAUSE FOR YOU TO ANSWER]

Examiner:	And Candidate A, what about you?
Candidate A:	I like to work with other students. If there's something I don't understand, sometimes they can help. And if it's something they find difficult, I can explain it to them. I think this helps me learn the subject better.
Examiner:	Thank you.

Part 2

Track 38

Examiner:	Now, I'd like each of you to talk on your own about something. I'm going to give each of you a photograph and I'd like you to talk about it. Candidate A. Here is your photograph. It shows people having their photograph taken. Please tell us what you can see in the photograph. Candidate B, you just listen.
Candidate A:	In this photograph, there are six people being photographed. It looks like a family as there are younger and older people in the group and they seem to have a lovely relationship. I think they might be grandparents, parents and children. They're dressed in casual clothes like jeans and T-shirts and look very happy and relaxed. I don't think they're at home as there isn't much furniture, so I imagine they're in a studio. There are two large lights that are making the room very bright. On the left, you can see the photographer. He's wearing jeans and a striped shirt. He's on one knee and it looks like he's actually taking the photographs.
Examiner:	Thank you.

Examiner:	Candidate B. Here is your photograph. It shows a man running. Please tell us what you can see in the photograph. Candidate A, you just listen.

[PAUSE FOR YOU TO ANSWER]

Examiner:	Thank you.

Part 3

Track 39

Examiner:	Now, in this part of the test you are going to talk about something together for about two minutes. I'm going to describe a situation to you. A girl is about to leave home to attend her first day at high school. Here are some things she could take to school. Talk together about the different things she could take and say which one would be best. All right? Now talk together.
Candidate A:	OK, would you like to start?

[PAUSE FOR YOU TO ANSWER]

Candidate A:	That's true. The sandwiches are important, but she might want to see what the school dinners are like. Do you think she should take her own food?

[PAUSE FOR YOU TO ANSWER]

Candidate A:	I think the pen is really important. She'll definitely have to write things during the day. If she doesn't take it, she'll have to ask the teacher for one. That could be embarrassing.

[PAUSE FOR YOU TO ANSWER]

Candidate A:	That's right. So, we have three things then – the phone, money and the pen. What do you think?

[PAUSE FOR YOU TO ANSWER]

Candidate A:	OK. Let's say the phone.
Examiner:	Thank you.

Part 4

Track 40

Examiner:	Candidate A, do you like to take your own food to school?
Candidate A:	I tried the school dinners when I first went to my school, but I didn't like a lot of the dishes, so now I take sandwiches or buy something on the way to school.
Examiner:	And what about you, Candidate B?

[PAUSE FOR YOU TO ANSWER]

Examiner:	Candidate B, is there anything important that you always take to school?

[PAUSE FOR YOU TO ANSWER]

Examiner:	And how about you, Candidate A?

Audio scripts

Candidate A: I'm the same. I feel a bit lost if I don't have my phone. Our teachers allow us to use the phones in class when we have to look up information. If you don't have one with you, it's a problem.
Examiner: Candidate B, do you ever cycle to school?
[PAUSE FOR YOU TO ANSWER]
Examiner: And what about you, Candidate A?
Candidate A: I like to cycle to school if it's a sunny morning, but if it's raining, I catch the bus. The roads are OK where I live and there are cycle paths all the way to my school.
Examiner: Thank you. That is the end of the test.

TEST 6 LISTENING

Part 1

Track 41

Preliminary English Test for Schools, Listening.
There are four parts to the test. You will hear each piece twice.
We will now stop for a moment.
Please ask any questions now, because you must not speak during the test.
Now look at the instructions for Part 1.
For each question, choose the correct answer.
Look at Question 1.

1 *Which activity takes place on a Thursday?*

Announcer: If any young people listening are looking for somewhere to go in their free time, I have some good news. The leisure centre is now running art classes every week through the summer holidays. After the success of the dance group that takes place on Wednesdays, they've decided to offer art on Thursdays. So, you have no excuse to feel bored as you now have dance and art classes as well as Saturday's film club to look forward to.

Now listen again.

2 *When is Grandad's birthday?*

Boy: You haven't forgotten it's Grandad's birthday soon, have you? We need to get him a present.
Girl: Yes, I know. I always get his mixed up with Granny's. Hers is on Wednesday, and we've already bought her something. It's getting delivered to their house, so that's done.
Boy: Well, his is on Thursday, so we need to get something before we see him on Friday.
Girl: We have all week to decide. He won't mind getting his present a day later, will he?

Now listen again.

3 *What is the boy doing on Friday?*

Boy: Tom, it's Jason here. I'm just calling about this Friday. I've got to stay late at school to study, so I won't make it. I can still come round on Saturday if that's OK. I told you I've still got those free tickets for the football match, didn't I? Maybe we could go to see that, or we could go into town. I've got to collect my laptop from the repair shop, so that would be useful too. Let me know what you want to do.

Now listen again.

4 *What has the girl forgotten to bring with her?*

Girl: Oh no! Can you turn the car round and go back? I've left something at home.
Father: Not your keys, I hope. I'm working late this afternoon, remember. You won't be able to get in without them.
Girl: No, I've got them here. I've left my phone in my bedroom. I've looked in my bag and I can't find it.
Father: OK, but next time can you pay a bit more attention when you're leaving?
Girl: Yes, sorry. I was in a hurry. Thanks, Dad!

Now listen again.

5 *What did the boy do for the first time today?*

Mother: So, how was school today?
Boy: It was OK. It didn't start very well. We're supposed to have maths with that new teacher, but she was sick. The one we had last year had to take the class. He's a bit boring, to be honest. We had lunch in the new café, though. That was good. It only opened today. I stayed late to watch the basketball team. They won for the first time this year.

Now listen again.

6 *Where is the boy now?*

Boy: Hi Dad. It's me. The brakes have stopped working on my bike.
Father: Oh no! Where are you? You're not trying to ride it, are you? It's too dangerous.
Boy: No, don't worry. I'm still at school. One of the teachers is looking at it to see if he can fix it. If he can't, I'll leave it here and get the bus home.
Father: OK. I'll tell Mum you're going to be home a little later.

Now listen again.

7 *Why has tomorrow's music lesson been cancelled?*

Woman: Hello, Ashley? It's Mrs Amberley, the secretary from school. I'm phoning to tell you that we've had to cancel tomorrow's music lesson. You probably know Mr Clements is off sick. Well, we were able to get another teacher to take the class, but we've now discovered the electricity in the music room isn't

Audio scripts

working. Someone is coming tomorrow to fix it. Hope you're OK and enjoying the snow. Take care.

Now listen again.

That is the end of Part 1.

Part 2

Track 42

Now look at Part 2.
For each question, choose the correct answer.

8 *You will hear two friends talking about a holiday.*

Girl: Welcome back! Did you have a nice holiday?
Boy: Yes, it was great. We went to the south of Spain. We had a lovely time.
Girl: What did you do?
Boy: We spent most of the time on the beach. The sea was so warm and I went swimming every day. The hotel was OK, but I wish we'd chosen somewhere nearer the beach. It was right at the top of a hill. There wasn't even a view of the sea, and it was a long walk back to the hotel every day.

Now listen again.

9 *You will hear two friends talking about homework.*

Boy: How are you getting on with the maths homework we were given?
Girl: Not too badly. I've nearly finished, but it's taking longer than I thought. I usually get it done quite quickly. How about you?
Boy: I worked on it last night and got it done before I went to bed. Don't forget you need to hand it in tomorrow.
Girl: I know. I've got homework from two other teachers to finish as well. That can be handed in next week, though, so I'll finish maths this evening and start the rest tomorrow.

Now listen again.

10 *You will hear a mother and her son talking about a book.*

Mother: I'm reading that book you recommended. It's good, isn't it?
Boy: I told you it was exciting. I've never been a big fan of science fiction, but the film was so good I thought I'd try the book.
Mother: I didn't see the film and I've only read half of it, so don't tell me what happens.
Boy: Don't worry. I won't say a word. I don't want to spoil it for you. I wasn't expecting the ending. It's not quite the same as the film and I was a bit shocked at how it finished.

Now listen again.

11 *You will hear two friends talking about basketball.*

Girl: I was talking to some of your friends earlier. They said you played really well on Saturday. Well done!
Boy: That's kind of you. Thanks. I really enjoyed the game. I haven't played very well the past few weeks because I was injured. But I felt much better on Saturday.
Girl: You weren't badly injured then?
Boy: Not really. It's a problem with my shoulder. It doesn't stop me playing, but I just don't feel very comfortable. I hope as long as I take things easy, it will be completely OK soon.

Now listen again.

12 *You will hear two friends talking about a clothes shop.*

Girl: I went into town earlier. There are so many shops that are no longer open.
Boy: I know. I was a bit worried about that clothes shop I like. One of my friends told me that there was a sale there. I went past it on the way home from school and there was no sale, but there's a notice in the window saying they're moving to a new location. Somewhere nearer the station.
Girl: That's good. I know you like the clothes from that shop.

Now listen again.

13 *You will hear two friends talking about the journey to school.*

Girl: I'm getting so annoyed with the trains. The one I get to school was cancelled this morning.
Boy: What, again? What was the reason this time?
Girl: I don't know. But each time it happens, I have to run to catch the bus or I'll be late for the first lesson. The bus was also late this morning, and I didn't get to class on time. I'm going to see if my dad will take me on his way to work. I was thinking about cycling to school. But my mum wouldn't let me as the roads are so busy.

Now listen again.

That is the end of Part 2.

Part 3

Track 43

Now look at Part 3.
For each question, write the correct answer in the gap.
Write one or two words or a number or a date or a time.
Look at Questions 14 to 19 now. You have 20 seconds.
You will hear a student give a presentation about how she helped her youth club.

Student: Hello. I'd like to tell you about a recent activity I took part in with my friends. My local youth club needed new sports equipment, but didn't have enough money to buy any. So, my friends and

Audio scripts

I decided to try to make the money ourselves.

We spent a while trying to decide what to do, but we couldn't agree as we all had different ideas. In the end, we decided to organise our own activities. I decided to make cakes and to sell them to friends and relatives. Plus, a local library offered to buy some from me to sell in their café.

We all agreed to do the activities on the same weekend so we could advertise them as one big event. We used social media to tell people about it, and we were even mentioned in our local newspaper. It all seemed to help as lots of people were talking about it in advance.

I spent the days before making the cakes and made exactly 230! I don't think I could have done it without help from my sister. On Saturday and Sunday, I managed to sell almost all of them. Afterwards, I put the ones that were left on a table outside my house and sold them to people who were walking past. Altogether I managed to collect over £80. It cost me about £25 to buy all the ingredients, so I made quite a lot of money. On the Sunday evening, we all met at the youth club to add up what we had raised. We were amazed. We had managed to make £725 altogether. This was much more than we thought we'd get, and the club was able to buy the new equipment.

Now listen again.

That is the end of Part 3.

Part 4

Track 44

Now look at Part 4.
For each question, choose the correct answer.
Look at Questions 20 to 25 now.
You have 45 seconds.
You will hear an interview with a woman called Amanda Wright, who runs a local leisure club.

Interviewer: Today I'm speaking with Amanda Wright from Sparks Leisure Club. Thanks for coming in, Amanda. Can you start by telling us something about the leisure club?

Amanda: Certainly. Well, the club's celebrating its twentieth anniversary next month. We used to be part of the sports centre, but a couple of years ago we moved to our own building. We spent the first year getting it ready for visitors as it was in poor condition. Then we started offering activities last year.

Interviewer: What do people do there?

Amanda: We've tried to offer things that don't cost us too much. We sell tea and coffee in the morning and run drawing and painting sessions, that kind of thing. Another organisation hires the main room to hold their own dance classes. We're planning to offer lots of activities in the future, like visits to local art galleries, when we have the volunteers to help.

Interviewer: Who usually attends the club?

Amanda: It's mainly those in their sixties and seventies who want somewhere to go to meet others. Some of them have fantastic skills and want to pass on their knowledge to the younger generation. Luckily, we were recently given a large sum of money from a charity to buy equipment and tools to make things from wood and metal. We now hope to offer classes to teenagers.

Interviewer: So, what kind of things will people be able to make?

Amanda: Well, now that we have this amazing equipment, members can make a variety of wooden things, like bird tables, bird boxes and containers for plants. Unfortunately, we don't yet have anyone to run jewellery-making classes, and we're looking for someone who can help us teach people about working safely with electrical equipment.

Interviewer: Do you think young people will be interested in these activities?

Amanda: I think there's a general feeling that young people aren't interested in them. But there are lots of online video channels where people are making things from wood or metal. Some of them have huge numbers of fans. In fact, as soon as some younger people found out about the new equipment we have, they asked us if they could join the club.

Interviewer: Great. So, is there anything you'd like to tell people?

Amanda: Well, as I said before, we already have several people who have offered their time to help, but we need another volunteer. If anyone is free in the morning, we need someone to sign new members up. Fortunately, we've just found someone to manage the kitchen and make snacks.

Now listen again.

That is the end of Part 4.

You now have six minutes to write your answers on the answer sheet.

That is the end of the test.

TEST 6 SPEAKING

Part 1

Track 45

Examiner:	Good morning. Can I have your mark sheets, please? I'm David Porter and this is Jenny Lawler.
Examiner:	What's your name, Candidate A? How old are you?
Candidate A:	My name's Cristin and I'm fourteen years old.
Examiner:	And what's your name, Candidate B? How old are you?
[PAUSE FOR YOU TO ANSWER]	
Examiner:	Candidate B, where do you come from?
[PAUSE FOR YOU TO ANSWER]	
Examiner:	And where do you come from, Candidate A?
Candidate A:	My family live in Paris, but I'm staying with a host family in London.
Examiner:	Candidate A, what's your favourite time of the day?
Candidate A:	It's definitely not the morning. It takes me a long time to wake up. I think I prefer the afternoon when I get home from school. It's nice to lie on the sofa for a while and relax.
Examiner:	And Candidate B, what about you?
[PAUSE FOR YOU TO ANSWER]	
Examiner:	Candidate A, do you watch many programmes on TV?
Candidate A:	I don't watch TV very often in France, but I do in the UK. My host family enjoy watching quiz shows and comedies and I like to sit with them.
Examiner:	Candidate B, what about you?
[PAUSE FOR YOU TO ANSWER]	
Examiner:	Candidate B, what do you like to eat for breakfast?
[PAUSE FOR YOU TO ANSWER]	
Examiner:	And Candidate A, what about you?
Candidate A:	I usually have cereal and a cup of coffee. I don't like eating a big breakfast. I prefer to wait till lunchtime and have something then.
Examiner:	Thank you.

Part 2

Track 46

Examiner:	Now I'd like each of you to talk on your own about something. I'm going to give each of you a photograph and I'd like you to talk about it. Candidate A. Here is your photograph. It shows people dancing. Please tell us what you can see in the photograph. Candidate B, you just listen.
Candidate A:	In this photograph, I can see a group of young people dancing. They all look around eighteen or nineteen years old and they're at a music festival. I think this is true because they're outside, and in the background, you can see lots of tents. It looks quite busy there. The girl nearest the camera is wearing a colourful red top with a white T-shirt underneath and blue jeans. She's smiling and it looks like she's having a lovely time. I think it must be spring or summer because the boy in the photo is wearing a T-shirt.
Examiner:	Thank you.
Examiner:	Candidate B. Here is your photograph. It shows people in a cinema. Please tell us what you can see in the photograph. Candidate A, you just listen.
[PAUSE FOR YOU TO ANSWER]	
Examiner:	Thank you.

Part 3

Track 47

Examiner:	Now, in this part of the test you are going to talk about something together for about two minutes. I'm going to describe a situation to you. A teacher at your school is leaving and you want to buy her a present. Here are some things you could give her. Talk together about the different things you could give her and say which one would be best. All right? Now talk together.
Candidate A:	Well, these are all nice presents. Are there any that you wouldn't want to give her?
[PAUSE FOR YOU TO ANSWER]	
Candidate A:	No, let's forget them. What about the flowers? They're pretty, but they don't last very long, do they? Maybe just a few days.
[PAUSE FOR YOU TO ANSWER]	
Candidate A:	That could be useful, but you might not know the things she likes to read. A pen is a nice present, especially for a teacher. She'd use it every day.
[PAUSE FOR YOU TO ANSWER]	

Audio scripts

Candidate A:	OK. That means we have the pen and the mug. I can't decide which one I prefer. If I were the teacher, I think I'd like to have the pen. I just think it's a nicer present.
[PAUSE FOR YOU TO ANSWER]	
Candidate A:	OK. We've decided to get the pen.
Examiner:	Thank you.

Part 4

Track 48

Examiner:	Candidate A, have you ever bought a teacher who is leaving a present?
Candidate A:	No, I haven't. A teacher left the school last year and I think the other teachers gave her something, but not the students.
Examiner:	And what about you, Candidate B?
[PAUSE FOR YOU TO ANSWER]	
Examiner:	Candidate B, is there a teacher at your school whose lessons you really enjoy?
[PAUSE FOR YOU TO ANSWER]	
Examiner:	And how about you, Candidate A?
Candidate A:	We have lots of great teachers at my school, but I suppose my favourite lesson is art. The teacher is very kind and always encourages you by saying positive things about your work.
Examiner:	Candidate B, what makes a good teacher?
[PAUSE FOR YOU TO ANSWER]	
Examiner:	And what about you, Candidate A?
Candidate A:	I agree. I think it's important for a teacher to be able to communicate clearly. They also need to be a little strict to make sure all the students behave well. But they also need to be fun.
Examiner:	Thank you. That is the end of the test.

TEST 7   LISTENING

Part 1

Track 49

Preliminary English Test for Schools, Listening.
There are four parts to the test. You will hear each piece twice.
We will now stop for a moment.
Please ask any questions now, because you must not speak during the test.
Now look at the instructions for Part 1.
For each question, choose the correct answer.
Look at Question 1.

1   What is the boy going to buy?

Girl:	Have you bought anything with the birthday money you were given?
Boy:	Not yet. I was thinking of saving it for a new phone. I don't have enough for the one I want.
Girl:	There's nothing wrong with the phone you've got. Why not get yourself some clothes? A shirt or something?
Boy:	I'll get a pair of trainers, I think. My toes have nearly made a hole in these. I got a few shirts for my birthday.

Now listen again.

2   When does the Business English course start?

Woman:	Hello. I'm just calling you back about our next English course. You asked about the advanced course in February, but that's fully booked now. We have another course starting in March, but that's for students who want to learn Business English, so I don't think that's any good for you. The next one after that is in April and I can put your name on the list for that if you're interested. If you call me back, I can give you more information.

Now listen again.

3   Which trip did the boy like best?

Girl:	Are you looking forward to the school trip to Oxford?
Boy:	I am, yes. I went with the school last year too, but I had a cold that day and I didn't really enjoy myself.
Girl:	I thought the last trip to Cambridge was good, though. That was a lovely day.
Boy:	Yes, it was. It was really hot. It was much better than that trip to Stratford. It rained the whole time we were there.

Now listen again.

4   What does the girl plan to do when she finishes school?

Boy:	Have you thought about what you want to do when you leave school?
Girl:	Well, my mum and dad are hoping I go to university. They both think it's important to get a degree, but I'd like to have a break from education for a while. My brother has just joined the police, which is an interesting profession. I might just get a job as a waitress for a while to earn some money while I decide to what to do.

Now listen again.

5   How many students are taking part in the event?

Announcer:	And just before the news and weather, a few words about the wonderful students from St Giles' School. Their teacher has been on the phone to tell us that a group of them are collecting money for charity on the 13th. There are twenty of them who are going to do a marathon dance in the city centre to collect money for gym equipment. They plan to dance for five hours and you can see the event from 2.00 p.m. on Saturday.

Now listen again.

6 *Which competition is the girl planning to enter?*

Boy: Well done for your win on Saturday. I bet you're really pleased!
Girl: I am. I really wanted to win that event because I was swimming for the school team.
Boy: Are you going to relax now for a while? You always seem to be doing something every weekend.
Girl: I've now got the running event to sign up for. That's this Saturday. After that's done, I can forget about competitions and start going to the football with you.

Now listen again.

7 *What has the boy forgotten?*

Boy: Hello. I'd like to change this shirt for another one if possible.
Assistant: That's fine. If you give me the receipt, I'll give you a refund.
Boy: Here you are. I made sure that I didn't forget that. The one I want instead costs £1.00 more. I didn't remember to bring any money with me, so can I pay the extra by credit card?
Assistant: That's OK. I'll make the refund and then you can pay for the new shirt with your card.

Now listen again.

That is the end of Part 1.

Part 2

Track 50

Now look at Part 2.
For each question, choose the correct answer.

8 *You will hear a mother and her son talking about ordering a present online.*

Mother: Have you bought anything for Dad's birthday yet?
Boy: I ordered a few books for him online yesterday. I hope there wasn't a problem when I tried to pay.
Mother: Why? Did something go wrong?
Boy: I entered my card details and pressed 'Pay now'. But nothing happened. The screen didn't change. I thought about pressing the button again, but I didn't want to pay twice. So, I closed the website.
Mother: Have you checked your bank account to see if the money has gone?
Boy: I only ordered the books last night, so the money probably hasn't come out yet.

Now listen again.

9 *You will hear two friends talking about a writing competition.*

Boy: Have you decided whether to enter that writing competition you were talking about?
Girl: I'm not sure I want to. I probably won't win anything.
Boy: Don't be silly. You write really well. Anyway, it doesn't matter if you win or not. If you enter, you can practise your writing, which is really important. You won't get better if you don't work at it.
Girl: Yes, that's true.
Boy: And you said they'd give the best five entries some help with their writing. So, if you don't win, you still have a good chance of getting support from an expert.

Now listen again.

10 *You will hear two friends talking about booking a tennis court.*

Boy: I'm looking forward to playing you at tennis on Saturday.
Girl: Me too. I haven't booked the court yet. I don't think it will be a problem, though. I've booked the same day before and it's always been OK.
Boy: Don't leave it too late this time. The weather's going to be really good this weekend, so it might get busy.
Girl: OK. I'll go there after college this afternoon. I could phone them up to book, but I don't think they open until midday, so I can't do anything this morning.

Now listen again.

11 *You will hear two friends talking about a party.*

Girl: Are you going to Anna's party next week?
Boy: I'm not sure. When is it?
Girl: It was going to be on Friday, but I spoke to her the other day and she's changed her mind. She's having it on Sunday afternoon now.
Boy: That's a strange time for a party. Why Sunday?
Girl: She told me she doesn't want lots of people to go. She just wants a few of her best friends there. Her parents will be there as well, so she just wants a quiet barbecue. I feel very lucky that she's invited us.

Now listen again.

12 *You will hear a father and his daughter talking about a TV programme.*

Father: Are you in tonight or going out with your friends?
Girl: I'm staying in. Why?
Father: There's something I want to watch. I'm just checking there's nothing else you want to see.

Audio scripts

Girl:	That's OK. I've got homework to do. What's it about?
Father:	It's a documentary about the fishing industry. It was on last night, but I was working on something on the laptop at the same time. I didn't really pay attention. Luckily, I recorded it. It looked really interesting. Maybe we can watch it together.
Girl:	Maybe. If I finish my homework.

Now listen again.

13 *You will hear two friends talking about some apps.*

Boy:	I've downloaded a few apps to help me with my English.
Girl:	Are they any good?
Boy:	There's one for vocabulary. It's really well designed, but I know almost all of the words. There's another for listening practice. That's good, but you can only listen to British speakers. I'd like to listen to different accents, like American, for example.
Girl:	Have you tried that dictionary app I told you about yet?
Boy:	I've got it on my phone now, but I haven't had a look at it yet. There's a website I use that I quite like.

Now listen again.

That is the end of Part 2.

Part 3

Track 51

Now look at Part 3.
For each question, write the correct answer in the gap.
Write one or two words or a number or a date or a time.
Look at Questions 14 to 19 now. You have 20 seconds.
You will hear a radio announcer talking about tours of a new stadium.

Announcer: Finally, some really exciting news about the new stadium. The builders have been working on it for three years and like me, you've probably seen it grow bigger and bigger each month. Well now, starting in May, you'll have the chance to look inside!

The company are running tours of the whole stadium, and these should be a great way to spend a morning or afternoon. The tour starts with a look around the athletes' area, including the training rooms, where you'll see the modern fitness facilities, and other areas that the public are rarely allowed to see. I'm sure that will be really interesting. You'll then have the chance to look around the main stadium area, and even try some of the sports. Walk or run around the track, or see how far you can get in the long jump. There will even be experts available to show you how it's done.

The stadium also has a fantastic café which is now open to the public, and you'll be able to get something to eat before you leave. You really should do that as well, because food and drink is included in the price of the tour. Keep your ticket to prove you are on the tour.

There are four tours during the weekend, in the morning and the afternoon of Saturday and Sunday. Tickets cost £25.00 for adults and £12.00 for children under the age of 16. Family tickets can be bought for £60.00. And parking is free in the huge car park.

If you're interested, you can book at the ticket office. This is at the west end of the stadium, opposite the station. Unfortunately, bookings cannot be made online as the website isn't live yet.

Now listen again.

That is the end of Part 3.

Part 4

Track 52

Now look at Part 4.
For each question, choose the correct answer.
Look at Questions 20 to 25 now.
You have 45 seconds.
You will hear an interview with a woman called Zoe Staines, who works in student services.

Interviewer:	In the studio today I have Zoe Staines, who is here to talk about careers in student services. Zoe, how did you get into this area of work?
Zoe:	I didn't have a clear career plan like some of my friends. Even at university, I wasn't sure what I wanted to do. But during my time there, I had lots of help from student services. When I saw an advert for a job in this area, I decided to apply. Luckily, I got the job at a local college.
Interviewer:	I suppose student services are the first people students have contact with?
Zoe:	Yes, that's right. That's why it's such an important job. Colleges like to make their information as clear as possible, but talking to someone can often help if a student is confused. We might not be experts in the different subjects, but we know how to find information about the courses the college offers.
Interviewer:	And what are the main issues you have when dealing with students?

Zoe:	All sorts of things, really. Students don't often complain about their courses or their teachers, but it happens sometimes. It's more common for students to come to us if they're feeling stressed or unhappy. I think they just like having someone to talk to.
Interviewer:	Do you have to work with the other departments in the college?
Zoe:	Yes. We have to keep up to date with new courses or those that aren't running anymore. That's usually important at the beginning of the year. During term time, our main job is dealing with absent students. Not just keeping details on the computer system, but calling them to check they're OK.
Interviewer:	What skills do people need to work in student services?
Zoe:	You'll need basic IT skills, although you get training in using the college computer system. You need to be organised and to be able to work in a team. But I think the main thing is to have great customer service skills. This is essential when dealing with current students and those thinking of joining the college.
Interviewer:	So finally, what do you enjoy most about your job?
Zoe:	Well, it's the perfect job for me. I like people and I enjoy supporting them during an exciting part of their lives. The students have important decisions to make about their courses, and sometimes need someone to talk to while they're studying. I can't always be the one to help them, but I can at least introduce them to someone who can.

Now listen again.

That is the end of Part 4.

You now have six minutes to write your answers on the answer sheet.

That is the end of the test.

TEST 7   SPEAKING

Part 1

Track 53

Examiner:	Good morning. Can I have your mark sheets, please? I'm Bill Mizen and this is Greta Manley.
Examiner:	What's your name, Candidate A? How old are you?
Candidate A:	My name's Adriana and I'm thirteen years old.
Examiner:	And what's your name, Candidate B? How old are you?
[PAUSE FOR YOU TO ANSWER]	
Examiner:	Candidate B, where do you come from?
[PAUSE FOR YOU TO ANSWER]	
Examiner:	And where do you come from, Candidate A?
Candidate A:	I come from Alicante in Spain.
Examiner:	Candidate A, what's the weather like where you live in the winter?
Candidate A:	We're lucky as the weather isn't too bad in the winter. It's cooler than the summer, but we still have lots of sunny days.
Examiner:	And Candidate B, what about you?
[PAUSE FOR YOU TO ANSWER]	
Examiner:	Candidate A, how often do you see your friends?
Candidate A:	I see my school friends every day and we meet at weekends. We usually go into the town centre and look in the shops.
Examiner:	Candidate B, what about you?
[PAUSE FOR YOU TO ANSWER]	
Examiner:	Candidate B, at the weekend, do you like to get up early or spend more time in bed?
[PAUSE FOR YOU TO ANSWER]	
Examiner:	And Candidate A, what about you?
Candidate A:	Well, I don't have to get up early as there's no school, so I stay in bed a little longer. But I like to get up before it's too late so I can enjoy the weekend.
Examiner:	Thank you.

Part 2

Track 54

Examiner:	Now I'd like each of you to talk on your own about something. I'm going to give each of you a photograph and I'd like you to talk about it. Candidate A. Here is your photograph. It shows people buying something. Please tell us what you can see in the photograph. Candidate B, you just listen.
Candidate A:	OK, there are three people in this photo. I think two of them are buying a new car. It looks like a husband and wife. The husband's wearing a blue shirt and jeans and the woman's wearing a white blouse and trousers. The other person is the salesman, who's wearing a grey suit. He's standing on the left of the photo and he's

Audio scripts

giving the man the key for the car. It's difficult to see which car the two people have bought, but they're standing next to a white one, so it might be that one. The man and woman look very happy and are probably excited about the new car.

Examiner: Thank you.
Examiner: Candidate B. Here is your photograph. It shows people by a river. Please tell us what you can see in the photograph. Candidate A, you just listen.

[PAUSE FOR YOU TO ANSWER]

Examiner: Thank you.

Part 3

Track 55

Examiner: Now, in this part of the test you are going to talk about something together for about two minutes. I'm going to describe a situation to you. A relative has moved to a new house and your family want to buy her a present for her garden. Here are some things you could give her. Talk together about the different things you could give her and say which one would be best. All right? Now talk together.

Candidate A: Would you like to start?

[PAUSE FOR YOU TO ANSWER]

Candidate A: I agree, especially if it's a small garden. I like the tree. That's something that the person could look at for years and enjoy it as it gets taller.

[PAUSE FOR YOU TO ANSWER]

Candidate A: Yes, let's forget the chair. The plants are OK, but personally, I prefer the tree. What about the barbecue? That's a really good present.

[PAUSE FOR YOU TO ANSWER]

Candidate A: Yes, I do. So, that means we've chosen the barbecue and the tree. Have you got one that you prefer?

[PAUSE FOR YOU TO ANSWER]

Candidate A: OK. Let's choose the barbecue, then. It's a great present.

Examiner: Thank you.

Part 4

Track 56

Examiner: Candidate A, do you like to spend time in a garden?
Candidate A: Yes, I really do. My family live in an apartment, so we don't have one. I think people who have a place outside are really lucky.

Examiner: And what about you, Candidate B?

[PAUSE FOR YOU TO ANSWER]

Examiner: Candidate B, is there a garden or a park near where you live that you go to?

[PAUSE FOR YOU TO ANSWER]

Examiner: And how about you, Candidate A?
Candidate A: Yes, we have a lot of parks too. I walk to school through a park every day and see lots of other people walking their dog or doing exercise.

Examiner: Candidate B, what do you think is the perfect garden?

[PAUSE FOR YOU TO ANSWER]

Examiner: And what about you, Candidate A?
Candidate A: I agree. If you have a big garden, you can have things like the table tennis table we saw before. Flowers are important, though, and a barbecue is nice when you have guests.

Examiner: Thank you. That is the end of the test.

TEST 8 LISTENING

Part 1

Track 57

Preliminary English Test for Schools, Listening.
There are four parts to the test. You will hear each piece twice.
We will now stop for a moment.
Please ask any questions now, because you must not speak during the test.
Now look at the instructions for Part 1.
For each question, choose the correct answer.
Look at Question 1.

1 Which exhibition takes place this weekend?

Announcer: Are you looking for something to do this weekend to get away from the computer screen? Well, there are some interesting things going on at the exhibition centre in town. After the success of the skateboard show last month, the people at the centre have decided to repeat the idea for cyclists. Experts will be available to help with the skills you need to stay safe and become a better cyclist.

Now listen again.

2 How much was the skirt previously?

Girl: Hello. I'm interested in buying this skirt. I was wondering about the price.
Assistant: Yes, how can I help you?
Girl: I'm sure I saw the same skirt here last week and it was £30.00. I see it's now reduced to £20.00. Is there anything wrong with it?

Assistant: No, nothing at all. We've just reduced prices on some of our less popular items. In fact, you can get two skirts in that design for £35.00 until the end of the week.

Now listen again.

3 *What does the girl want her brother to collect?*

Girl: Are you coming straight home from school later?

Boy: Yes, why?

Girl: Mum asked me to get dinner organised as she'll be home late. I've got to collect two books from the library on my way home, so could you go to the shoe shop around the corner for me? I've ordered a pair of shoes and they're ready to pick up. We can have burgers for tea. I'll get some from the supermarket.

Boy: OK. I'll get them on the way home.

Now listen again.

4 *What is the woman afraid of?*

Woman: I've just seen another spider in the bath! That's the fourth one I've caught this week. It's lucky I'm not scared of them.

Boy: Well done! You used to hate going anywhere near spiders. Dad always had to get rid of them for you.

Woman: I know. I used to be the same when I saw a mouse, but they don't really worry me now either. Snakes are different. I'm sure I wouldn't be happy near one of them.

Now listen again.

5 *What does the dance teacher need?*

Teacher: Hello, it's Christine, your dance teacher here. I hope you're still able to come to the session tonight. We have some new students attending. I think that advertisement I put in the dance magazine has worked. Can you remember to bring in the sports bag you borrowed last week? We don't have any spare ones, and it's always useful to have one here. And don't forget your dance shoes this week! You can't do the steps without them and trainers are not suitable.

Now listen again.

6 *How is the man getting to work?*

Father: Sorry, but I won't be able to give you a lift to school this morning.

Girl: I know. Mum already told me. When are you getting your car back from the garage?

Father: I don't know. I'll call them later. A colleague offered to take me to work today, but he drives too fast. I think I'll use public transport. The bus stops right outside the office, but the train will be better. The traffic is always terrible at this time of day and the bus will be late.

Now listen again.

7 *What time does the party start?*

Boy: Just checking: the party's on Friday, right?

Girl: Yes, Friday evening. I've told everyone to get here by half past seven. I'm really looking forward to it.

Boy: I'll be a bit late. I'll probably be there at about 8.00. I've got somewhere else to go first.

Girl: That's OK. I don't think you'll miss anything interesting. People like to come late to parties, so I expect lots of people will arrive at 8.30.

Now listen again.

That is the end of Part 1.

Part 2

Track 58

Now look at Part 2.
For each question, choose the correct answer.

8 *You will hear two friends talking about eating snacks.*

Boy: Can we stop at the supermarket on the way to school? I want to buy some snacks for lunchtime.

Girl: Yes, we have plenty of time. I'm not going to get anything. I've decided to try to save money and just have the sandwiches I bring. I worked out how much I spend on crisps and sweets each week. It's such a waste of money.

Boy: That's a good idea. I might do the same.

Girl: We could go out at the weekend and spend what we've saved. We'll definitely have enough to go the cinema.

Now listen again.

9 *You will hear a conversation between a father and his daughter about passwords.*

Father: I can't get into my account. I've forgotten my password.

Girl: Just click 'Get a new password'. They'll send you one. Do you have a different password for all your accounts?

Father: I do now. I used to have the same one before, just so I could remember it. When I started using different ones, I thought about writing them down in a notebook. But a mate at work told me that wasn't a good idea.

Girl: No, don't do that. Someone else might find it.

Father: Life was much easier when I was younger. We didn't have passwords to worry about then.

Now listen again.

10 *You will hear two parents talking about how to travel on holiday.*

Woman: I'm so pleased we've booked a holiday. How are we going to get there?

213

Audio scripts

Man:	I was going to drive. I usually do.
Woman:	The children were saying they'd like to go by train. I agree with them. It might be a bit more expensive, but it probably won't take as long as it will by car, especially if there are traffic jams.
Man:	The car might be useful if we want to go sightseeing.
Woman:	True, but you know how stressed you get driving on busy roads. Let's leave the car at home, shall we?

Now listen again.

11 *You will hear two friends talking about cooking a meal.*

Girl:	Have you got a favourite meal?
Boy:	I don't know, really. It's hard to say. Some days I look forward to having a curry, especially at the weekend. But other days I enjoy something less spicy, like pasta.
Girl:	Do you ever cook at home?
Boy:	Not very often. My mum's taught me how to make a few meals, like pasta, for example. She says mine is better than the one she makes. I'd like to learn how to cook more meals, though. I think I'd be quite good at it if I practised more.

Now listen again.

12 *You will hear two friends talking about going swimming.*

Boy:	Do you still want to go swimming later? I've got no other plans.
Girl:	OK. It gets quite crowded today, but I fancy a swim. We can go after school. I'll need to go home first to get my swimming costume. Shall I meet you there?
Boy:	OK. I'll be there about 4.30. Do we need to book a session?
Girl:	I don't think so. I've never had to do that before. But I'll phone them at lunchtime to find out.

Now listen again.

13 *You will hear two friends talking about using the internet.*

Girl:	I'll never get my homework done at home. Our internet connection was really bad last night.
Boy:	My dad said there's a problem in the whole area.
Girl:	Really? I suppose I could stay late and do it in the library.
Boy:	Why not go to a café that has an internet connection? You could enjoy a nice drink and cake while you're studying.
Girl:	That sounds like a great idea, but I'd spend all my time watching people and not doing any work. Plus, it would be a bit noisy.

Now listen again.

That is the end of Part 2.

Part 3

Track 59

Now look at Part 3.
For each question, write the correct answer in the gap. Write one or two words or a number or a date or a time. Look at Questions 14 to 19 now. You have 20 seconds. You will hear a teacher talking about the school's 'International Day'.

Teacher:	Hello everyone. I just want to let you know more about the International Day celebrations on 13th June. We have students here from all over the world and previous events have been a great success. There are various things you can do to take part.
	Of course, we have the party in the evening, but more about that in a minute. We'd like you to provide the food. Why not cook something from your country? It could be a main meal, like a curry or pasta, or something sweet, like cakes. The school café have said they're happy for you to use the kitchen area and to keep food overnight in their refrigerators.
	During the day in the lessons, we're asking you to give presentations about your country. You can do this in small groups or on your own, it's up to you. If you have any documents you need to share with the other students, speak to your teacher, who will get them printed.
	As I said earlier, we have the party in the evening, when we can try your delicious food. There will be a disco, and also the chance to hear Mr James give one of his famous performances on the keyboards! The party is due to finish at 10.00 p.m., so please let your family know if they're picking you up. The school bus will take anyone who hasn't got a lift home, and it will depart at 10.15 p.m.
	We're leaving the day before International Day free of lessons so you can have time to prepare. You can use the IT room to practise your presentations, and the kitchen area will be available for cooking. If you need to speak to me about anything, I'll be in my office the whole day.

Now listen again.

That is the end of Part 3.

Part 4

Track 60

Now look at Part 4.
For each question, choose the correct answer.
Look at Questions 20 to 25 now.

You have 45 seconds.

You will hear an interview with a man called Hugh Treadwell, who teaches art.

Interviewer: Today we welcome back Hugh Treadwell, who is giving us tips on how to draw. Today you're talking about drawing faces, is that right?

Hugh: Yes. The last time I came on the show, I explained the importance of light and using your pencil to create shade and shadows in your picture to make it look more natural. I told everyone to practise, using something simple like an apple or a vase.

Interviewer: So, are we ready to draw a face?

Hugh: I think the best method is to practise drawing individual bits of the face first, rather than trying to copy a photo of someone straightaway. Use a photo, but focus on drawing one eye. Do it again and again. Then try with a nose. Repeat this until you feel more confident. This will allow you to focus on the shape and on how shade works.

Interviewer: Is it a good idea to copy from a photo?

Hugh: Yes. When you're ready to try a whole face, find a photo where the person is looking directly at the camera rather than showing the side of their face. Most of the photographs you'll find are in colour, but it can help to copy from a black and white one as the shadows are easier to see.

Interviewer: How do we make sure we get everything in the right place?

Hugh: Well, we all have different faces, of course, and nobody's face is exactly the same on each side. But there are general rules you can follow. For example, eyes are usually halfway down the face, and the nose and the mouth are usually halfway between the two eyes. Drawing lines on the paper to show where these are is a good start.

Interviewer: Is it important to get things correct the first time?

Hugh: Not at all. The great thing about drawing is the fact that it's quite easy to rub a bit out if you're not happy with it, rather than starting all over again. This isn't quite so easy when you're working with paints. Just make sure you have a very thin rubber so you can get into small spaces.

Interviewer: Have you got any advice for those of us who hate what we draw?

Hugh: Yes. Don't forget that drawing is supposed to be fun. You'll notice how relaxed you feel when you're drawing and you really don't want to make yourself feel unhappy or stressed about what you've created. Be pleased with what you've drawn well, and practise those areas you're not happy with.

Now listen again.

That is the end of Part 4.

You now have six minutes to write your answers on the answer sheet.

That is the end of the test.

TEST 8   SPEAKING

Part 1

Track 61

Examiner: Good morning. Can I have your mark sheets, please? I'm Sam Gregory and this is Lisa Martin.

Examiner: What's your name, Candidate A? How old are you?

Candidate A: My name's Gunther and I'm fifteen years old.

Examiner: And what's your name, Candidate B? How old are you?

[PAUSE FOR YOU TO ANSWER]

Examiner: Candidate B, where do you live?

[PAUSE FOR YOU TO ANSWER]

Examiner: And where do you live, Candidate A?

Candidate A: I live in Frankfurt in Germany.

Examiner: Candidate A, what's the most important thing you own?

Candidate A: I think I have to say my phone. I use it all the time, and if I didn't have it, I wouldn't be able to keep in contact with my friends or family or use the internet easily.

Examiner: And Candidate B, what about you?

[PAUSE FOR YOU TO ANSWER]

Examiner: Candidate A, how often do you go to the cinema?

Candidate A: I don't go very often. Sometimes my parents take me and my brother, and occasionally I go with my friends. But I like watching films at home on my laptop or on TV.

Examiner: Candidate B, what about you?

[PAUSE FOR YOU TO ANSWER]

Examiner: Candidate B, do you have any pets?

[PAUSE FOR YOU TO ANSWER]

Examiner: And Candidate A, what about you?

Candidate A: We have two. My dad bought a parrot recently and he's trying to teach it to say some words. We also have a cat. My mum said it

Audio scripts

	wouldn't be a good idea to have a cat and a bird in the same room, but they seem OK.
Examiner:	Thank you.

Part 2

Track 62

Examiner:	Now I'd like each of you to talk on your own about something. I'm going to give each of you a photograph and I'd like you to talk about it. Candidate A. Here is your photograph. It shows a family painting. Please tell us what you can see in the photograph. Candidate B, you just listen.
Candidate A:	In this picture there are three people. I think it's a family: a father and his two children. The younger one has long hair, so it might be a girl, but I think it's a boy. They're all wearing jeans and T-shirts and they're decorating a room. There are lots of tins of paint on the floor, and I think they're trying to find a colour that they like. The older boy is trying a colour on the wall. It's a kind of green paint. I can't see clearly what the man and the younger boy are doing, but it looks like the boy is holding a stick, so he might be stirring the paint.
Examiner:	Thank you.
Examiner:	Candidate B. Here is your photograph. It shows a family. Please tell us what you can see in the photograph. Candidate A, you just listen.

[PAUSE FOR YOU TO ANSWER]

Examiner:	Thank you.

Part 3

Track 63

Examiner:	Now, in this part of the test you are going to talk about something together for about two minutes. I'm going to describe a situation to you. A school wants to invite someone to give a talk about their job. Here are some occupations they could think about. Talk together about the different ones and say which one would be best. All right? Now talk together.
Candidate A:	OK, so we have to choose one of these people. Would you like to start?

[PAUSE FOR YOU TO ANSWER]

Candidate A:	That's true. Obviously, the police officer would have lots of interesting stories, so we should think about that one. What about the nurse or the chef?

[PAUSE FOR YOU TO ANSWER]

Candidate A:	OK, so far that's the police officer and the nurse. What about the hairdresser? It might be a good job, but not very interesting to talk about.

[PAUSE FOR YOU TO ANSWER]

Candidate A:	That leaves the dentist. Do you think she'd be a good speaker?

[PAUSE FOR YOU TO ANSWER]

Candidate A:	OK. Let's choose the police officer. It's a really important job, and I'm sure the speaker will be very interesting.
Examiner:	Thank you.

Part 4

Track 64

Examiner:	Candidate A, are there any jobs you'd like to consider for a career?
Candidate A:	Actually, I'd really like to be a doctor. I know it takes a long time to get the qualifications, but it's something I'd like to do.
Examiner:	And what about you, Candidate B?

[PAUSE FOR YOU TO ANSWER]

Examiner:	Candidate B, are there any jobs that you really wouldn't enjoy?

[PAUSE FOR YOU TO ANSWER]

Examiner:	And how about you, Candidate A?
Candidate A:	I agree. An office job would be quite boring. I enjoy meeting people and I'd hate to spend all day working on a computer and not meeting anyone.
Examiner:	Candidate B, is it important to you to earn a lot of money?

[PAUSE FOR YOU TO ANSWER]

Examiner:	And what about you, Candidate A?
Candidate A:	Yes, I totally agree. As long as I had enough to be comfortable, I'd be happy. It's nice to have lots of money in the bank, but it's not the most important thing.
Examiner:	Thank you. That is the end of the test.

Sample answer sheets

Preliminary for Schools Reading Candidate Answer Sheet

Instructions
Use a PENCIL (B or HB)
Rub out any answer you want to change with an eraser.

For Parts 1, 2, 3, 4 and 5:
Mark ONE letter for each answer.
For example: If you think A is the right answer to the question, mark your answer sheet like this:

Turn over for Part 6:
Write your answers clearly in the spaces next to the numbers (27 to 32) on Page 2.

Reproduced with permission of Cambridge Assessment English © copyright UCLES 2022.

Sample answer sheets

For Part 6:
Write your answers clearly in the spaces next to the numbers (27 to 32) like this:

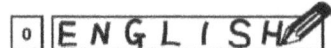

Write your answers in CAPITAL LETTERS.

Part 6	
27	
28	
29	
30	
31	
32	

Sample answer sheets

Cambridge Assessment English

Candidate Name:
Centre Name:
Examination Title:
Candidate Signature:

Candidate Number:
Centre Number:
Examination Details:
Assessment Date:

Supervisor: If the candidate is ABSENT or has WITHDRAWN shade here ○

Preliminary for Schools Listening Candidate Answer Sheet

Instructions
Use a PENCIL (B or HB). Rub out any answer you want to change with an eraser.

For Parts 1, 2 and 4:
Mark one letter for each answer. For example: If you think **A** is the right answer to the question, mark your answer sheet like this:

For Part 3:
Write your answers clearly in the spaces next to the numbers (14 to 19) like this:

`0 | E N G L I S H`

Write your answers in CAPITAL LETTERS.

Part 1
1. A B C
2. A B C
3. A B C
4. A B C
5. A B C
6. A B C
7. A B C

Part 2
8. A B C
9. A B C
10. A B C
11. A B C
12. A B C
13. A B C

Part 3
14.
15.
16.
17.
18.
19.

Part 4
20. A B C
21. A B C
22. A B C
23. A B C
24. A B C
25. A B C

Reproduced with permission of Cambridge Assessment English © copyright UCLES 2022.

Answer key

Answer key for the Reading and Listening papers

This is the Answer key for the Reading and Listening papers of Tests 1–8.

TEST 1

Paper 1 Reading Test

Part 1
1 A
2 C
3 A
4 B
5 A

Part 2
6 D
7 F
8 G
9 A
10 C

Part 3
11 B
12 D
13 C
14 B
15 A

Part 4
16 F
17 B
18 H
19 D
20 A

Part 5
21 C
22 A
23 D
24 A
25 B
26 C

Part 6
27 in
28 are
29 the
30 for
31 being
32 what

Paper 2 Listening Test

Part 1
1 C
2 A
3 A
4 B
5 B
6 A
7 A

Part 2
8 C
9 C
10 C
11 A
12 B
13 B

Part 3
14 eleven / 11
15 studio
16 photographs
17 Thief
18 reception
19 prices

Part 4
20 A
21 C
22 B
23 C
24 B
25 A

TEST 2

Paper 1 Reading Test

Part 1
1 B
2 A
3 A
4 C
5 B

Part 2
6 C
7 A
8 F
9 D
10 G

Part 3
11 A
12 B
13 C
14 A
15 C

Part 4
16 G
17 C
18 B
19 D
20 E

Part 5
21 A
22 C
23 B
24 D
25 A
26 B

Part 6
27 was
28 most
29 that / which
30 for
31 to
32 more

Paper 2 Listening Test

Part 1
1 A
2 B
3 C
4 A
5 C
6 C
7 A

Part 2
8 C
9 C
10 B
11 C
12 A
13 B

Part 3
14 takeaway
15 recording
16 weekends
17 café / cafe
18 lunch box
19 report

Part 4
20 A
21 B
22 B
23 A
24 A
25 C

Answer key

TEST 3

Paper 1 Reading Test

Part 1
1 A
2 A
3 B
4 B
5 C

Part 2
6 H
7 G
8 E
9 A
10 B

Part 3
11 B
12 C
13 D
14 D
15 B

Part 4
16 C
17 F
18 H
19 A
20 D

Part 5
21 D
22 A
23 B
24 C
25 A
26 C

Part 6
27 the
28 who
29 by
30 when
31 the
32 than

Paper 2 Listening Test

Part 1
1 C
2 C
3 A
4 A
5 B
6 A
7 B

Part 2
8 B
9 A
10 B
11 C
12 C
13 C

Part 3
14 month
15 (new) school / (new) building
16 video
17 Friday
18 (leaving) card
19 golf

Part 4
20 C
21 A
22 B
23 A
24 A
25 B

TEST 4

Paper 1 Reading Test

Part 1
1 C
2 B
3 C
4 A
5 B

Part 2
6 C
7 H
8 B
9 G
10 E

Part 3
11 C
12 D
13 B
14 C
15 A

Part 4
16 F
17 A
18 D
19 H
20 B

Part 5
21 D
22 A
23 C
24 A
25 B
26 D

Part 6
27 in
28 if
29 by
30 one
31 without
32 many

Paper 2 Listening Test

Part 1
1 A
2 A
3 C
4 B
5 A
6 A
7 C

Part 2
8 B
9 A
10 B
11 B
12 A
13 B

Part 3
14 park
15 tree
16 signs
17 May
18 Strong winds
19 bridge

Part 4
20 C
21 C
22 A
23 A
24 B
25 B

223

Answer key

TEST 5

Paper 1 Reading Test

Part 1
1 C
2 A
3 C
4 A
5 B

Part 2
6 E
7 F
8 D
9 B
10 H

Part 3
11 C
12 A
13 A
14 C
15 C

Part 4
16 H
17 B
18 A
19 F
20 E

Part 5
21 B
22 A
23 D
24 C
25 B
26 A

Part 6
27 they
28 if / when
29 an
30 are / have
31 in
32 between

Paper 2 Listening Test

Part 1
1 B
2 B
3 C
4 A
5 B
6 C
7 A

Part 2
8 A
9 C
10 B
11 B
12 A
13 C

Part 3
14 qualified
15 beginners
16 9.00 (a.m.)
17 Video
18 £13.00 / £13
19 date

Part 4
20 C
21 A
22 C
23 A
24 B
25 C

Answer key

TEST 6

Paper 1 Reading Test

Part 1
1 C
2 B
3 B
4 B
5 A

Part 2
6 E
7 H
8 C
9 F
10 A

Part 3
11 D
12 C
13 A
14 A
15 C

Part 4
16 G
17 B
18 E
19 A
20 H

Part 5
21 A
22 D
23 B
24 B
25 C
26 A

Part 6
27 It
28 is
29 on
30 which
31 the
32 from

Paper 2 Listening Test

Part 1
1 A
2 B
3 C
4 A
5 C
6 B
7 A

Part 2
8 A
9 A
10 B
11 C
12 A
13 C

Part 3
14 sports
15 library
16 social media
17 sister
18 table
19 £725

Part 4
20 A
21 A
22 B
23 A
24 B
25 B

Answer key

TEST 7

Paper 1 Reading Test

Part 1
1 B
2 C
3 B
4 C
5 A

Part 2
6 C
7 F
8 A
9 H
10 E

Part 3
11 B
12 B
13 C
14 C
15 D

Part 4
16 G
17 E
18 A
19 H
20 C

Part 5
21 D
22 A
23 B
24 D
25 A
26 C

Part 6
27 to
28 how
29 in
30 so
31 one
32 as

Paper 2 Listening Test

Part 1
1 C
2 B
3 B
4 B
5 C
6 A
7 B

Part 2
8 C
9 A
10 C
11 B
12 C
13 A

Part 3
14 May
15 training
16 Experts
17 ticket
18 £60.00 / £60
19 west

Part 4
20 B
21 B
22 A
23 C
24 C
25 C

TEST 8

Paper 1 Reading Test

Part 1
1 A
2 B
3 A
4 B
5 A

Part 2
6 E
7 C
8 F
9 H
10 A

Part 3
11 C
12 A
13 B
14 B
15 C

Part 4
16 B
17 G
18 C
19 H
20 D

Part 5
21 B
22 A
23 D
24 A
25 C
26 A

Part 6
27 about
28 these / them
29 a
30 where
31 in
32 is

Paper 2 Listening Test

Part 1
1 A
2 B
3 C
4 C
5 C
6 A
7 A

Part 2
8 C
9 B
10 C
11 B
12 A
13 B

Part 3
14 13th / 13 June
15 kitchen (area)
16 printed
17 keyboards
18 10.15 p.m. / 22.15
19 IT room

Part 4
20 A
21 C
22 C
23 B
24 A
25 B

Model answers: Writing

Model answers for the Writing papers

These are the model answers for the Writing papers of Tests 1–8.

TEST 1

Part 1

Question 1

Hi Steve,
Thanks for your wishes! No party this year. I just spent the day with my family.
Your project sounds interesting. Saturdays and Sundays in my country are quite similar. The shops are open both days, so people usually go into the city centre and look around. They close earlier on Sunday, though, so we have time later in the day to get ready for work or school on Monday.
Actually, my favourite day is Friday. We finish school early and I can look forward to the weekend. I also often see my friends on Friday evening, which is always good fun.
I'm free on Wednesday evening if you'd like to chat then.
Looking forward to speaking soon!

Part 2

Question 2

It's not very exciting, I know, but the place I find very relaxing is my bedroom. I'm lucky because I have my own room and my mum and dad have decorated it just how I like it. I have some dried flowers and indoor plants on the shelves, which make the room smell nice, and a soft rug on the floor that feels lovely under my feet. My favourite place of all is sitting in the armchair by the bedroom window. I love to look out at the garden, especially on a sunny day. And in the evening, I can put the lamp on and lie in bed reading until I go to sleep.

Question 3

I was sitting on the bus on the way to school one Monday. It was the first day of our summer term and I was looking forward to seeing my friends again after the holiday. Every time the bus stopped for passengers to get on, I looked carefully to see if any of my friends were there. It seemed strange that there were no children with their school bags, just older people going into town to do their shopping or work. In fact, I got all the way to school and didn't see another student at all. It was then that I remembered. Monday was a teacher training day and school didn't start until Tuesday!

TEST 2

Part 1

Question 1

Dear Miss Phillips,
Thanks for your email. I am really looking forward to the party. Thank you for organising it. I have told my parents that I will be home a little later and they said that was fine.
It might be a good idea to have one or two games, but I think my classmates would also like to chat about things. Perhaps we could have a quiz in teams?
I eat anything, so you don't have to worry about me. I know there are some vegetarians in our class, though.
I will be very happy to help clean up after the party and I am sure other students will be pleased to help as well.
Best wishes

Part 2

Question 2

I'm really keen on history and my parents have paid for a history magazine that comes out once every month. It gets delivered to our apartment and I always look forward to it arriving in the post. It has articles about famous historical events, information about how people lived, some of the strange customs that existed, and lots of other interesting facts. I like it because it looks at different subjects that we study at school, but I can just enjoy finding out things without having to take an exam about them at the end.

Question 3

I knew what it was before I opened the parcel. My dad had promised me something special for my seventeenth birthday and Mum had told me he was going to get me a new laptop for when I started college. The parcel was quite heavy and as I took the paper off, I could see the box that the laptop was in. Once all the paper was off and the laptop was out of the box and on the table, I was able to try it out. It was shiny and very fast and I couldn't wait to explore all the apps and software.

TEST 3

Part 1

Question 1

> Hi Anna,
> I can't believe your dad is going to visit my city! Tell him not to worry. The airport is quite close to the centre and there are plenty of trains, buses and taxis.
> It can get quite hot in August, so he needs summer clothes and a jacket in case it rains.
> There are lots of places to see, but everything is very busy in August, with long queues to get in everywhere. I'd recommend walking around one of the parks as these are lovely in the summer. When your dad gets hungry, he could try a curry. We have lots of great Indian restaurants here.
> Best wishes

Part 2

Question 2

I have an app on my phone that I have used ever since I started running. It helps me in so many different ways. Most important of all, it tells me how fast I have managed to run, and not only the time for the whole run but also for each kilometre, which is very helpful. It also shows me a map of the run I have completed, as well as the runs of other people. This is really useful because you can leave a comment on your friends' runs and send them congratulations if they have had a good one.

Question 3

I was looking forward to the trip to the coast. I was going to the seaside with the school the next day. I hadn't been near the sea for a few years, so I knew it was going to be a lovely day out. We had to bring our own food, so I spent the night before making sandwiches and getting my backpack ready for the next morning. This included my swimming costume, sun cream and a towel to lie on at the beach. I went to bed that night feeling very excited and thinking of the fun I was going to have with my friends.

Model answers: Writing

TEST 4

Part 1

Question 1

> Dear Mr Gilbert,
> Thank you for organising the film club. Yes, I would be interested in joining when it starts.
> I watch quite a lot of films with my friends, and I think it would be better if students could choose which one to see sometimes. Maybe you can also suggest films if you think we would like them.
> As students have lessons in the afternoon, I don't think they would feel relaxed if they saw films at lunchtime. After school would be much better.
> I think half an hour for a discussion would be enough time so students can get home before it gets late.
> Many thanks

Part 2

Question 2

I've known my friend Michael since we started high school. That was about three years ago. We sat next to each other in our English class and quickly became friends. His house is near mine as well, so we also see each other a lot after school.
There are a few reasons why I like him. To begin with, he is really good fun and makes me laugh a lot. As well as that, he's very kind and always thinks of other people. He also supports the same team as me and we spend ages talking about football. He's a good friend and I'm lucky I met him.

Question 3

It was two o'clock and the class was about to start. Suddenly, we heard the fire alarm and had to leave the building. Our teacher led us out to the playground, where we all had to meet.
We had been there for about 30 minutes when someone came out to tell us there had been a small fire in the kitchen, but that it was now safe to go back to our rooms. By the time we got back to the classroom, there were only 15 minutes left of the lesson. As maths wasn't my favourite subject, I wasn't very disappointed that I had missed most of the lesson!

TEST 5

Part 1

Question 1

> Dear Mrs Elliot,
> Thank you for your email. I'd love to give my opinion.
> I go to the café every day. I arrive at school early in the morning because I like to get a drink before lessons begin. I also have lunch there every day.
> I've always enjoyed the food and I like most of the meals they serve. They don't often make pasta meals, though, which I love. Apart from that, the vegetables are sometimes cold, but that's the only problem I have with the food.
> I think white walls are all right for a café, but perhaps they can put some paintings by the art students on the wall.
> Thanks for asking for my opinion!
> Best wishes

Model answers: Writing

Part 2

Question 2

Most people prefer to see a blue sky when they look out of the window, and I enjoy sunny days too. But I like it most when it rains, and especially when it pours down.

My country is very hot and the sun shines almost all the time. So, when it rains it is always exciting and everyone runs outside to enjoy the change in the weather. When I was younger, I used to love going out in the rain and running around until I got very wet. Now I am older, I prefer to have an umbrella, but I still like to feel the rain on my face occasionally.

Question 3

I switched on the light, but nothing happened. It was 7.00 in the evening and it was dark outside, so it was difficult to see anything. I put my hand out to help me find my way to the kitchen. Suddenly, another light came on and there were people all around me shouting 'Happy birthday!' My mum and dad had organised a surprise party and all my friends and relations were there. It took me a few minutes to recover, but it was such a lovely surprise and I had a great time celebrating my special day.

TEST 6

Part 1

Question 1

> Hi Dominika,
> It's good to hear from you. We're all well, thanks. It's exciting to hear you're getting a pet, and of course I'll try to help.
> A dog is definitely lots of fun. You can take it to the park for a walk and play with it. Unfortunately, you can't do this with a cat.
> However, cats are better if you all go to school or work because they can stay inside until you get home. It isn't very kind to leave a dog indoors all day as it gets lonely.
> As you have to take more care of a dog, I think a cat would be best.
> Write back soon!
> Steph

Part 2

Question 2

There are lots of restaurants where I live, but the one I like most of all is called *Pasta Di Piazza*. As you can tell from the name, it's an Italian restaurant and serves the kind of food many people have heard of, like spaghetti and pizza. However, there are lots of other dishes as well and I always try something new when I go.

Apart from the delicious food, the reason I like this restaurant is because the staff are very friendly and helpful. It's owned by two brothers and they are always there to welcome you and check that everything is all right.

Question 3

I woke up early as it was my first day back at school. I was really looking forward to seeing my friends after the summer holiday. I also knew we were going to have two new teachers and I wanted to find out what they were like. After breakfast, I had a shower, got dressed and left home to catch the bus. Some of my friends were already at the bus stop and we spent time telling each other what we had done during our holiday. The bus arrived and we all got on, excited about our first day together in the new school year.

Model answers: Writing

TEST 7

Part 1

Question 1

> Dear Mr Simmonds,
> Thank you for your email. Yes, I will be happy to help on sports day. Thank you for asking me.
> All my lessons on that day are in the morning. I have an appointment with my teacher in the afternoon, but I will ask her if I can change the date.
> I would love to be a manager. I am the captain of my football team and I know how to get people to try their best.
> Unfortunately, I can't go to the party at the end of the day as I have to go straight home after school.
> Best wishes

Part 2

Question 2

I enjoy cycling a lot and use my bike nearly every day. But if I have to go on a long journey, my favourite way of travelling is by train.
I don't often travel this way because I go to school on the bus or go out with my mum and dad in their car. I think this is the reason I like the train so much. It's an unusual experience for me and I always feel a little excited when the train comes into the station. I love looking out of the window as we go past the houses and countryside, and looking at the people on the train is always interesting.

Question 3

As I was getting ready to do my homework, my phone rang. It was a bit of a surprise as I usually only get text messages. I was even more surprised when I answered it. It was my older brother. He told me someone had given him two tickets for the football match on Saturday and wanted to know if I'd like to go with him. I said 'yes' immediately. I loved spending time with my brother, but we had never been to a game together before. I spent the rest of the week looking forward to seeing him and I hoped to see a great match.

TEST 8

Part 1

Question 1

> Hi Camilla,
> It was great to get your email. I'm doing OK at school, thanks. Of course I'll try to help!
> I'm sorry to hear you're finding maths hard. I had the same problem and that's why I took the evening class. It was hard work, but I only took evening classes for one term and they helped me understand the subject a lot better.
> My main tip is to get plenty of sleep. Don't stay up late on your phone, for example. If you do, you'll be too tired to study well during the day and too tired to take the evening class.
> Write back soon!
> Olivia

Part 2

Question 2

I spend a lot of time on the internet and there are some websites I use every day. However, I think my favourite one is AllMyPop.

This site contains millions of videos. Some are made by professionals like record companies, and others are made by ordinary people like me.

I enjoy using it because I love music and it's a great way to see my favourite musicians. AllMyPop also recommends other videos that are similar to those you have searched for. This means you discover music that you might not know about. The only problem with the website is that you can spend far too much time on it!

Question 3

The train was late and we were in a hurry. I was going to the airport with my family and we needed to be there by 10.00. It was 8.30, the train was delayed and we were all feeling stressed. Suddenly, there was an announcement that all trains were cancelled because of a problem on the line. We ran out of the station to look for a taxi, but there were none. I was beginning to think that we would miss our flight to Greece when someone called out 'John. It's time to get up'. I was so happy when I realised it had all been a dream.

Model answers: Speaking

Model answers for the Speaking papers

The model answers for the Speaking papers of Tests 1–8 are highlighted in grey here. You can listen to these model answers online at www.collins.co.uk/eltresources. Please note some of the model answers refer to colours; if you have a colour photo in the exam, you can refer to colours in your answer.

Test 1

Speaking Part 1

05a

Examiner:	Good afternoon. Can I have your mark sheets, please? I'm Jenny Wright and this is Steve Saunders.
Examiner:	What's your name, Candidate A? How old are you?
Candidate A:	My name's Sara Fernandez and I'm twelve years old.
Examiner:	And what's your name, Candidate B? How old are you?
Candidate B:	My name's Artur Bauman and I'm fourteen years old.
Examiner:	Candidate B, where do you live?
Candidate B:	I live in Germany. I live with my mum and dad in Munich in the south of the country.
Examiner:	And Candidate A, where do you live?
Candidate A:	I live in Madrid. I live with my mum, dad and my younger brother. We live in a house just outside the city centre.
Examiner:	Candidate A, what do you like to do at weekends?
Candidate A:	I enjoy going to my friend's house. We play music and watch videos. We both like dancing as well.
Examiner:	Candidate B, what do you do to relax?
Candidate B:	I love playing football. If the weather is nice, I meet my friends in the park and we play all afternoon.
Examiner:	Candidate A, tell me what you like about where you live.
Candidate A:	I think I'm lucky. We live near the city, so I can go into town with my friends if I want to. But there's also some lovely countryside nearby, so I sometimes go for long walks with my family there too.
Examiner:	Candidate B, is your area a nice place to live?
Candidate B:	Yes. I like it a lot. We don't live close to the city centre, but there are lots of shops and places to go to near my house. There's also a good train and bus service if I want to go into the centre.
Examiner:	Thank you.

Speaking Part 2

06a

Examiner:	Now I'd like each of you to talk on your own about something. I'm going to give each of you a photograph and I'd like you to talk about it. Candidate A. Here is your photograph. It shows somebody buying something. Please tell us what you can see in the photograph. Candidate B, you just listen.
Candidate A:	This photograph was taken in a clothes shop. There are two people, a man and a woman. One of them is buying something and the other person is taking their money. It's difficult to say who is the customer and which person works in the shop, but I think the man is the cashier. He's giving her two bags with the things she has bought, and she's passing her credit card to him. There are some shoes or trainers on the shelves behind the man, and in the background, I can see some clothes on hangers. They both seem to be very happy and are smiling at each other.
Examiner:	Thank you.
Examiner:	Candidate B. Here is your photograph. It shows some young people in a classroom. Please tell us what you can see in the photograph. Candidate A, you just listen.

Model answers: Speaking

Candidate B:	This photograph shows a group of children who are sitting around a table. I think they're in a library because there are shelves of books behind them. There are five children altogether, two boys and three girls. They all look about five or six years old. There's another child on the right of the photo, but you can only see this child's arm. It looks like they're doing school work. They all have books in front of them on the table. Two of the girls are writing in them and some of the others are reaching out for pencils that are in a container. They all look like they're interested in what they're doing and are having a lot of fun.
Examiner:	Thank you.

Speaking Part 3

Examiner:	Now, in this part of the test you are going to talk about something together for about two minutes. I'm going to describe a situation to you. A girl is having her bedroom decorated. Her parents want to buy her something for the room. Here are some things they could buy. Talk together about the different things she could get and say which one would be best. All right? Now, talk together.
Candidate A:	So, we need to decide what the parents could buy for their daughter. I think some of these things are useful. What do you think?
Candidate B:	The TV would be great, but a lot of teenagers now watch things on a laptop, don't they? And the alarm clock might not be useful if she has a mobile phone.
Candidate A:	Yes, that's true. The TV is a lovely present, but it costs a lot of money. What about the picture? I don't think that's a good idea because they might not choose something the girl likes.
Candidate B:	No, I wouldn't suggest the picture. The flowers are nice, but they won't last very long, will they? It would be better to buy something that lasts a long time.
Candidate A:	Yes, I agree. So, that leaves the chair, the mirror and the lamp. I think the mirror would be best. It's nice to be able to look at ourselves when we're trying on clothes. That's a nice big one.
Candidate B:	Yes, let's say the mirror. She probably has a lamp in the bedroom anyway, and she can sit on her bed.
Examiner:	Thank you.

Speaking Part 4

Examiner:	Candidate A, do you like spending time in your bedroom?
Candidate A:	Yes. I usually do my homework in my bedroom. I have a desk and it's quiet. I can concentrate on my work.
Examiner:	And what about you, Candidate B?
Candidate B:	Yes, I like my bedroom too. I like lying on my bed and watching things on my laptop. It's only a small room, but I like it because it's mine and I can make it look the way I like.
Examiner:	Candidate B, what kind of things have you got in your room?
Candidate B:	Apart from the bed, I have some posters of singers on the wall and a wardrobe for my clothes. I've also put up lots of little lights around the room that look lovely at night.
Examiner:	And how about you, Candidate A?
Candidate A:	I told you about my desk. I've also got shelves with my books on them, and there's a lamp on the table that I use for studying. I've also got lots of posters of people on my walls, pop stars and actors.
Examiner:	Candidate B, many people keep their phones, tablets and laptops in their bedrooms. Do you think this is a good thing to do?
Candidate B:	I think it's a good idea to turn them all off a little while before you go to sleep. It's easy to stay up too late while you're on your laptop or phone, which isn't good for you.
Examiner:	And what about you, Candidate A?
Candidate A:	We could leave our laptops and phones downstairs so we can forget about studying or chatting with friends. I think if they're near you at night, they might stop you sleeping.
Examiner:	Thank you. That is the end of the test.

Model answers: Speaking

Test 2 SPEAKING

Speaking Part 1

Examiner:	Good morning. Can I have your mark sheets, please? I'm Carol Partridge and this is Steve Hilton. What's your name, Candidate A? How old are you?
Candidate A:	My name's Cristine Garcia and I'm fifteen years old.
Examiner:	And what's your name, Candidate B? How old are you?
Candidate B:	My name's Lukasz Nowak and I'm sixteen years old.
Examiner:	Candidate A, where do you come from?
Candidate A:	I come from Brazil, but I'm living in London at the moment.
Examiner:	And where do you come from, Candidate B?
Candidate B:	I come from Warsaw, the capital of Poland.
Examiner:	Candidate B, what food do you like to eat?
Candidate B:	I like all kinds of food, to be honest. But my favourite meal is pizza. We have a really good pizza restaurant where I live and I often go there with my friends.
Examiner:	And what food do you like, Candidate A?
Candidate A:	I like Italian food too and we eat pasta a lot in my house. I also like chocolate. I probably eat too much.
Examiner:	Candidate A, do you do any sport?
Candidate A:	Yes, I do. I play volleyball for my school. We play every month against other schools near where I live and I also go training once a week.
Examiner:	Candidate B, what about you?
Candidate B:	I don't do much sport. I like to play football with my friends after school, but it isn't very serious. I'd like to find a sport that I really like because I know it would be good for me.
Examiner:	Candidate A, tell us about a lesson you like at school.
Candidate A:	I think my favourite lesson is art. I really enjoy painting and we learn lots about the subject from our teacher. It's also relaxing and feels different to when I'm in a lesson like maths or history.
Examiner:	Candidate B, do you have a favourite lesson?
Candidate B:	I like art too, but the best lesson in the week for me is music. I play the piano and it's great to spend an hour with my music teacher learning new songs and playing with other students.
Examiner:	Thank you.

Speaking Part 2

Examiner:	Now I'd like each of you to talk on your own about something. I'm going to give each of you a photograph and I'd like you to talk about it. Candidate A. Here is your photograph. It shows people preparing food. Please tell us what you can see in the photograph. Candidate B, you just listen.
Candidate A:	This photograph shows two people working together in the kitchen. There's a man on the left holding a large spoon and he's mixing a salad in a bowl. There's a woman on the right cutting red peppers. There are lots of other vegetables on the table in front of them. I can see a bowl of tomatoes, some carrots and lots of mushrooms. I don't know the word, but they're both wearing something to keep their clothes clean. People wear these in the kitchen when they're preparing food and cooking.
Examiner:	Thank you. Candidate B. Here is your photograph. It shows people looking at a map. Please tell us what you can see in the photograph. Candidate A, you just listen.
Candidate B:	This photograph was taken on a sunny day. There are three people, I think it's a family: a mum, a dad and their son. I think they're standing on a road somewhere

Model answers: Speaking

and they're looking at a map, which the boy and the father are holding. I think they're probably on holiday and are trying to find a place they want to visit. The boy is about ten years old and he's wearing a shirt with white and blue stripes. The father has a light blue T-shirt on with a green bag over his shoulder. The woman looks like she's wearing the same kind of T-shirt as her husband.

Examiner: Thank you.

Speaking Part 3

Examiner: Now, in this part of the test you're going to talk about something together for about two minutes. I'm going to describe a situation to you.
A family are going to the beach. They are trying to decide what to take with them. Here are some things they could take.
Talk together about the different things they could take and say which one would be best. All right? Now talk together.

Candidate A: So, the family are going to the beach. What do you think they should take? A lot of these things are useful, aren't they?

Candidate B: Yes, that's true. It's difficult to say which ones aren't important. They can buy food and drink when they're there, so they don't really need water or the sandwiches. What do you think?

Candidate A: I agree. If they're only going for a little while, they could put the sun cream on before they go out. Then they wouldn't need to take that.

Candidate B: Yes, that's true. What about the sunglasses? Are they important? I don't usually wear them, so I don't think so. What do you think? Shall we forget them?

Candidate A: Yes, I agree. The towel and the swimsuits go together, really, don't they? If they go swimming, they need both of them. I can't really decide which one of those is most important.

Candidate B: I know. If they don't go swimming and just stay on the beach, they don't need them. And if it's very sunny, the hats will be useful to protect them from the sun. Shall we say the hats? What do you think?

Candidate A: Yes, the hats are a good idea. Let's choose them.

Examiner: Thank you.

Speaking Part 4

Examiner: Candidate A, have you been on a holiday recently?

Candidate A: Yes, I went to a place near where we live with my family a few months ago. The weather was really nice and we spent our time on the beach or swimming.

Examiner: And what about you, Candidate B?

Candidate B: I haven't had a family holiday for a while, but I went on a school trip to Paris last year. We went for the weekend and I had a great time. We saw all the famous buildings and practised speaking French.

Examiner: Candidate B, is there anywhere you would like to visit?

Candidate B: I'd love to visit Edinburgh. Some members of my family live there and it would be great to see them. And London is an interesting city to visit as well.

Examiner: And how about you, Candidate A?

Candidate A: I'd like to go to the USA. I've seen so many places there on TV, but it would be nice to go there and actually see them. It's quite expensive there, though, so I'd need to save up some money first.

Examiner: Candidate B, what do you like to do when you go on holiday?

Candidate B: I like going somewhere that has lots of shops and places of interest. I enjoy spending time on the beach, but that gets boring after a while and it's nice to have interesting places to see.

Examiner: And what about you, Candidate A?

Candidate A: I'm the same. I really enjoy walking around the shops in a different city. I'm not really interested in visiting old buildings or museums, though. I think I prefer lying on the beach to doing that.

Examiner: Thank you. That is the end of the test.

Model answers: Speaking

Test 3

Speaking Part 1

Examiner:	Good afternoon. Can I have your mark sheets, please? I'm Karen Taylor and this is Martin Brindley.
Examiner:	What's your name, Candidate A? How old are you?
Candidate A:	My name's Vera Bohren and I'm fourteen years old.
Examiner:	And what's your name, Candidate B? How old are you?
Candidate B:	My name's Andrei Sukhov and I'm fourteen years old as well.
Examiner:	Tell me about what you like to do in your spare time, Candidate B.
Candidate B:	Well, I enjoy reading. I like reading novels and short stories. I'm also keen on baking. I make a lot of different cakes at home.
Examiner:	Who do you live with, Candidate B?
Candidate B:	I live with my parents and my brother.
Examiner:	Candidate A, what about you? What do you like doing in your spare time?
Candidate A:	I enjoy listening to music and going to concerts because I really love live music.
Examiner:	Who do you live with, Candidate A?
Candidate A:	I also live with my parents. I don't have any brothers or sisters.
Examiner:	Candidate A, do you enjoy studying English?
Candidate A:	Yes, I do. I enjoy studying all languages. I also speak a little French, and I'd like to learn Chinese in the future.
Examiner:	Candidate B, what about you?
Candidate B:	It's OK. It's not my favourite subject at school. I prefer my history and maths classes. But English is important for work and for holidays, so I'm pleased I can study it.
Examiner:	Can you tell me something about the area where you live, Candidate B?
Candidate B:	I live in a small town near Moscow. It's quite a busy place and we have lots of shops and facilities near my house.
Examiner:	Candidate A, what about you?
Candidate A:	We live in the country. My parents are farmers and we live in a small village in the south of Germany. There are one or two shops in the village, but we have to drive into the nearest town when we want to go shopping.
Examiner:	Thank you.

Speaking Part 2

Examiner:	Now I'd like each of you to talk on your own about something. I'm going to give each of you a photograph and I'd like you to talk about it. Candidate A. Here is your photograph. It shows some people in a gym. Please tell us what you can see in the photograph. Candidate B, you just listen.
Candidate A:	Well, this photograph reminds me of my sports class at school. It shows teenagers playing volleyball. There are two teams, but they're all wearing the same clothes: white vests and blue shorts. I think this must be the sports kit that children wear in the school. They have numbers on the back of the vests, though, so there is some difference. The teams have boys and girls in them. The boy nearest the camera is about to hit the ball and there are boys and girls standing near the net waiting to play. They're all concentrating and want to win.
Examiner:	Thank you.
Examiner:	Candidate B. Here is your photograph. It shows people at an airport. Please tell us what you can see in the photograph. Candidate A, you just listen.
Candidate B:	OK, so this shows a group of people at the airport. There are a few people in the background, but the main people seem to be from the same family. There's a tall man wearing jeans, and I think that's his daughter in a blue shirt and trousers. They're with two older people. I think these must be the girl's grandmother and grandfather.

Model answers: Speaking

	The grandmother has a suitcase in her hand, so they've probably just arrived and their son and granddaughter were waiting for them. They all look very happy to see each other and they're hugging each other.
Examiner:	Thank you.

Speaking Part 3

Examiner:	Now, in this part of the test you're going to talk about something together for about two minutes. I'm going to describe a situation to you. A girl of sixteen wants to take up a hobby. Her parents have suggested some things she could do. Here are some things they have suggested. Talk together about the different things she could do and say which one would be best. All right? Now talk together.
Candidate A:	OK, well these are all popular hobbies, aren't they? Are there any that you think she probably wouldn't like?
Candidate B:	Well, it's nice to learn to play a musical instrument, but her parents might not be able to afford a piano, and I wouldn't be interested in playing chess. What do you think?
Candidate A:	I agree. A bicycle would be cheaper and she'd get fit if she started cycling. But she might not be keen on keeping fit. What about photography or dancing? Would these be interesting?
Candidate B:	I'm not sure, really. I think it would be good if she learned how to knit. It doesn't cost very much, and she could make things for herself and other people. But most of all, it's very relaxing. That's the thing I'd like to learn. What do you think?
Candidate A:	That's a good idea. I can imagine it's something she can do in the evening after she has finished her homework that isn't hard work.
Candidate B:	The only other idea is learning to paint. What do you think about that as a hobby? It's relaxing as well.
Candidate A:	That's true. But I think I prefer your idea of her learning to knit. She probably has art classes at school, so painting wouldn't really be a new hobby.
Candidate B:	OK. Let's say she could learn to knit.
Examiner:	Thank you.

Speaking Part 4

Examiner:	Candidate A, is there a hobby or activity you'd like to start doing?
Candidate A:	Actually, I like the idea of learning to knit. My grandmother is very good at it, and every time we visit her, she's making something for someone. I think it would be very relaxing as well.
Examiner:	And what about you, Candidate B?
Candidate B:	I can't think of anything that I really want to do. I sometimes imagine doing a sport like swimming or football, but I prefer things like reading and baking.
Examiner:	Candidate B, are some hobbies better for younger people rather than older people?
Candidate B:	I don't think so. Older people aren't as fit as teenagers, but most of them still want to keep fit. So, exercise is good for all ages. And more relaxing interests can be done by people of any age.
Examiner:	And how about you, Candidate A?
Candidate A:	Yes, I agree. Some things might be dangerous for older people, like mountain climbing, for example. But apart from activities like that, I think younger and older people are able to have the same interests and hobbies.
Examiner:	Candidate B, is it important for people to have a hobby or interest?
Candidate B:	I suppose it is, yes. If you have something you like doing in your spare time, it means you can forget about work or your studies and concentrate on something that's fun.
Examiner:	And what about you, Candidate A, what do you think?
Candidate A:	I agree. It's also possible to meet new people if you have a hobby. You might have the chance to play football in a team, or join a club to do a hobby like painting, and you might make new friends.
Examiner:	Thank you. That is the end of the test.

239

Model answers: Speaking

Test 4

Speaking Part 1

Examiner:	Good morning. Can I have your mark sheets, please? I'm Marcus Holliday and this is Sarah Davidson.
Examiner:	What's your name, Candidate A? How old are you?
Candidate A:	My name's Daniel Bassot and I'm fifteen years old.
Examiner:	And what's your name, Candidate B? How old are you?
Candidate B:	My name's Carla Rossi and I'm fourteen years old.
Examiner:	Candidate B, where do you live?
Candidate B:	I live in Italy, in Milan.
Examiner:	And where do you live, Candidate A?
Candidate A:	I live in Marseille with my mother, father and my sister.
Examiner:	Candidate A, did you do anything interesting last weekend?
Candidate A:	Not really. The weather wasn't very good, so I stayed indoors and watched football on TV. My grandparents visited us on Sunday, so that was good fun.
Examiner:	And Candidate B, did you do anything interesting at the weekend?
Candidate B:	I met my friends in the city centre on Saturday and we went shopping for some clothes. I stayed at home and did my homework on Sunday.
Examiner:	Candidate A, what is your favourite time of year?
Candidate A:	I definitely like spring best. I love seeing the trees turning green and flowers appearing in people's gardens. I think people start to feel happier when the weather gets warmer.
Examiner:	Candidate B, what about you?
Candidate B:	I like spring too, but I also like autumn. There's some lovely countryside where I live and the leaves on the trees start to turn red and yellow and look really beautiful.
Examiner:	Candidate B, do you prefer to eat at home or to go to a restaurant?
Candidate B:	I actually prefer eating at home. I like my mum's cooking and I always eat everything she gives me. I don't mind takeaways either, but I'm not fond of eating in a restaurant.
Examiner:	And Candidate A, what about you?
Candidate A:	I like any kind of food, so it doesn't matter if I eat it at home or in a restaurant. I love Italian food, so I always feel excited if my parents take me to an Italian restaurant.
Examiner:	Thank you.

Speaking Part 2

Examiner:	Now I'd like each of you to talk on your own about something. I'm going to give each of you a photograph and I'd like you to talk about it. Candidate A. Here is your photograph. It shows people selling things. Please tell us what you can see in the photograph. Candidate B, you just listen.
Candidate A:	In this photograph, I can see a man and a woman and two children. I think the woman and her kids are having a garage sale. They're selling some of the things they don't want anymore. I imagine that the man is passing the house and is looking to see if there's anything he wants to buy. In the photo, he's looking at a book. There are quite a lot of things for sale. There are some suitcases and a guitar on the ground in front of the table, some clothes just behind the man and a barbecue. There are also some chairs on the right of the photo, but I don't know if these are for sale or if the family are using them to sit on.
Examiner:	Thank you.
Examiner:	Candidate B. Here is your photograph. It shows some people with an animal. Please tell us what you can see in the photograph. Candidate A, you just listen.
Candidate B:	In this photograph, I can see a young girl and her mother. They're both wearing very colourful summer clothes. They're probably in a zoo or somewhere that takes care of

Model answers: Speaking

	animals. The girl is holding her hand out to an elephant. I don't know if she's feeding him something or just saying hello. The elephant is standing in water, and in the background, there's another one walking away from the camera. There's a fence between the girl and the elephant to stop people falling in, and she looks safe and very happy to be there. Her mum is smiling and doesn't seem to be worried about the elephant.
Examiner:	Thank you.

Speaking Part 3

Examiner:	Now, in this part of the test you are going to talk about something together for about two minutes. I'm going to describe a situation to you. A family want to do something together with their young children this weekend. Here are some things they could do together. Talk together about the different things they could do and say which one would be best. All right? Now talk together.
Candidate A:	OK, would you like to start?
Candidate B:	Yes, OK, well, we know the children are young, so I don't think going climbing is a good idea, do you?
Candidate A:	No, even the parents might not want to do something that difficult. Going for a walk can be good fun, but sometimes young children get tired and start to complain.
Candidate B:	Yes, that's true. The parents might enjoy fishing, but if they catch something, it might upset young children, so I think we should leave that one. What about seeing a film?
Candidate A:	I'm not sure about that. It's not very special, is it? Everyone likes food, so a barbecue or a picnic would be a good idea. I'm sure the children would enjoy that.
Candidate B:	I know. Cycling is a good activity to do if they all have bikes. I think it would be enjoyable to cycle somewhere in the country and then have a picnic when they arrive. But we can only choose one thing. What do you think is best?
Candidate A:	OK, let's say the picnic. They can do that in a local park, can't they? Or even in the garden if they have one.
Examiner:	Thank you.

Speaking Part 4

Examiner:	Candidate A, what do you like to do for a special occasion?
Candidate A:	I said before that I like going to a restaurant. I always feel excited before I go and look forward to eating something I haven't tried before, or a meal that I've had before and loved.
Examiner:	And what about you, Candidate B?
Candidate B:	I often go for walks in the country with my friends. There are lots of hills near where I live and we like to go out for the day and see how many we can manage to walk up.
Examiner:	Candidate B, does the weather affect what we can do for a special occasion?
Candidate B:	Yes, if you plan to do something outside, you need good weather. For example, if you want to have a barbecue, it's best to choose a sunny day or nobody will enjoy it.
Examiner:	And how about you, Candidate A?
Candidate A:	I agree. I think the best activities are often outside, so the weather is really important. Unfortunately, there are lots of rainy days where I live, so we have to be careful when we want to do something outside.
Examiner:	Candidate B, if you could do any activity at all this weekend, what would it be?
Candidate B:	I'd like to go to a different city and look around the shops with my family or my friends. It would be great to go somewhere I've never been before, like a city in another country.
Examiner:	And what about you, Candidate A?
Candidate A:	I think I'd like to get some tickets for me and my friends to see a football match. I'd like to see a game between two of our best teams and get really good seats in the stadium.
Examiner:	Thank you. That is the end of the test.

Model answers: Speaking

Test 5

Speaking Part 1

Examiner:	Good morning. Can I have your mark sheets, please? I'm James Huntley and this is Jayne Mathiewson.
Examiner:	What's your name, Candidate A? How old are you?
Candidate A:	My name's Ingrid and I'm fifteen years old.
Examiner:	And what's your name, Candidate B? How old are you?
Candidate B:	My name's Rui and I'm fourteen years old.
Examiner:	Candidate B, where do you come from?
Candidate B:	I come from Portugal. My family live in Lisbon.
Examiner:	And where do you come from, Candidate A?
Candidate A:	I'm from Zurich in Switzerland.
Examiner:	Candidate A, when did you start learning English?
Candidate A:	We had English lessons in my primary school. I think I was about six when I had my first lesson. My mum speaks good English, so she also taught me some words when I was little.
Examiner:	And Candidate B, when did you start learning English?
Candidate B:	We had English lessons at school, but I also went to classes on Wednesday afternoon when I was quite young. I didn't really want to go because that was a half day at school and I wanted to relax.
Examiner:	Candidate A, what do you like to do when you're on holiday?
Candidate A:	I enjoy walking around the shops, especially if they're different from the ones we have at home. I don't think I'd like a holiday in the countryside because I wouldn't be able to do that.
Examiner:	Candidate B, what about you?
Candidate B:	I'm the same. I love shopping and if I'm in another country, all the shops seem very exciting. I also like visiting historic buildings and taking photographs.
Examiner:	Candidate B, in class, do you prefer to work on your own or in a group of other students?
Candidate B:	It depends on what I have to do. When I have to concentrate on something difficult, I like to be on my own so that I can think. But I also enjoy discussions with other people in a group.
Examiner:	And Candidate A, what about you?
Candidate A:	I like to work with other students. If there's something I don't understand, sometimes they can help. And if it's something they find difficult, I can explain it to them. I think this helps me learn the subject better.
Examiner:	Thank you.

Speaking Part 2

Examiner:	Now I'd like each of you to talk on your own about something. I'm going to give each of you a photograph and I'd like you to talk about it. Candidate A. Here is your photograph. It shows people having their photograph taken. Please tell us what you can see in the photograph. Candidate B, you just listen.
Candidate A:	In this photograph, there are six people being photographed. It looks like a family as there are younger and older people in the group and they seem to have a lovely relationship. I think they might be grandparents, parents and children. They're dressed in casual clothes like jeans and T-shirts and look very happy and relaxed. I don't think they're at home as there isn't much furniture, so I imagine they're in a studio. There are two large lights that are making the room very bright. On the left, you can see the photographer. He's wearing jeans and a striped shirt. He's on one knee and it looks like he's actually taking the photographs.
Examiner:	Thank you.
Examiner:	Candidate B. Here is your photograph. It shows a man running. Please tell us what you can see in the photograph. Candidate A, you just listen.

Model answers: Speaking

Candidate B: In this photograph, I can see a man running along a road towards the camera. He might actually be running across a bridge as there are metal fences each side of him. He's wearing a tracksuit with a red top and grey trousers. He has headphones on and is probably listening to music. There are no other runners in the photograph, and I think he's training on his own because he looks very serious. There are trees on each side of the road, and in the background on the right, you can see lots of cars. There are also buildings in the distance, so I think this must be a city somewhere.

Examiner: Thank you.

Speaking Part 3

39a

Examiner: Now, in this part of the test you are going to talk about something together for about two minutes. I'm going to describe a situation to you.
A girl is about to leave home to attend her first day at high school.
Here are some things she could take to school.
Talk together about the different things she could take and say which one would be best. All right? Now talk together.

Candidate A: OK, would you like to start?

Candidate B: Yes, OK, well, a lot of the things here are quite useful, but I don't think the watch is important. If she takes the phone, she can use that to tell the time.

Candidate A: That's true. The sandwiches are important, but she might want to see what the school dinners are like. Do you think she should take her own food?

Candidate B: Personally, I'd prefer to see what the food at school is like. And she can probably get water there too. So, I wouldn't take sandwiches. Let's forget about them. What about the pen and paper?

Candidate A: I think the pen is really important. She'll definitely have to write things during the day. If she doesn't take it, she'll have to ask the teacher for one. That could be embarrassing.

Candidate B: Yes, that's true, and she should leave the bike at home. The school might not have anywhere to put it. But she should take some money with her. What do you think?

Candidate A: That's right. So, we have three things then – the phone, money and the pen. What do you think?

Candidate B: Well, they're all important, but I'd take the phone. Just in case there was an emergency.

Candidate A: OK. Let's say the phone.

Examiner: Thank you.

Speaking Part 4

40a

Examiner: Candidate A, do you like to take your own food to school?

Candidate A: I tried the school dinners when I first went to my school, but I didn't like a lot of the dishes, so now I take sandwiches or buy something on the way to school.

Examiner: And what about you, Candidate B?

Candidate B: Our school dinners are OK. You have lots of things to choose from and most of the food is tasty. I take sandwiches sometimes when I want to be healthy, but that's not very often.

Examiner: Candidate B, is there anything important that you always take to school?

Candidate B: I think like most people, my phone is the most important thing. Even though we aren't allowed to use it in class, I like to have it during my lunch break to check social media.

Examiner: And how about you, Candidate A?

Candidate A: I'm the same. I feel a bit lost if I don't have my phone. Our teachers allow us to use the phones in class when we have to look up information. If you don't have one with you, it's a problem.

Examiner: Candidate B, do you ever cycle to school?

Candidate B: I'd like to, but the roads are too busy between my house and the school. If they were quieter, I'd definitely use my bike.

Examiner: And what about you, Candidate A?

Candidate A: I like to cycle to school if it's a sunny morning, but if it's raining, I catch the bus. The roads are OK where I live and there are cycle paths all the way to my school.

Examiner: Thank you. That is the end of the test.

Model answers: Speaking

Test 6
Speaking Part 1

Examiner:	Good morning. Can I have your mark sheets, please? I'm David Porter and this is Jenny Lawler.
Examiner:	What's your name, Candidate A? How old are you?
Candidate A:	My name's Cristin and I'm fourteen years old.
Examiner:	And what's your name, Candidate B? How old are you?
Candidate B:	My name's Liu and I'm sixteen years old.
Examiner:	Candidate B, where do you come from?
Candidate B:	I come from China, but I'm living in London at the moment.
Examiner:	And where do you come from, Candidate A?
Candidate A:	My family live in Paris, but I'm staying with a host family in London.
Examiner:	Candidate A, what's your favourite time of the day?
Candidate A:	It's definitely not the morning. It takes me a long time to wake up. I think I prefer the afternoon when I get home from school. It's nice to lie on the sofa for a while and relax.
Examiner:	And Candidate B, what about you?
Candidate B:	I like the afternoon too, but just after we leave school. My friends and I often go straight to the park and have a game of football before we go home.
Examiner:	Candidate A, do you watch many programmes on TV?
Candidate A:	I don't watch TV very often in France, but I do in the UK. My host family enjoy watching quiz shows and comedies and I like to sit with them.
Examiner:	Candidate B, what about you?
Candidate B:	Not really. I spend my free time watching videos online. There are more things to choose from. I can also watch films and documentaries from my own country on the internet, which I can't do on our TV.
Examiner:	Candidate B, what do you like to eat for breakfast?
Candidate B:	During the week when I have to go to school, I have something simple like toast. But at the weekend, I usually have a cooked breakfast. My favourite breakfast is omelette.
Examiner:	And Candidate A, what about you?
Candidate A:	I usually have cereal and a cup of coffee. I don't like eating a big breakfast. I prefer to wait till lunchtime and have something then.
Examiner:	Thank you.

Speaking Part 2

Examiner:	Now I'd like each of you to talk on your own about something. I'm going to give each of you a photograph and I'd like you to talk about it. Candidate A. Here is your photograph. It shows people dancing. Please tell us what you can see in the photograph. Candidate B, you just listen.
Candidate A:	In this photograph, I can see a group of young people dancing. They all look around eighteen or nineteen years old and they're at a music festival. I think this is true because they're outside, and in the background, you can see lots of tents. It looks quite busy there. The girl nearest the camera is wearing a colourful red top with a white T-shirt underneath and blue jeans. She's smiling and it looks like she's having a lovely time. I think it must be spring or summer because the boy in the photo is wearing a T-shirt.
Examiner:	Thank you.
Examiner:	Candidate B. Here is your photograph. It shows people in a cinema. Please tell us what you can see in the photograph. Candidate A, you just listen.
Candidate B:	This photo was taken in a cinema. There are quite a few young people in the audience, and some of them appear to be with their mum or dad. The film has probably started or they're all watching advertisements. The cinema is quite dark, and you can see

Model answers: Speaking

	the light from the film shining on their faces. The woman who is sitting nearest the camera has a little girl on her lap. The woman is smiling, and it looks like she's enjoying the film. The little girl is drinking something from a large paper cup, and she also seems to be having a good time.
Examiner:	Thank you.

Speaking Part 3

Examiner:	Now, in this part of the test you are going to talk about something together for about two minutes. I'm going to describe a situation to you. A teacher at your school is leaving and you want to buy her a present. Here are some things you could give her. Talk together about the different things you could give her and say which one would be best. All right? Now talk together.
Candidate A:	Well, these are all nice presents. Are there any that you wouldn't want to give her?
Candidate B:	I think it's nice to get something that will last. Something that will help her remember the student who gave it to her. So, I wouldn't buy the cake or the chocolates. Do you agree?
Candidate A:	No, let's forget them. What about the flowers? They're pretty, but they don't last very long, do they? Maybe just a few days.
Candidate B:	True, so no flowers. I think a card is a good idea, but that's not really a present. Normally you give someone a card and a gift. What about a book?
Candidate A:	That could be useful, but you might not know the things she likes to read. A pen is a nice present, especially for a teacher. She'd use it every day.
Candidate B:	Yes, I agree, but I also like the mug. Whenever she had a cup of tea or coffee, she'd remember the time she spent at the school. I think that would be a great gift.
Candidate A:	OK. That means we have the pen and the mug. I can't decide which one I prefer. If I were the teacher, I think I'd like to have the pen. I just think it's a nicer present.
Candidate B:	I actually prefer the mug, but I agree with you that the pen is a lovely thing to give her.
Candidate A:	OK. We've decided to get the pen.
Examiner:	Thank you.

Speaking Part 4

Examiner:	Candidate A, have you ever bought a teacher who is leaving a present?
Candidate A:	No, I haven't. A teacher left the school last year and I think the other teachers gave her something, but not the students.
Examiner:	And what about you, Candidate B?
Candidate B:	No, I haven't either. We once bought a very big card for a teacher who was moving to another city. We all signed it and wrote a short message in it. She loved it.
Examiner:	Candidate B, is there a teacher at your school whose lessons you really enjoy?
Candidate B:	Our sports teacher is a lot of fun. His name is Mr King and he's got a strong Scottish accent. At first, he seems a bit scary, but when you get to know him, he's very funny.
Examiner:	And how about you, Candidate A?
Candidate A:	We have lots of great teachers at my school, but I suppose my favourite lesson is art. The teacher is very kind and always encourages you by saying positive things about your work.
Examiner:	Candidate B, what makes a good teacher?
Candidate B:	I think a good teacher needs to know a lot about their subject, but they also need to be able to explain things clearly.
Examiner:	And what about you, Candidate A?
Candidate A:	I agree. I think it's important for a teacher to be able to communicate clearly. They also need to be a little strict to make sure all the students behave well. But they also need to be fun.
Examiner:	Thank you. That is the end of the test.

Model answers: Speaking

Test 7

Speaking Part 1

Examiner:	Good morning. Can I have your mark sheets, please? I'm Bill Mizen and this is Greta Manley.
Examiner:	What's your name, Candidate A? How old are you?
Candidate A:	My name's Adriana and I'm thirteen years old.
Examiner:	And what's your name, Candidate B? How old are you?
Candidate B:	My name's Sergei and I'm fifteen years old.
Examiner:	Candidate B, where do you come from?
Candidate B:	I come from Moscow.
Examiner:	And where do you come from, Candidate A?
Candidate A:	I come from Alicante in Spain.
Examiner:	Candidate A, what's the weather like where you live in the winter?
Candidate A:	We're lucky as the weather isn't too bad in the winter. It's cooler than the summer, but we still have lots of sunny days.
Examiner:	And Candidate B, what about you?
Candidate B:	Unfortunately, winter in Moscow is very cold. The temperature is often minus 10 degrees Celsius and we get a lot of snow.
Examiner:	Candidate A, how often do you see your friends?
Candidate A:	I see my school friends every day and we meet at weekends. We usually go into the town centre and look in the shops.
Examiner:	Candidate B, what about you?
Candidate B:	I'm the same. I see them Monday to Friday at school and at weekends. I also have friends at another school that I see when I can.
Examiner:	Candidate B, at the weekend, do you like to get up early or spend more time in bed?
Candidate B:	I stay in bed longer on Saturday because I don't have a reason to get up early. But I play football on Sunday mornings and I have to be there at 9.00 a.m., so I can't lie in bed too long.
Examiner:	And Candidate A, what about you?
Candidate A:	Well, I don't have to get up early as there's no school, so I stay in bed a little longer. But I like to get up before it's too late so I can enjoy the weekend.
Examiner:	Thank you.

Speaking Part 2

Examiner:	Now I'd like each of you to talk on your own about something. I'm going to give each of you a photograph and I'd like you to talk about it. Candidate A. Here is your photograph. It shows people buying something. Please tell us what you can see in the photograph. Candidate B, you just listen.
Candidate A:	OK, there are three people in this photo. I think two of them are buying a new car. It looks like a husband and wife. The husband's wearing a blue shirt and jeans and the woman's wearing a white blouse and trousers. The other person is the salesman, who's wearing a grey suit. He's standing on the left of the photo and he's giving the man the key for the car. It's difficult to see which car the two people have bought, but they're standing next to a white one, so it might be that one. The man and woman look very happy and are probably excited about the new car.
Examiner:	Thank you.
Examiner:	Candidate B. Here is your photograph. It shows people by a river. Please tell us what you can see in the photograph. Candidate A, you just listen.
Candidate B:	There are two people in this photo. There's a woman nearest the camera on the left and a man in the background. The woman is wearing a white shirt and blue jeans and

Model answers: Speaking

Examiner: the man also has a white shirt on and dark blue or black trousers. They're both at the side of a river, which you can see on the right. It looks like they're collecting litter that people have left behind when they have visited. They both have blue plastic bags and it looks like they've collected a lot of rubbish. There's paper on the sand and the woman is putting a plastic bottle in the bag.
Examiner: Thank you.

Speaking Part 3

Examiner: Now, in this part of the test you are going to talk about something together for about two minutes. I'm going to describe a situation to you.
A relative has moved to a new house and your family want to buy her a present for her garden.
Here are some things you could give her.
Talk together about the different things you could give her and say which one would be best.
All right? Now talk together.
Candidate A: Would you like to start?
Candidate B: OK. Well, it would be great to play table tennis in the garden, but a table tennis table is probably too big. What do you think?
Candidate A: I agree, especially if it's a small garden. I like the tree. That's something that the person could look at for years and enjoy it as it gets taller.
Candidate B: Yes, that's true. I'm not sure one chair is a good present. You need at least two chairs in case you have a visitor.
Candidate A: Yes, let's forget the chair. The plants are OK, but personally, I prefer the tree. What about the barbecue? That's a really good present.
Candidate B: Yes, I prefer that to the sculpture. She might not like that in her garden. And I think the table isn't very useful without chairs. Do you agree?
Candidate A: Yes, I do. So, that means we've chosen the barbecue and the tree. Have you got one that you prefer?
Candidate B: I think I prefer the barbecue. The tree is a lovely idea, but we don't know what the garden is like. It might not be suitable for a tree.
Candidate A: OK. Let's choose the barbecue, then. It's a great present.
Examiner: Thank you.

Speaking Part 4

Examiner: Candidate A, do you like to spend time in a garden?
Candidate A: Yes, I really do. My family live in an apartment, so we don't have one. I think people who have a place outside are really lucky.
Examiner: And what about you, Candidate B?
Candidate B: I'm the same. We don't have a garden either, unfortunately. I think it's a lovely place to relax and enjoy the fresh air and nature. Learning about plants would also be nice.
Examiner: Candidate B, is there a garden or a park near where you live that you go to?
Candidate B: Yes, we have a few parks near my house. Some of them are beautiful. They have a wide range of flowers and I enjoy walking around them with my family.
Examiner: And how about you, Candidate A?
Candidate A: Yes, we have a lot of parks too. I walk to school through a park every day and see lots of other people walking their dog or doing exercise.
Examiner: Candidate B, what do you think is the perfect garden?
Candidate B: Gardens are usually quite small, so I think they just need a lot of different colourful plants and flowers and somewhere to sit to enjoy them.
Examiner: And what about you, Candidate A?
Candidate A: I agree. If you have a big garden, you can have things like the table tennis table we saw before. Flowers are important, though, and a barbecue is nice when you have guests.
Examiner: Thank you. That is the end of the test.

Model answers: Speaking

Test 8

Speaking Part 1

Examiner:	Good morning. Can I have your mark sheets, please? I'm Sam Gregory and this is Lisa Martin.
Examiner:	What's your name, Candidate A? How old are you?
Candidate A:	My name's Gunther and I'm fifteen years old.
Examiner:	And what's your name, Candidate B? How old are you?
Candidate B:	My name's Yuki and I'm fourteen years old.
Examiner:	Candidate B, where do you live?
Candidate B:	I live in Tokyo in Japan.
Examiner:	And where do you live, Candidate A?
Candidate A:	I live in Frankfurt in Germany.
Examiner:	Candidate A, what's the most important thing you own?
Candidate A:	I think I have to say my phone. I use it all the time, and if I didn't have it, I wouldn't be able to keep in contact with my friends or family or use the internet easily.
Examiner:	And Candidate B, what about you?
Candidate B:	My phone's very important as well. My laptop is also very useful. I need it for school, and I spend a lot of my time watching videos on it. I think both those things are important for me.
Examiner:	Candidate A, how often do you go to the cinema?
Candidate A:	I don't go very often. Sometimes my parents take me and my brother, and occasionally I go with my friends. But I like watching films at home on my laptop or on TV.
Examiner:	Candidate B, what about you?
Candidate B:	I like going to the cinema. I prefer seeing the film on a big screen. I go with my friends quite a lot, maybe every month.
Examiner:	Candidate B, do you have any pets?
Candidate B:	No, I don't. I like dogs and I'd love to have one, but we live in an apartment and it isn't really suitable to keep a pet like that.
Examiner:	And Candidate A, what about you?
Candidate A:	We have two. My dad bought a parrot recently and he's trying to teach it to say some words. We also have a cat. My mum said it wouldn't be a good idea to have a cat and a bird in the same room, but they seem OK.
Examiner:	Thank you.

Speaking Part 2

Examiner:	Now I'd like each of you to talk on your own about something. I'm going to give each of you a photograph and I'd like you to talk about it. Candidate A. Here is your photograph. It shows a family painting. Please tell us what you can see in the photograph. Candidate B, you just listen.
Candidate A:	In this picture there are three people. I think it's a family: a father and his two children. The younger one has long hair, so it might be a girl, but I think it's a boy. They're all wearing jeans and T-shirts and they're decorating a room. There are lots of tins of paint on the floor, and I think they're trying to find a colour that they like. The older boy is trying a colour on the wall. It's a kind of green paint. I can't see clearly what the man and the younger boy are doing, but it looks like the boy is holding a stick, so he might be stirring the paint.
Examiner:	Thank you.
Examiner:	Candidate B. Here is your photograph. It shows a family. Please tell us what you can see in the photograph. Candidate A, you just listen.

248

Model answers: Speaking

Candidate B: This is another family photograph and there are also three people in this one: the dad, the mum and their young daughter. This is a definitely a girl because you can tell by her hair. She's wearing a grey T-shirt like her dad, and the mother is wearing a blue top and jeans. It looks like the man is wearing shorts as I can see his knee. He's playing the guitar and his daughter is watching very carefully. He might be teaching her how to play, but she's very young, so I think he's just playing it and maybe singing to her. This is probably what's happening because the mum is clapping.

Examiner: Thank you.

Speaking Part 3

63a

Examiner: Now, in this part of the test you are going to talk about something together for about two minutes. I'm going to describe a situation to you.
A school wants to invite someone to give a talk about their job.
Here are some occupations they could think about.
Talk together about the different ones and and say which one would be best.
All right? Now talk together.

Candidate A: OK, so we have to choose one of these people. Would you like to start?

Candidate B: Well, I think it would be good to have someone who can talk about a job that's interesting, or it might be boring to listen to. I don't think the postman would have much to say.

Candidate A: That's true. Obviously, the police officer would have lots of interesting stories, so we should think about that one. What about the nurse or the chef?

Candidate B: They're both interesting jobs, I suppose. I think I'd choose the nurse.

Candidate A: OK, so far that's the police officer and the nurse. What about the hairdresser? It might be a good job, but not very interesting to talk about.

Candidate B: No, or the butcher. And there might be vegetarians in the class, so he wouldn't be a good idea.

Candidate A: That leaves the dentist. Do you think she'd be a good speaker?

Candidate B: Perhaps yes, the dentist is the best job out of all of them. Well, what I mean is the dentist earns the most money. But I think we should choose between the police officer or the nurse. What do you think?

Candidate A: OK. Let's choose the police officer. It's a really important job, and I'm sure the speaker will be very interesting.

Examiner: Thank you.

Speaking Part 4

64a

Examiner: Candidate A, are there any jobs you'd like to consider for a career?

Candidate A: Actually, I'd really like to be a doctor. I know it takes a long time to get the qualifications, but it's something I'd like to do.

Examiner: And what about you, Candidate B?

Candidate B: I haven't really decided yet. I love animals and I'd love a job taking care of them in a zoo or a safari park. That would be great.

Examiner: Candidate B, are there any jobs that you really wouldn't enjoy?

Candidate B: I don't think I'd enjoy working in an office. I prefer to be outside and being active. I don't think I'd be happy sitting at a desk all day long.

Examiner: And how about you, Candidate A?

Candidate A: I agree. An office job would be quite boring. I enjoy meeting people and I'd hate to spend all day working on a computer and not meeting anyone.

Examiner: Candidate B, is it important to you to earn a lot of money?

Candidate B: Money is important. We have to pay our bills and have money to buy clothes and food for ourselves. But I also think it's important to enjoy what you do.

Examiner: And what about you, Candidate A?

Candidate A: Yes, I totally agree. As long as I had enough to be comfortable, I'd be happy. It's nice to have lots of money in the bank, but it's not the most important thing.

Examiner: Thank you. That is the end of the test.

Speaking: Questions

Speaking paper: Additional practice by topic

This section will give you extra practice in the sorts of questions the examiner may ask you in the Speaking test. Listen to the audio and practise answering the questions. Some of the questions mean quite similar things, but the words used in the question are different; this gives you more speaking practice and shows you how different questions are formed. Remember, in this part of the test, the examiner will choose what questions to ask you and won't ask you lots of questions about the same topic.

When you are practising, try to give a longer answer even if you want to just say *No*. Imagine the question is followed by *Why?* or *Why not?* Doing this will help you make your answer longer. For example, you may not watch films very often, but if the question is *Do you like watching films about the future?* and your real answer is *No*, you can say something like *No, I don't like watching films about the future because I think some of them are frightening.*

Once you are feeling confident, it would be a good idea not to look at the book – just listen to the audio and answer the questions. Also look at the **How to prepare for the test** and **Model answers for Speaking** sections of the book for good example answers to Part 1 Speaking questions. When you have practised with the audio a few times, it would be a good idea to work with a 'study buddy'. Take turns to ask each other the questions and answer them, trying to make your answers a bit longer each time. Choose questions about different topics as that is what the examiner will do in the Speaking test. And keep practising!

The questions are grouped under different topic headings: celebrations; clothes; daily life; education; entertainment and media; the environment; food and drink; free time; health, medicine and exercise; house and home; language; people; personal feelings, experiences and opinions; places and buildings; services; shopping; sport; technology; the natural world; transport; travel and holidays; weather; work.

Celebrations

65

Now let's talk about celebrations.
Tell us about the last time you celebrated something with your friends.
Did you have birthday parties when you were younger? Tell us about them.
What kind of food do children usually eat at a birthday party?
Tell us about the games children play at parties.
Do you prefer to go to a party in someone else's home or to have one in your own home?
Is there an event in your local area that people celebrate?
Do people ever have outdoor celebrations in your country? Tell us about them.
Have you ever celebrated something at your school?
Are there any national holidays in your country to celebrate an event? Tell us about it.
What is the most important cultural celebration in your country?
Have you ever been to a festival in another country?
Is there a festival in your country that tourists like to see? Tell us about it.

Clothes
66

Now let's talk about clothes.
Do you like going shopping for clothes? Why? / Why not?
What is your favourite shop to buy clothes?
What problems are there with buying clothes online?
Do you like to wear bright colours? Why? / Why not?
Do you read fashion magazines? Why? / Why not?
What do you wear in the winter?
What did you wear yesterday?
Do you ever wear a hat or a cap?
Are there any types of clothes you don't like?
Do you always try clothes on before you buy them in a shop?
How often do you wear smart clothes?

Have you received any clothes as a present recently?
How often do you wear jeans?

Daily life
Let's talk about your daily life.
Do you enjoy getting up early in the morning? Why? / Why not?
How soon do you check your phone after you wake up?
What is your favourite time of the day?
Do you like to get to school early? Why? / Why not?
How long does it take you to get to school?
What is your busiest day of the week?
Do you have any habits you want to change? Tell us about them.
What do you like to do in the evening?
Which day of the week do you look forward to most?
Do you take your phone to bed with you? Why? / Why not?
What time do you go to sleep?
How many hours' sleep do you usually have?

Education
Now let's talk about education.
How do you get to school?
Do you have to wear a school uniform?
Which subjects did you like most when you were younger?
Which subject are you best at now?
Does your school have a library?
Have you got a favourite place to study at home?
Do you like to study alone or with other students in class?
Are you allowed to use your phone in class to study?
What time does your school finish?
How much homework do you get?
When do you usually do your homework?
Have you ever forgotten to do your homework?

Entertainment and media
Now let's talk about entertainment and media.
What do people like to do at weekends in your country?
What is the most popular form of entertainment in your country?
When do you like to listen to music?
Have you got a favourite kind of music?
Do you watch many programmes on TV with your family?
When did you last go to the cinema?
What was the last book you read?
What kind of things do you like to read?
Do you ever use your local library? Why? / Why not?
Have you got a favourite actor?
Have you been to a party lately?
What did you do the last time you went out with your friends?

Environment
Now let's talk about the environment.
Is there any nice countryside where you live? Tell us about it.
What wildlife do you have in your area?
Is it important to you to protect the environment? Why? / Why not?
What kind of problems with the environment are there in your country?
Is air pollution a problem where you live?
Are young people concerned about the environment in your country?

Speaking: Questions

Do you try to reduce the paper you use? Why? / Why not?
Why do you think people drop litter?
Are there any rules in your country to stop people dropping litter?
What kind of things do you recycle?
Do you discuss the environment at your school?
Have you had any projects about the environment at school?

Food and drink
Now let's talk about food and drink.
How often do you eat chocolate?
What is your favourite snack?
When did you last buy any sweets for yourself?
Is there a restaurant you go to near where you live? Tell us about it.
Do you ever eat food from other countries?
Was there any food you didn't like when you were younger?
What are you going to have for dinner later?
Do you like spicy food?
How often do you eat dinner in front of the TV?
When was the last time you had a takeaway meal?
How much water do you drink every day?
Have you got a favourite drink?

Free time
Let's talk about your free time.
Do you find it easy to relax? Why / Why not?
What do you like to do to relax?
Do you have much free time in the evenings?
What do you do during your breaks at school?
Are you free to do what you want at weekends?
Do you prefer to be busy or have nothing to do?
How often do you feel bored?
What do you do if you feel bored?
Do you like to spend time lying in bed?
Do you like to spend all your free time with your friends?
Did you have more free time when you were younger?
Who do you like to spend your free time with?

Health, medicine and exercise
Now let's talk about health, medicine and exercise.
Is good health important to you? Why? / Why not?
Do you try to avoid eating fast food?
What do you do to keep healthy?
Do you like to eat healthy food?
When was the last time you went to the dentist?
Do you check the ingredients on packets of food?
How often do you do exercise?
What kind of exercise do you do?
Are you an active person?
Do you enjoy exercising? Why? / Why not?
Do you think you get enough sleep?
What do you think is the best form of exercise?
Do you have any lessons at school about keeping healthy?

Hobbies and leisure
Now let's talk about hobbies and leisure.
What facilities are there for young people where you live?

Did you have a hobby when you were younger?
Does anyone in your family have a hobby or interest?
Have you ever collected anything? Tell us about it.
Is there a hobby you would like to start? Tell us about it.
What are some popular hobbies in your country?
What clubs are there for young people where you live?
Have you ever gone to a youth club?
Do you enjoy taking photographs?
Are you keen on drawing or painting?
Do you enjoy going to museums?
How often do you buy magazines?

House and home
Now let's talk about accommodation.
Do you live in a house or an apartment?
How often do you see your neighbours?
What can you see from your windows?
Have you always lived in the same place?
Do you do any housework?
Where do you like to do your homework?
How often do you wash the dishes?
Have you got your own bedroom or do you share?
What shops are there near where you live?
How many floors are there in your home?

Language
Now let's talk about language.
How many languages can you speak?
Do you find learning another language interesting? Why? / Why not?
What is the most difficult thing about learning another language?
Do you speak English with your friends?
Do many people speak English in your country?
Do any members of your family speak English?
Have you got any friends from an English-speaking country?
Which language do you like to listen to?
How often do you watch films or programmes in English?
Why do people learn English in your country?
Do you have any friends who speak another language?
How do you try to learn new words?
When did you start learning English?

People
Now let's talk about people.
Tell us about your family.
Who do you look like most in your family?
Have you got a favourite aunt or uncle?
Do you ever have family parties?
How often do you visit other people in your family?
How long have you known your best friend?
Where did you meet your friends?
When did you last go out with your friends?
What do you like about your close friends?
Do you prefer to be around quiet people or people who talk a lot?
Are your friends similar to or different from you?
Have you got a friend who makes you laugh a lot?

Speaking: Questions

Personal feelings, experiences and opinions
Let's talk about your feelings, experiences and opinions.
What kind of things make you laugh?
Do you ever cry at sad films?
How reliable are you?
Tell us about a time you were lucky.
Do you think it's important to earn a lot of money? Why? / Why not?
Have you ever done something that was very challenging?
When was the last time someone surprised you?
Are you good at telling jokes?
What kind of things make you nervous?
Do you like to spend time alone?
Tell us about the last time you felt excited.

Places and buildings
Let's talk about places and buildings.
Are there many historic buildings where you live?
Do you like modern buildings?
Do you like the architecture where you live?
Have you ever visited a museum?
Have you always lived in the same place?
When did you last visit another city?
What is your favourite city?
Which city would you like to visit most?
Are there any nice parks near where you live?
How often do you go to a park?
What do you like doing in a park?

Services
Let's talk about services.
How often do you go to a hairdresser's?
Is it easy to get an appointment to see a doctor where you live?
Are there many hotels in your local area?
When did you last go to an art gallery?
Have you got many cinemas or theatres where you live?
Do you ever use your local bank?
Have you got an online bank account?
Do you prefer using the internet or going to a shop?
When did you last go to a swimming pool?
Are there lots of facilities in your area for people who want to keep fit?
Do you get many visitors to your local town or city?
Have you got a favourite café or restaurant where you live?
How often do you use the post office?

Shopping
Now let's talk about shopping.
Have you got a favourite shop you like to use?
Is there a shop near you which is good for buying people presents? Tell us about it.
How often do you shop online?
Do you think it's safe to shop online?
Have you ever taken something back for a refund?
Have you ever made a complaint about something you have bought?
Do you ever buy things you don't really need?
How often do you go to busy shopping centres?
When did you last buy some new clothes?

Are you going shopping this weekend?
Tell us about any new shops that have opened in your area.
Have you got a friend that you like to go shopping with?

Sport

Let's talk about sport.
When did you last take part in any sport?
Is there a sport you would like to start doing?
Is there any sport you have tried and didn't enjoy?
Do you have any exercise apps?
What sports do you do at school?
Have you ever been to a gym?
What is the most unusual sport you have ever tried?
Is it important to you to be fit?
Have you ever taken part in a sports competition?
Have you ever been to a sports event?
Are there any important sports events in your country?
Did you have swimming lessons at school?

Technology

Now let's talk about technology.
What was the last piece of technology you bought?
Do you spend much money on technology?
Do you like to have the latest phone or laptop?
Which website do you use most often?
When did you last order something online?
Which are the most popular websites in your country?
When do you listen to music on your phone?
Which items of technology do you often use at school?
What is your favourite way of communicating online?
How often do you take photographs on your phone?
Do you use social media often?
Are there any social media websites you don't use?

The natural world

Let's talk about the natural world.
Have you ever visited a farm?
Are there any farms near where you live?
When did you last spend time in the countryside?
Do you like spending time in the countryside?
Is there much wildlife in your area of the country?
Have you ever been to a zoo?
What is the most exciting creature you have ever seen?
Are you scared of spiders?
Have you got a favourite animal?
Have you ever spent time in the mountains? Tell us about it.
Do you like to watch programmes about nature on TV? Why? / Why not?

Transport

Let's talk about transport.
Do many people cycle in your country?
Is it safe to cycle on the roads where you live?
Do you enjoy travelling by plane? Why? / Why not?
Where did you go the last time you travelled by train?
Have you got an app on your phone to help you with your travel plans? Tell us about it.

Speaking: Questions

Are the buses and trains reliable in your country?
When was the last time you were late for something?
What kind of transport do you use most often?
Have you ever been on a boat or ship?
Do you ever get travel sick?
What is the traffic like in the morning where you live?
Are there many lorries on the road where you live?

Travel and holidays
Now let's talk about travel and holidays.
When did you last go on holiday?
Do you enjoy sightseeing?
Have you ever swum in the sea?
What is the most popular place in your country for tourists?
Have you ever bought a souvenir?
What is your favourite holiday activity?
Have you ever had a holiday in another country?
When was the last time you went on a school trip?
Do you miss home when you go on holiday?
Do you take a lot of luggage with you when you go on holiday?
Have you ever been camping?
Have you ever been on holiday with a friend?

Weather
Let's talk about the weather.
What is the weather like in the summer where you live?
Do you like it when the weather is hot?
Does the weather make a difference to how you feel?
Do you ever check the weather forecast online?
What is your favourite kind of weather?
What do you like to do when it's sunny?
Does the weather change frequently in your country?
Do you like to go out in the rain? Why? / Why not?
Is there any dangerous weather in your country?
Do you know what the weather forecast is for this weekend?
What will you do this weekend if it's warm and sunny?

Work
Let's talk about work.
Have you ever had a part-time job? Tell us about it.
How easy is it for young people to find jobs where you live?
What kind of jobs do young people do in your country?
Are many people out of work where you live?
What jobs do your friends want to do when they finish their education?
What job would you like to do?
Do you plan to go to university before starting a career?
Which jobs are well paid in your country?
Do you want a job that pays a lot of money? Why? / Why not?
Does anyone in your family have an interesting job? Tell us about it.
Would you prefer to work inside or outside?
What kind of holiday jobs are there in your country?